THE ART INSTITUTE OF CHICAGO

THE ESSENTIAL GUIDE

THE ART INSTITUTE OF CHICAGO

THE ESSENTIAL GUIDE

Foreword by
James Rondeau

THE ART INSTITUTE OF CHICAGO

The Art Institute of Chicago gratefully acknowledges the Elizabeth F. Cheney Foundation for its early support of this publication.

Fourth edition
Printed in China
ISBN: 978-0-86559-301-5

Published by
The Art Institute of Chicago
111 South Michigan Avenue
Chicago, Illinois 60603-6404
www.artic.edu

Produced by the Department of Publishing of the Art Institute of Chicago, Greg Nosan, Executive Director. *Entries written by* the curatorial staff of the Art Institute of Chicago. *Edited by* Robert V. Sharp, Wilson McBee, and Maia Rigas. *Production by* Sarah E. Guernsey, Joseph Mohan, and Lauren Makholm. *Photography research by* Katie Levi
Photography by the Department of Imaging, Christopher Gallagher.
Third edition designed and typeset by Jena Sher
Fourth printing design updates by Beata Hosea
Separations by Professional Graphics, Rockford, Illinois
Printing and binding by Oceanic Graphics, China

Front covers: Edward Hopper, *Nighthawks* (detail), 1942 (p. 41). Katsushika Hokusai, *The Great Wave off Kanagawa* (detail), 1830/31 (p. 114). Archibald John Motley, *Nightlife* (detail), 1943 (p. 42). Georgia O'Keeffe, *Sky above Clouds IV* (detail), 1965 (p. 44). Georges Seurat, *A Sunday on La Grande Jatte—1884* (detail), 1884 (p. 186).
Gallery: Rosalba Carriera, *A Young Lady with a Parrot* (detail), c. 1730 (p. 310). Kolomon Moser, designer, *Poppyheads (Dress or Furnishing Fabric)* (detail), 1900 (p. 347). *Shell Ritual Mask* (detail), Teotihuacan, Mexico, 300/600 (p. 92). *Attachments Depicting Busts of Silenoi* (detail), Roman, mid-1st century BC/mid-1st century AD (p. 55). Claude Monet, *Water Lilies* (detail), 1906 (p. 194). Tosa Mitsuoki, *Flowering Cherry and Autumn Maples with Poem Slips* (detail), 1654/81 (p. 110). Jacob Halder, *Portions of a Field Armor* (detail), 1588/90 (p. 127). Kerry James Marshall, *Many Mansions* (detail), 1994 (p. 270).
Frontispiece: Winslow Homer, *Croquet Scene* (detail), 1866 (p. 19)
Back covers: Harry Callahan, *Chicago* (detail), 1950 (p. 295). Joan Mitchell, *City Landscape* (detail), 1955 (p. 240). Georgia O'Keeffe, *Sky above Clouds IV* (detail), 1965 (p. 44). *Bishamon*, Japanese, 11th century (p. 106). Charles White, *Harvest Talk* (detail), 1953 (p. 327).
For other details and photography credits, see pages 351–52.

CONTENTS

"To the east were the moving waters as far as the eye could follow. To the west a sea of grass as far as wind might reach." With these words the Chicago writer Nelson Algren began his portrait *Chicago: City on the Make* (1951), locating his hometown in the heart of the continent, bordered by the Great Lakes and the Great Plains.

As Chicago rapidly rebuilt after the Great Fire of 1871, it expanded its cultural ambitions. Local leaders and museum patrons alike saw the arts as an essential aspect of metropolitan life—they imagined their city as a source of culture and learning, as something more than a market for livestock and grain, a manufacturing center, or a transportation hub. In 1879 the Chicago Academy of Fine Arts was established to accomplish "the founding and maintenance of schools of art and design, the formation and exhibition of collections of objects of art, and the cultivation and extension of the arts by any appropriate means." The academy changed its name to the Art Institute of Chicago, which it announced in December 1882 when it moved from rented rooms into a building that it soon purchased on the southwest corner of Michigan Avenue and Van Buren Street. Five years later, it commissioned Burnham & Root to design an entirely new structure on the same site. Quickly outgrowing these quarters, in 1893 it moved into a building designed by Shepley, Rutan & Coolidge on Michigan Avenue at Adams Street, which it occupies to this day. The Art Institute officially opened on December 8, 1893, after having served as a venue of the World's Columbian Exposition earlier that year. At that time, the museum was an empty hope chest, and its leaders began an ambitious campaign to fill it. In the succeeding 130 years, it has acquired artworks of every kind, place, time, and style.

As the very form of the modern city was invented across Michigan Avenue in the towering skyscrapers of Chicago, the Art Institute set in motion its dual commitment to collect the art of the past and the present while training and inspiring the artists of the future. What makes our early history unique—what cannot be said about other major American museums—is that the acquisition of historical artworks was accompanied by an equally aggressive push by forward-thinking collectors interested in contemporary art. These men and women were deeply invested in the avant-garde, and they introduced Chicagoans to the work of artists such as Claude Monet, Georges Seurat, and Vincent van Gogh, which was then unfamiliar to American audiences. Eventually these pioneers donated their paintings to the Art Institute, which as a result boasts one of the finest Impressionist and Post-Impressionist collections in the world. The transformative gifts and bequests from individuals such as Bertha Honoré Palmer (1922), Frederick Clay and Helen Birch Bartlett (1926), Arthur Jerome Eddy (1931), Martin A. Ryerson (1933), Lindy and Edwin Bergman (1983), and most recently, Stefan Edlis and Gael Neeson (2015) have built the museum as it is today— both encyclopedic and contemporary.

The Art Institute has continued to be a lively home for the best new art of each subsequent generation, and it remains committed to championing voices that reflect our visitors, our city, and our world. The 2009 opening of the Renzo Piano–designed Modern Wing—the largest addition in the museum's history—enabled us to present our collections of modern and contemporary painting, sculpture, photography, film and video, and architecture and design in more effective and compelling ways. This expansion introduced new narratives to our audiences, showcasing recently acquired works by artists from more than nineteen different countries, including Brazil, China, India, Japan, Korea, and Sudan. Other recent gallery renovations and reinstallations have inspired us to reconsider the presentation of numerous areas of the collection, including African art; ancient and Byzantine art; European medieval and Renaissance art; the arts of the Americas; Indian, Southeast Asian, and Himalayan art; Japanese art; and Islamic art. These collections, and many more, are presented in a variety of contexts intended to provide the viewer with a meaningful experience and foster learning and understanding. Distinguished holdings of architectural renderings, photography, prints and drawings, and textiles—materials sensitive to light and atmosphere—have their own galleries and study facilities where rotations of objects can be enjoyed by all. This access encourages new research, generating knowledge that is at once clearer and broader.

Today, while we serve our communities with the collections we foster, and as an institution dedicated to inquiry and experimentation, research, and teaching, we also aspire to more. The Art Institute aims to be a space not separate from the world but integrally and dynamically engaged with it—what our third president and one of our most influential leaders, Charles Hutchinson, referred to at the beginning of the twentieth century as a "museum of living thought." A knowledgeable and sympathetic guide can be a tremendous resource in nurturing discovery and the exchange of ideas. It is our wish that this new edition of *The Art Institute of Chicago: The Essential Guide* will be just such a companion, providing introductions to many of our most celebrated landmarks and encouraging you to strike out on your own to explore secondary trails that stimulate your imagination.

An endeavor such as this publication is realized only with the participation, direct and indirect, of the entire museum staff. In particular, we have relied upon the extensive research and writing of current and former members of the curatorial departments, whose efforts at understanding and maintaining every aspect of our holdings are the cornerstone of this institution. *The Essential Guide* is intended to help you make the Art Institute your own during your visit and remind you of favorite works once you have departed. More importantly, we hope that experiencing original works of art firsthand will make you want to return to seek out fresh experiences. We invite you to help us shape the museum in the present and for the future.

James Rondeau
President and Eloise W. Martin Director
The Art Institute of Chicago

CORNELIUS KIERSTEDE American, 1674–1757
Two-Handled Covered Cup, 1698/1720
New York, New York

Silver; 12.7 × 20.3 × 12.7 cm (5 ³/₈ × 8 ⁵/₈ × 5 ³/₄ in.)

Restricted gift of Mrs. James W. Alsdorf, Pauline Seipp Armstrong, Marshall Field, Charles C. Haffner III, Mrs. Burton W. Hales, Mrs. Harold T. Martin, Mrs. C. Phillip Miller, Mr. and Mrs. Milo M. Naeve, Mrs. Eric Oldberg, and Mrs. Frank L. Sulzberger, and the Ethel T. Scarborough Fund, 1984.1132

This luxurious vessel, by one of New York's foremost early silversmiths, was used to serve syllabub, a sweetened or flavored wine, cider, beer, or ale into which milk was whipped. The cover helped preserve the frothy drink and also, using its three equidistant handles as legs, could be inverted into a stand for the cup. The vessel bears the mark *CK*, standing for Cornelius Kierstede, a third-generation New York silversmith of Dutch descent. Kierstede opened a shop around 1698 in New York, where he worked, off and on, until moving to New Haven, Connecticut, in the early 1720s. Like the Van Cortlandt family, who commissioned this cup and whose coat of arms it bears, and the Stuyvesant family, whose descendants owned the object until the Art Institute acquired it, the majority of Kierstede's patrons were wealthy Dutch colonists. This cup is one of four nearly identical pieces made during the same period by Kierstede and two other well-known New York silversmiths. Evolved from English prototypes, all four have the same nearly straight sides, scroll-like handles, and slightly domed cover as well as variations of the embossed acanthus-leaf ornament.

JOHN SINGLETON COPLEY American, 1738–1815
Mrs. Daniel Hubbard (Mary Greene), c. 1764
Oil on canvas; 127.6 × 100.9 cm (50 ¼ × 39 ¾ in.)
The Art Institute of Chicago Purchase Fund, 1947.28

America's foremost portrait painter before the Revolutionary War, John Singleton
Copley had completed his first compositions by the age of fifteen. Largely self-taught,
the Boston painter often relied, as did English artists, on European prints for compositional models and, in particular, on the print collection of his stepfather and teacher,
Peter Pelham, a mezzotint engraver. For this rendering of a wealthy merchant's wife,
Copley emulated the pose, gown, and background of an English noblewoman in a
mezzotint portrait. Standing on a balcony or terrace, Mrs. Hubbard rests her arm
on an embroidered cloth placed over a pedestal. As in the print, draperies and clouds
billow behind her. Even the cherub carved in relief on the parapet is borrowed from
the mezzotint. Nevertheless, the penetrating directness, vigorous execution, and
precision of detail are Copley's own; this particular indigenous sensibility was much
appreciated throughout the colonies. The wealthy merchants and professionals Copley
painted included Mrs. Hubbard's husband (whose portrait is also in the Art Institute),
as well as some of the colonies' most influential personages, such as patriots Samuel
Adams, John Hancock, and Paul Revere. Copley left America for England on the eve
of the American Revolution and never returned.

ATTRIBUTED TO JOHN TOWNSEND American, 1732–1809
Bureau Table, c. 1770
Newport, Rhode Island
Mahogany, chestnut, and tulip poplar; 86.6 × 93.4 × 58 cm (34 ⅛ × 36 ¾ × 20 in.)
Gift of Jamee J. and Marshall Field, 1984.1387

This elegant piece epitomizes the Late Baroque style that flourished in Newport, Rhode Island. It is one of six bureaus that can be attributed to the celebrated cabinetmaker John Townsend on the basis of similar construction and design features in labeled pieces by the maker. For example, the carved shells have central C-scrolls featuring petals and crosshatched baskets, all motifs that are indicative of Townsend's work. In addition, the top is integrated into the case by cove-and-bead molding, with smaller cavetto molding underneath. The blocking of the upper drawer continues through the side drawers and into the graceful double scroll of the bracket feet, creating an unbroken visual plane that unifies the design elements.

   Kept in bedchambers, bureau tables most likely functioned as dressing tables. They were particularly popular among the Quaker citizens of Newport, who appreciated the wide array of storage possibilities they offered. According to oral tradition, Samuel Fowler originally owned this bureau. A successful merchant, Fowler frequently conducted business with the Townsend family. In 1786 and 1787, John Townsend purchased hinges, nails, and sundries from Fowler. This relationship bolsters the argument that Fowler owned this bureau, since patronage loyalty resulting from familial, religious, and trading ties was typical in eighteenth-century Newport.

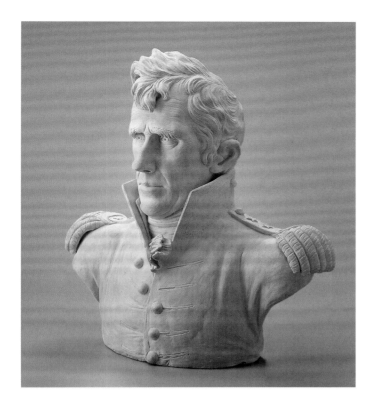

WILLIAM RUSH American, 1756–1833
General Andrew Jackson, 1819
Terra-cotta; 50.5 × 47.9 × 22.2 cm (19 ⁷/₈ × 18 ⁷/₈ × 8 ³/₄ in.)
Restricted gift of Jamee J. and Marshall Field; the Brooks and Hope B. McCormick
Foundation, and Bessie Bennett, W. G. Field, Ada Turnbull Hertle, Laura T. Magnuson, and
Major Acquisitions funds, 1985.251

Andrew Jackson was described by a contemporary as having "an erect military bearing, and a head set with considerable *fierté* [pride] upon his shoulders. . . . His eye is of a dangerous fixedness; . . . [and] the instant his lips close, a visor of steel would scarcely look more impenetrable." William Rush rendered a remarkably similar depiction of the general. Demonstrating a blend of naturalism, subtlety, and strength, Rush avoided grandiosity in this terra-cotta portrait bust of the fifty-two-year-old military hero, who, ten years later, would begin to serve the first of two consecutive terms as president of the United States. The artist's only concession to idealization was the replacement of the general's well-known stiff, wiry hair with the soft curls that signify noble qualities in Neoclassical sculpture. Since there is no documentation that Jackson formally posed for Rush, the artist, a prominent resident of Philadelphia, may have observed the general during his three-day visit to the city in 1819. This sculpture achieved critical and commercial success, with one reviewer ranking it as "Rush's masterpiece." Hoping to benefit from Jackson's popularity, Rush followed the European custom of producing plaster replicas of the bust.

MARTIN JOHNSON HEADE American, 1819–1904
Magnolias on Light Blue Velvet Cloth, 1885/95
Oil on canvas; 38.6 × 61.8 cm (15 1/4 × 24 3/8 in.)
Restricted gift of Gloria and Richard Manney; Harold L. Stuart Endowment, 1983.791

This sensuous and decorative image dates from the later part of Martin Johnson Heade's long, varied, and peripatetic career. Traveling through much of the United States, to England and continental Europe, and (three different times) to Brazil, he produced work ranging from pristine views of East Coast salt marshes and lush tropical landscapes to pictures of exotic hummingbirds and orchids. At the age of sixty-four, Heade settled in Saint Augustine, Florida. There he began painting detailed arrangements of native flowers, including the Cherokee rose, orange blossom, and magnolia. Stretched out like an odalisque on blue velvet cloth, the curvaceous magnolia was meticulously rendered in pale, subtle hues and illuminated by a light so sharp that the image evokes the hyperintensity of a dream. The warm, steamy atmosphere is almost palpable, as is the blossom's heady, pungent scent. The Art Institute's *Magnolias* is one of a number of compositions by the artist featuring this dramatic yet delicate white flower.

FREDERIC EDWIN CHURCH American, 1826–1900
View of Cotopaxi, 1857
Oil on canvas; 62.2 × 92.7 cm (24 ½ × 36 ½ in.)
Gift of Jennette Hamlin in memory of Mr. and Mrs. Louis Dana Webster, 1919.753

One of the leading American landscape painters in the mid-nineteenth century, Frederic Edwin Church approached his subject matter as both an artist and a scientist. Inspired by the writings of the German naturalist and explorer Alexander von Humboldt, Church visited the mountainous terrain of South America twice, in 1853 and 1857. In this untamed "New World"—and particularly in what was then the highest active volcano in the world, the mighty Ecuadorian Cotopaxi—Church saw the perfect symbol of primeval nature and the spiritual renewal it could bring to civilization. This view of the smoldering cone of Cotopaxi was completed after Church's first trip to South America. A dazzling compendium of minutely rendered wildlife, vegetation, and terrain, the scene illustrates the fascinating contrasts indigenous to this locale: from the calm water to the explosive cascades and from the lush, green foliage to the frozen, barren peak. The elevated vantage point, which makes the viewer feel suspended in midair, heightens these evocative juxtapositions. One of at least ten finished canvases featuring the Andean volcano that Church executed over the course of almost two decades, this painting represents an intermediate vision between his more naturalistic early pieces and the dramatic, transcendental works of his later years.

EMMA STEBBINS American, 1815–1882
Machinist's Apprentice and *Machinist*, c. 1859
Marble; left: 74.9 × 29.9 × 22.9 cm (29 ½ × 11 ¾ × 9 in.); right: 74.9 × 29.2 × 29.2 cm
(29 ½ × 11 ½ × 11 ½ in.)
Gift of the Antiquarian Society, 2000.13.1–2

Emma Stebbins was a member of the community of women sculptors in Rome. Like their male colleagues, these women emulated the statues of antiquity, seeing in them the highest form of art. This rare pair of marble statues portrays a laborer and his apprentice, an unusual theme in mid-nineteenth-century American sculpture. Stebbins's innovative conceit was to render a modern subject—the profession of the machinist—in the refined, Neoclassical visual language traditionally used to depict biblical, historical, and mythological subjects. Both figures can be identified as machinists by their clothing: cap, work shirt, leather apron, and long pants. The senior machinist holds a forging hammer and toothed gear, the means and ends of his labor; the young apprentice demonstrates his ability to improve on his teacher's experience with a compass and drawing stylus. By using a Neoclassical idiom to represent a new, machine-based profession practiced by two generations of workers, Stebbins celebrated the possibilities of innovation and suggested the peaceful coexistence of traditional labor and mechanization.

JOHN QUINCY ADAMS WARD American, 1830–1910
The Freedman, 1862–63
Bronze; 49.9 × 40 × 23.9 cm (19 ⁵/₈ × 15 ³/₄ × 9 ³/₈ in.)
Roger McCormick Endowment, 1998.1

A leader among the nation's second generation of sculptors, John Quincy Adams Ward played a significant role in elevating the medium in the United States, calling for a new realism to address moral concerns. Inspired by Abraham Lincoln's 1862–63 Emancipation Proclamation, *The Freedman* reflects not only Ward's aspiration to create relevant statements on pressing issues of the day but also his abolitionist sentiments. Using antiquity as his inspiration, he depicted a seminude man seated on a tree stump who has just been liberated from the shackles that bound him to slavery. Ward broke artistic convention by showing the former slave as master of his own destiny, not a man reliant on white men for freedom. The vestiges of chains, potent symbols of his bondage, dangle from both wrists, and his muscular body, turned to look over his shoulder, is contained within a formal, triangular composition. *The Freedman* was modeled from life and is generally considered the first and most accurate sculptural representation of an African American. Shortly after *The Freedman* was first exhibited in 1863, art critic James Jackson Jarves effectively summarized the work's power: "We have seen nothing in our sculpture more soul-lifting or more comprehensively eloquent. It tells in one word the whole sad story of slavery and the bright story of emancipation."

RAPHAELLE PEALE American, 1774–1825
Still Life—Strawberries, Nuts, &c., 1822
Oil on wood panel; 41.1 × 57.8 cm (16 ³/₁₆ × 22 ³/₄ in.)
Gift of Jamee J. and Marshall Field, 1991.100

Academic theory during Raphaelle Peale's time relegated still life to the bottom of the hierarchy of painting subjects. Yet Peale ignored its low status and is now acknowledged as America's first professional still-life painter and leading practitioner of the genre. Born into an artistic Philadelphia family, Raphaelle was the eldest son of Charles Willson Peale and the nephew of James Peale, both artists; his siblings were, like him, named after famous old master painters (e.g., he had brothers named Rembrandt, Titian, and Rubens). Characterized by crisp forms and serenely balanced compositions, most of Peale's still lifes portray food (mainly fruit), crockery, and glassware arranged on a plain shelf, parallel to the picture plane. In this particularly fine example, the rhythmic balance of fruit, nuts, and Chinese export porcelain is enlivened by the diagonal branch of raisins and orange leaf. These objects are brightly illuminated against a bare, dark background in the manner of the dramatic still-life compositions of seventeenth-century masters such as the Spanish painter Juan Sánchez Cotán (see p. 157). Peale may have seen Sánchez Cotán's work when it was shown at the Pennsylvania Academy of the Fine Arts in 1818.

WINSLOW HOMER American, 1836–1910
Croquet Scene, 1866
Oil on canvas; 40.3 × 66.2 cm (15 $^7/_8$ × 26 $^1/_{16}$ in.)
Friends of American Art Collection; Goodman Fund, 1942.35

One of America's foremost painters, Winslow Homer began his career as an illustrator during the Civil War. In the late 1860s, he turned his acute observational and technical skills toward oil painting, depicting figures bathed in sunlight out-of-doors. These early paintings, often executed in series, feature scenes of upper-class leisure pursuits—in this case, women and men competing with one another in the popular sport of croquet, which had recently been introduced to the United States from the British Isles. In *Croquet Scene*, one of five paintings Homer completed on the subject, progress on "the grand round" seems fairly advanced. The crouching male figure positions the ball belonging to the woman dressed in red. She is about to croquet (or "send up the country") another ball, probably belonging to the woman in the left foreground, who shields her eyes against the bright afternoon sun. Notable for its bold patterning, strong contours, and brilliant light effects, the painting epitomizes the spirit of a breezy summer afternoon.

JAMES MCNEILL WHISTLER American, 1834–1903
Nocturne: Blue and Gold—Southampton Water, 1872
Oil on canvas; 50.5 × 76 cm (19 ⅞ × 29 ¹⁵⁄₁₆ in.)
Stickney Fund, 1900.52

"Art should be independent of all clap-trap—should stand alone and appeal to the artistic sense of eye or ear," said the daringly unconventional painter James McNeill Whistler. Born in the United States, Whistler spent most of his adult life in Paris and London. To emphasize that his paintings have no narrative overtones—that they instead are aesthetic arrangements of color and shape on flat surfaces—he gave them titles derived from music, such as *arrangement, symphony,* and *nocturne.* One of his first such paintings, *Nocturne: Blue and Gold—Southampton Water,* depicts a hazy, moonlit night on an inlet of the English Channel, southwest of London. Although the work is based on his experience of the location, the specifics of place are inconsequential. Instead, Whistler was interested in the subtle harmony of shades of blue, punctuated by touches of gold. By blurring and obscuring the shapes of the distant boats, he made color and form the primary focus of the painting. Often misunderstood and sometimes openly ridiculed when they were first exhibited, Whistler's luminous nocturnal visions were forerunners of the experiments in abstraction that would follow in the next century.

DESIGN ATTRIBUTED TO EDWARD C. MOORE American, 1827–1891
TIFFANY & COMPANY American, founded 1838
Pitcher, 1878
New York, New York
Silver, gold, and copper; 20.3 × 12.7 × 15.2 cm (8 7/8 × 5 1/4 × 6 7/8 in.)
Restricted gift of Mrs. Frank L. Sulzberger, 1984.240

By the time this elegant pitcher was produced, Tiffany & Company had become one
of the largest and most accomplished silver manufacturers in the world. Likely conceived by the company's chief designer, Edward C. Moore, the vessel reflects the late
nineteenth-century fascination with Japan, a nation that had resumed full trade with
the outside world just two decades earlier. Moore formed one of the earliest collections
of Japanese art in the United States; here he emulated motifs found in Japanese
woodblock prints and the multiple metals and hammered surfaces used in Japanese
metalwork. Company records show that several dozen versions of this object were
made during the 1870s and 1880s and sold as far away as Russia. An identical version
received widespread acclaim when it was exhibited at the Exposition Universelle in
Paris in 1878, where Moore received a gold medal and the company's founder, Charles
Lewis Tiffany, was made a Knight of the French Legion of Honor. The London *Spectator*
lamented, "We confess we were surprised and ashamed to find that a New York firm,
Tiffany & Co., had beaten the old country and the old world in domestic silver plate."

HERTER BROTHERS American, 1864–1906
Cabinet, 1878/80
New York, New York
Rosewood with ebonized cherry, maple, walnut, satinwood, marquetry of various woods, brass, gilding, and paint; 134.6 × 180.3 × 40.6 cm (53 × 71 × 16 in.)
Restricted gift of the Antiquarian Society through the Capital Campaign, 1986.26

Herter Brothers, one of New York's foremost decorating firms during the 1870s and early 1880s, followed the lead of English designers intent on reforming an industry that produced poorly conceived and constructed work by advocating designs that were both beautiful and functional. Brothers Gustave and Christian Herter preferred bold, rectilinear shapes, which they often enlivened, as in this case, with exquisite surface decoration inspired by Japanese art, evidence of the Japanism that was prevalent throughout the West at this time. Here the painted roundels featuring flowers and insects at top left and right of the cabinet emulate Japanese lacquer, while the floral inlay across the facade is reminiscent of patterns found in Japanese screen paintings and textiles. Japanese family crests inspired the bands of inlay across the tops of the doors and above the side compartments, and Japanesque plum blossoms were carved in the arched spandrels on either side of the facade. Nevertheless, the overall form of the cabinet is Western, and the piece also includes such non-Japanesque elements as Egyptian-Revival paw feet. Aesthetic Movement designers such as Herter Brothers readily combined such eclectic motifs as long as they achieved a sense of visual harmony.

DANIEL PABST American, 1826–1910
Sideboard, 1868/80
Philadelphia, Pennsylvania
Walnut and burled elm; 256.5 × 185.4 × 62.2 cm (101 × 73 × 24 ½ in.)
Gift of the Antiquarian Society, 2005.51

Marking the height of the "modern Gothic" style in Philadelphia, this sideboard
resembles the furniture designed by notable architect Frank Furness, who frequently
collaborated with cabinetmaker Daniel Pabst. Although details of the piece's carving
tie it unmistakably to Pabst, the design cannot be attributed conclusively to a particular
hand. The designer was influenced by the writings of Christopher Dresser and Charles
Eastlake, British reformers who advocated honesty of construction and convention-
alized ornament. Instead of carving the decoration deeply in order to achieve a
naturalistic effect, Pabst used a cameo technique, cutting through the burled elm veneer
to reveal the darker walnut beneath and creating a striking color contrast and flattened style of decoration.

In the mid-nineteenth century, dining-room furniture typically featured ornament
that was intended to reinforce ideals of hospitality and gentility. Here the cabinet doors
display designs recounting Aesop's fable of the fox and the stork, a tale in which each
animal offers the other some food in a serving dish from which the guest cannot eat,
thus proving the importance of true hospitality. The panels are virtually identical to
images found on curtain designs illustrated in Eastlake's 1868 book *Hints on Household
Taste*, a text that was widely influential in the United States.

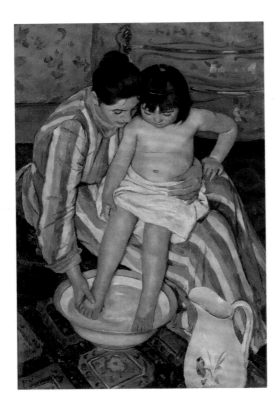

MARY CASSATT American, 1844–1926
The Child's Bath, 1893
Oil on canvas; 100.3 × 66.1 cm (39 ½ × 26 in.)
Robert A. Waller Fund, 1910.2

The only American artist to exhibit her work with the French Impressionists, Mary Cassatt was first invited to show with the group by Edgar Degas in 1877. By that time, she had become disenchanted with traditional academic painting. Like her friend Degas, Cassatt concentrated on the human figure in her Impressionist works, particularly on sensitive yet unsentimental portrayals of women and children. *The Child's Bath*, with its striking and unorthodox composition, is one of Cassatt's masterworks. Here she employed unconventional devices such as cropped forms, bold patterns and outlines, and a flattened perspective, all of which derived from her study of Japanese woodblock prints. The lively patterns play off one another and serve to accentuate the nakedness of the child, whose vulnerable white legs are as straight as the lines of the woman's striped dress. The elevated vantage point permits the viewer to observe, but not participate in, this most intimate scene. Cassatt's composition thereby reinforces her subject: the tender absorption of a woman with a child.

WINSLOW HOMER American, 1836–1910
The Herring Net, 1885
Oil on canvas; 76.5 × 122.9 cm (30 1/8 × 48 3/8 in.)
Mr. and Mrs. Martin A. Ryerson Collection, 1937.1039

In 1883 Winslow Homer moved to the small coastal village of Prouts Neck, Maine, where he created a series of paintings of the sea unparalleled in American art. Long inspired by the subject, Homer had spent summers visiting New England fishing villages during the 1870s, and in 1881–82 he made a trip to a fishing community in Cullercoats, England, that fundamentally changed his work and his life. The paintings he created after 1882 focus almost exclusively on humankind's age-old contest with nature. Here Homer depicted the heroic efforts of fishermen at their daily work, hauling in an abundant catch of herring. In a small dory, two figures loom large against the mist on the horizon, through which the sails of the mother schooners are dimly visible. While one fisherman hauls in the netted and glistening herring, the other unloads the catch. Utilizing the teamwork so necessary for survival, both strive to steady the precarious boat as it rides the incoming swells. Homer's isolation of these two figures underscores the monumentality of their task: the elemental struggle against a sea that both nurtures and deprives.

JOHN HENRY TWACHTMAN American, 1853–1902
Icebound, c. 1889
Oil on canvas; 64.2 × 76.6 cm (25 ¼ × 30 ⅛ in.)
Friends of American Art Collection, 1917.200

Around 1889, after years of training and travel, John Henry Twachtman purchased a seventeen-acre farm in Greenwich, Connecticut. During the next decade, he created some of his finest works there. Like the French Impressionists, whose style greatly influenced him, Twachtman found an inexhaustible source of subjects and inspiration in his local surroundings. *Icebound* illustrates a favorite theme: a stream descending from rocks to a serene pool surrounded by hemlock trees. In the hushed tranquility of this winter scene, Twachtman achieved a fine compositional balance between spontaneity and control. Movement is implied despite the frozen stillness suggested by the title and the muted tonal harmonies of the painting's limited white and blue palette. Sinuous arabesques of white snow against blue water accentuate the stream's descent. Thick brushstrokes of white and streaks of violet amid the blue of the water enliven the picture's surface. Vivid red-orange leaves serve both as distinctive accents against the dominant white and as reminders of an autumnal life that has not surrendered to the relentless change of seasons.

FREDERIC REMINGTON American, 1861–1909
The Bronco Buster, modeled 1895; cast 1899
Cast by Henry-Bonnard Bronze Company, New York
Bronze; 61 × 39.4 × 17.8 cm (24 × 15 ¹/₂ × 7 in.)
George F. Harding Collection, 1982.808

Although born, raised, and educated on the East Coast, Frederic Remington achieved considerable success as America's leading illustrator of life on the western frontier. In 1894 he turned his skill and energy to sculpture. This vigorous portrayal of a cowboy taming a wild horse was the artist's first effort in bronze, and with an illustrator's eye for drama, he captured the single most illuminating moment of the event. Although the horse and rider struggle against each other, they are pulled together at the instant of utmost exertion. As the bronco rears up, back arched and splayed tail snapping, the cowboy leans forward, his whip suspended in midair as he clutches the reins and horse's mane. This minutely rendered, spirited, and technically remarkable depiction of life in the Wild West became one of the most popular American bronzes of the early twentieth century. The Art Institute's version is one of nearly seventy made at the Henry-Bonnard Bronze Company of New York using the French sand-casting method.

FRANK LLOYD WRIGHT American, 1867–1959
Spindle Cube Chair, 1902/6

Poplar and leather; 73.7 × 73.7 × 73.7 cm (29 × 29 × 29 in.)

Restricted gift of the Antiquarian Society; Roger McCormick Purchase, Alyce and Edwin DeCosta and the Walter E. Heller Foundation, Robert Allerton Purchase Income, Ada Turnbull Hertle, and Mary Waller Langhorne Memorial funds; Robert Allerton Trust; Pauline Seipp Armstrong Fund; bequest of Ruth Falkenau Fund in memory of her parents; Wendell Fentress Ott Endowment, Bessie Bennett, Elizabeth R. Vaughn, and Gladys N. Anderson funds; Estate of Stacia Fischer; the Goodman Fund; Maurice D. Galleher Endowment; Samuel P. Avery and Charles U. Harris Endowed Acquisition funds; Estate of Cora Abrahamson; Charles R. and Janice Feldstein Endowment Fund for Decorative Arts, 2007.79

This elegant spindle cube chair is an early example from Frank Lloyd Wright's home and studio. In 1889 Wright built a house for his young family on Forest Avenue in Oak Park, a new suburb just west of Chicago; ten years later, he opened an attached studio and designed it and the home's interior in accordance with his philosophy of simplicity and integrity of materials. Among his furniture experiments were heavy, solid cube chairs. By the first decade of the twentieth century, Wright had refined his early design into that of this chair, adding spindles, a subtly tapering crest rail, and gently curving leg ends to produce an effect that is equal parts sophistication and simplicity. The spindles themselves were a legacy of William Morris–inspired ladder-back dining chairs, as well as the Arts and Crafts approach of contrasting positive and negative space. This chair was also influenced by the reticulated ceilings and walls of Japanese homes.

DESIGNED BY GEORGE GRANT ELMSLIE (OF PURCELL, FEICK AND ELMSLIE) American, born Scotland, 1871–1952
NIEDECKEN-WALBRIDGE American, 1907–38
Tall Clock, 1912

Mahogany with brass inlay; 213.3 × 66 × 40 cm
(84 × 26 × 15 ³/₄ in.)
Restricted gift of Mrs. Theodore D. Tieken,
1971.322

This handsome tall-case clock was designed by the firm of George Grant Elmslie and William Gray Purcell for the Henry Babson House in Riverside, Illinois. Although Louis Sullivan designed the house in 1907, a large part of the scheme—including the built-in and freestanding furniture—was actually executed by Elmslie, who was then working for Sullivan. In 1912 Elmslie and his firm made additions to the house, including eight pieces of furniture. This elegant clock, whose works and nine chimes were imported from Germany, dates from this later commission. Its hands were executed by Chicago metalsmith Robert Riddle Jarvie according to Elmslie's design. In his concern over creating an organic, harmonious relationship between the interior of a house and its exterior, the Scottish-born Elmslie found a staunch ally in designer George Niedecken, president of Niedecken-Walbridge, a firm based in Milwaukee, Wisconsin, which made the clock's mahogany case.

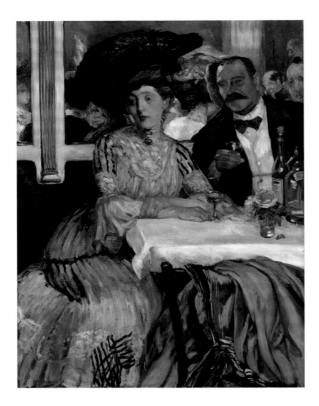

WILLIAM GLACKENS American, 1870–1938
At Mouquin's, 1905
Oil on canvas; 122.4 × 92.1 cm (48 ⅛ × 36 ¼ in.)
Friends of American Art Collection, 1925.295

William Glackens—a member of an association of artists called the Eight—was at the center of avant-garde American painting at the turn of the twentieth century. Rejecting the academic standards of the influential National Academy of Design in New York, Glackens and his fellow urban realists focused unflinchingly on the city around them, vividly recording the street life and leisure activities they encountered. Mouquin's was a fashionable New York restaurant frequented by Glackens and artists of his circle. Combining portraiture with genre painting, he depicted the restaurateur James B. Moore sharing a drink with Jeanne-Louise Mouquin, the wife of the proprietor. The artist's wife, Edith, and Charles Fitzgerald, a local art critic and champion of Glackens's work, are reflected in the large wall mirror. Mouquin is the focal point of the composition; not only is her dress and cloak rendered with fluid, eye-catching brushstrokes, but her mysterious, abstracted gaze also creates an unresolved tension within the work. Perhaps Glackens intended to make a social commentary; many contemporary writers maintained that anomie was one of the psychological consequences of rapid change in European and American cities. Criticized for its unabashed depiction of men and women drinking together, *At Mouquin's* suggests the pleasures and the perils of modern life.

JOHN SINGER SARGENT American, 1856–1925
The Fountain, Villa Torlonia, Frascati, Italy, 1907
Oil on canvas; 71.4 × 56.5 cm (28 ⅛ × 22 ¼ in.)
Friends of American Art Collection, 1914.57

As one of the most sought-after and prolific portraitists of international high society, American expatriate John Singer Sargent painted the cosmopolitan world to which he belonged with elegance and a bravura touch. Born to American parents residing in Italy, Sargent spent his early adult life in Paris, moving to London in the mid-1880s. The artist traveled frequently, and it was during these trips that he experimented most extensively with painting en plein air, or outdoors. Set in a sunlit garden in the central Italian town of Frascati, this charming double portrait depicts Sargent's friends and fellow artists Wilfrid and Jane Emmet de Glehn. The painting is filled with light, displaying Sargent's characteristically dazzling surface articulated with thick impasto and virtuoso brushwork. Jane described the work as a "most amusing and killingly funny picture" in a letter to her sister Lydia. She continued: "I am all in white with a white painting blouse and a pale blue veil around my hat. I look rather like a pierrot, but have a rather worried expression as every painter should who isn't a perfect fool, says Sargent. Wilfrid is in short sleeves, very idle and good for nothing and our heads come against the great 'panache' of the fountain."

GEORGE INNESS American, 1825–1894
The Home of the Heron, 1893
Oil on canvas; 76.2 × 115.2 cm (30 × 45 in.)
Edward B. Butler Collection, 1911.31

The landscape painter George Inness once explained, "The true purpose of the painter is simply to reproduce in other minds the impression which a scene has made upon him . . . to awaken an emotion." Inness sought, particularly in his later years, to record not so much the appearance of nature as its poetry. To achieve this, he limited his subject matter to, in his words, "rivers, streams, the rippling brook, the hillside, the sky, the clouds." For half a century, the artist captured these moisture-laden subjects in all seasons, during all hours of the day and night. First he made small, quick sketches in the field or wood, and then, in the seclusion of his studio, he used them to create the more than one thousand oils credited to him.

Inness completed *The Home of the Heron* near the end of his career, after he had finally achieved a degree of comfort and success. The painting is characteristic of his late work, with loosely rendered detail and dim objects that seem bathed in an almost incandescent glow. The picture's blurred outlines, broad handling, and delicate, subtle tonalities, as well as the solitary presence of the heron, masterfully evoke nature's stillness and mystery. With more than two dozen canvases by Inness, the Art Institute has one of the most comprehensive collections of the painter's work.

DESIGN ATTRIBUTED TO CLARA PIERCE WOLCOTT DRISCOLL
American, 1861–1944
TIFFANY STUDIOS American, 1902–32
Hanging Head Dragonfly Shade on Mosaic and Turtleback Base, by 1906
Favrile glass and bronze; 86.4 × 57.2 cm (34 × 22 ½ in.)

Roger and J. Peter McCormick Endowments; Robert Allerton Purchase Fund; Goodman Endowment for the Collection of the Friends of American Art; Pauline S. Armstrong Endowment; Edward E. Ayer Endowment in memory of Charles L. Hutchinson; restricted gift of the Antiquarian Society in memory of Helen Richman Gilbert and Lena Turnbull Gilbert, Sandra van den Broek, Mr. and Mrs. Henry M. Buchbinder, Quinn E. Delaney, Mr. and Mrs. Wesley M. Dixon, Jamee J. and Marshall Field, Celia and David Hilliard, Elizabeth Souder Louis, Mrs. Herbert A. Vance, and Mr. and Mrs. Morris S. Weeden, 2006.2

In the 1890s Louis Comfort Tiffany began using his opalescent Favrile glass to produce lamps, the decorative form for which he would become most famous. As the artistic director of Tiffany Studios located in Corona, New York, he approved all patterns but created relatively few lamps himself. Clara Driscoll, head of the Women's Glass Cutting Department, was likely responsible for this shade and base. Driscoll began working for Tiffany in 1888, and she designed the majority of the firm's lamps before she left the company in 1908 or 1909. Driscoll created at least eight dragonfly shades. This example is distinguished by its large size, glass cabochons, and the placement of insects' bodies along the lower edge. While Tiffany Studios mass-produced these shades and bases, the firm varied the color scheme of each object to heighten the sense of handcraftsmanship. This daring design became one of Tiffany's most popular and was made through 1924.

MARSDEN HARTLEY American, 1877–1943
Movements, 1913
Oil on canvas; 119.5 × 119 cm (47 × 46 ⁷/₈ in.)
Alfred Stieglitz Collection, 1949.544

Marsden Hartley painted *Movements* while living in Berlin, where he met Vasily Kandinsky (see p. 204), whose abstract and highly spiritual art influenced the American painter deeply. Hartley was a central figure of the American avant-garde that exhibited at 291, the New York gallery of Alfred Steiglitz (see p. 287). The title of this intense, vividly colored canvas suggests a musical analogy for its nearly abstract forms, which are rhythmically orchestrated around the central red circle and black triangle. Yet Hartley also drew on his experience of Berlin in *Movements*; the vigorous forms in the composition, bursting and overlapping in a riotous array, suggest the fast pace of life in the German capital. Although Hartley's art underwent frequent changes in style and subject, the charged, romantic energy seen here remained a constant presence.

JOSÉ CLEMENTE OROZCO Mexican, 1883–1949
Zapata, 1930
Oil on canvas; 198.8 × 122.6 cm (78 ¼ × 48 ¼ in.)
Gift of Joseph Winterbotham Collection, 1941.35

This dramatic canvas was painted during José Clemente Orozco's self-imposed exile in the United States, where he took up residence in 1927. He moved in part to escape political unrest but also because he felt that it was increasingly difficult to get commissions in his native land. A leader of the Mexican mural movement of the 1920s and 1930s, Orozco claimed to have painted *Zapata* to finance his trip back to New York after completing a mural commission in California. For liberal Mexicans, Emiliano Zapata became a symbol of the Mexican Revolution (1910–20) after his assassination in 1919. The charismatic Zapata crusaded to return the enormous holdings of wealthy landowners to Mexico's peasant population. Here his specterlike figure appears in the open door of a peasant hut. Despite the drama before him, the revolutionary hero seems solemn and unmoved. The painting is filled with menacing details—the bullets, the dagger, and especially the sword aimed at Zapata's eye—and the somber palette of dark reds, browns, and blacks further underscores the danger of the revolutionary conflict.

PAUL THEODORE FRANKL American, born Austria, 1886–1958
Skyscraper Cabinet, c. 1927
Painted wood; 213.4 × 83.8 × 40 cm (84 × 33 × 15 ³/₄ in.)
Gift of the Antiquarian Society through Mr. and Mrs. Thomas B. Hunter III and
Mr. and Mrs. Morris S. Weeden, 1998.567

Trained as an architect in Vienna and Berlin, Paul T. Frankl immigrated to New
York in 1914 and established his own gallery. There he began to design interiors and
champion the skyscraper as a source of a uniquely American modernist vision. The
impetus behind the *Skyscraper Cabinet*, however, was distinctly rural. Frankl spent
the summer of 1925 in Woodstock, New York, sketching ideas for new furniture designs
and renovating his cabin. In an effort to organize his books, he fitted boards together
to create a cabinet with "a rather large, bulky lower section and a slender, shallow
upper part going straight to the ceiling. It had a new look; the neighbors came and
said, 'It looks just like the new skyscrapers.'" From then on, Frankl experimented
with spare, geometric furniture that mimicked the setback contours of New York
skyscrapers. By 1926 these pieces were touted in *Good Furniture* magazine as the
"sky-scraper type of furniture, which is as American and as New Yorkish as Fifth
Avenue itself." The Art Institute's monumental cabinet epitomizes Frankl's designs.
Its geometric form rests on a sharply molded base and consists of a bottom cabinet
section surmounted by a series of compartments and shelves arranged in a pyramid-
like fashion. Smooth, unadorned surfaces exemplify the tenets of modernist design.

JOHN BRADLEY STORRS American, 1885–1956
Ceres, 1928
Copper alloy plated with nickel, then chrome; 67.3 × 16.2 × 12.4 cm (26 ½ × 6 ⅜ × 4 ⅞ in.)
Gift of John N. Stern, 1981.538

John Storrs was a leading American modernist sculptor in the 1920s and 1930s. Although he moved to Paris in 1911 and spent much of his career there, he grew up in Chicago and studied at the Chicago Academy of Fine Arts and the School of the Art Institute of Chicago. *Ceres* is a smaller version of the figure Storrs designed for the top of the Chicago Board of Trade Building. In his efforts to make the sculpture symbolic of the building's purpose, Storrs turned to the Classical subject of Ceres, the Roman goddess of grain, alluding to the board's activity as the world's biggest grain exchange. He depicted Ceres holding a sheaf of wheat in one hand and a grain sample bag in the other. Storrs also synchronized his sculpture with the building's Art Deco architecture, emphasizing the figure's streamlined form and employing modern materials. *Ceres* garnered a great deal of praise; a contemporary review stated that "this work has been described by some of the nation's leading architects as one of the finest pieces of architectural sculpture to be found in America." Perhaps in reaction to such favorable notices, Storrs produced smaller versions of the sculpture, such as this one.

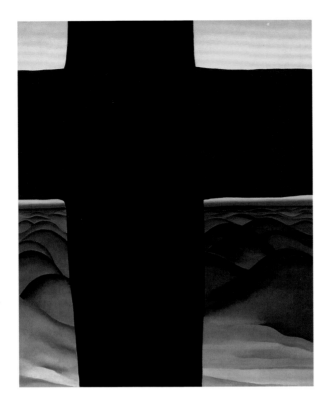

GEORGIA O'KEEFFE American, 1887–1986
Black Cross, New Mexico, 1929
Oil on canvas; 99.1 × 76.2 cm (39 × 30 in.)
Art Institute Purchase Fund, 1943.95

"I saw the crosses so often—and often in unexpected places—like a thin dark veil of the Catholic Church spread over the New Mexico landscape," said Georgia O'Keeffe about her first visit to Taos, New Mexico, in the summer of 1929. A member of the circle of avant-garde artists who exhibited at Alfred Stieglitz's gallery 291 in New York, O'Keeffe had married the progressive photographer and dealer (see p. 287) in 1924. What she encountered during late-night walks in the desert and then transformed into *Black Cross, New Mexico* were probably crosses erected near remote *moradas*, or chapels, by the secret Roman Catholic lay brotherhoods the Penitentes. As this pioneer of American modernism approached all of her subjects, whether buildings or flowers, landscapes or bones, here O'Keeffe magnified shapes and simplified details to underscore their essential beauty. She painted the cross just as she saw it: "big and strong, put together with wooden pegs," and behind it, "those hills . . . [that] go on and on—it was like looking at two miles of gray elephants." For O'Keeffe, "painting the crosses was a way of painting the country," a beloved region where, in 1949, she settled permanently and worked almost until her death at the age of ninety-eight.

GRANT WOOD American, 1891–1942
American Gothic, 1930
Oil on Beaver Board; 78 × 65.3 cm (30 ³/₄ × 25 ³/₄ in.)
Friends of American Art Collection, 1930.934

This familiar image was exhibited publicly for the first time at the Art Institute of Chicago, winning a three-hundred-dollar prize and instant fame for Grant Wood. The impetus for the painting came while Wood was visiting the small town of Eldon in his native Iowa. There he spotted a little wood farmhouse, with a single oversized window, made in a style called Carpenter Gothic. "I imagined American Gothic people with their faces stretched out long to go with this American Gothic house," he said. He used his sister and his dentist as models for a farmer and his daughter, dressing them as if they were "tintypes from my old family album." The highly detailed, polished style and the rigid frontality of the two figures were inspired by Flemish Renaissance art, which Wood studied during his travels to Europe between 1920 and 1928. After returning to settle in Iowa, he became increasingly appreciative of midwestern traditions and culture, which he celebrated in works such as this. *American Gothic*, often understood as a satirical comment on the midwestern character, quickly became one of America's most famous paintings and is now firmly entrenched in the nation's popular culture. Yet Wood intended it to be a positive statement about rural American values, an image of reassurance at a time of great dislocation and disillusionment. The man and woman, in their solid and well-crafted world, with all their strengths and weaknesses, represent survivors.

THOMAS HART BENTON American, 1889–1975

Cotton Pickers, 1945

Oil on canvas; 81.3 × 121.9 cm (32 × 48 in.)

Prior bequest of Alexander Stewart; Centennial Major Acquisitions Income and Welsley M. Dixon Jr. funds; Roger and J. Peter McCormick Endowments; prior acquisition of the George F. Harding Collection and Cyrus H. McCormick Fund; Quinn E. Delaney, American Art Sales Proceeds, Alyce and Edwin DeCosta and Walter E. Heller Foundation, and Goodman funds; prior bequest of Arthur Rubloff; Estate of Walter Aitken; Ada Turnbull Hertle and Mary and Leigh Block Endowment funds; prior acquisition of Mr. and Mrs. Frank G. Logan Purchase Prize; Marian and Samuel Klasstorner and Laura T. Magnuson Acquisition funds; prior acquisition of Friends of American Art Collection; Wirt D. Walker Trust; Jay W. McGreevy Endowment; Cyrus Hall McCormick Fund; Samuel A. Marx Purchase Fund for Major Aquisitions; Maurice D. Galleher Endowment; Alfred and May Tiefenbronner Memorial, Dr. Julian Archie, Gladys N. Anderson, and Simeon B. Williams funds; Capital Campaign General Aquisitions Endowment, and Benjamin Argile Memorial Fund, 2013.4

The American Regionalist Thomas Hart Benton painted *Cotton Pickers* based on notes of a trip he made to Georgia in the late 1920s. He depicted the dignity of the cotton pickers in the face of backbreaking labor and intense summer heat, rendering the dry fields and the working bodies in a sinuous, curvilinear style. Benton held progressive views on race, social relations, and politics, and he believed ardently that African American history was central to the understanding of American culture. Cotton sharecropping, an agricultural system that developed after the Civil War, allowed landowners to rent land to poor farmers in return for a share of the crops. Because sharecropping kept agricultural laborers impoverished, it became a symbol of a racially and economically unjust system. Cotton cultivation became one of Benton's most important subjects, especially as the rapid industrialization of the nation during World War II changed the American landscape.

EDWARD HOPPER American, 1882–1967
Nighthawks, 1942
Oil on canvas; 84.1 × 152.4 cm (33 ⅛ × 60 in.)
Friends of American Art Collection, 1942.51

Edward Hopper said that *Nighthawks* was inspired by "a restaurant on New York's Greenwich Avenue where two streets meet," but the image—with its carefully constructed composition and lack of narrative—has a timeless, universal quality that transcends its particular locale. One of the best-known images of twentieth-century art, the painting depicts an all-night diner in which three customers, all lost in their own thoughts, have congregated. Hopper's understanding of the expressive possibilities of light playing on simplified shapes gives the painting its beauty. Fluorescent lights had just come into use in the early 1940s, and the all-night diner emits an eerie glow, like a beacon on the dark street corner. Hopper eliminated any reference to an entrance, and the viewer, drawn to the light, is shut out from the scene by a seamless wedge of glass. The four anonymous and uncommunicative night owls seem as separate and remote from the viewer as they are from one another. (The red-haired woman was actually modeled by the artist's wife, Jo.) Hopper denied that he purposefully infused this or any other of his paintings with symbols of human isolation and urban emptiness, but he acknowledged that in *Nighthawks* "unconsciously, probably, I was painting the loneliness of a large city."

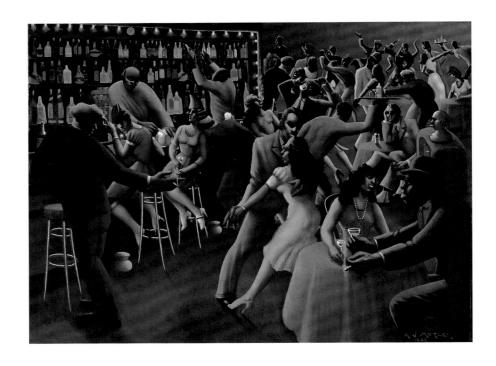

ARCHIBALD JOHN MOTLEY, JR. American, 1891–1981
Nightlife, 1943
Oil on canvas; 91.4 × 121.3 cm (36 × 47 ³/₄ in.)
Restricted gift of Mr. and Mrs. Marshall Field, Jack and Sandra Guthman, Ben W. Heineman, Ruth
Horwich, Lewis and Susan Manilow, Beatrice C. Mayer, Charles A. Meyer, John D. Nichols, and
Mr. and Mrs. E. B. Smith, Jr.; James W. Alsdorf Memorial Fund; Goodman Endowment, 1992.89

Chicago painter Archibald Motley represented the vibrancy of African American
culture, frequently portraying young, sophisticated city dwellers out on the town.
Nightlife depicts a crowded cabaret in the South Side neighborhood of Bronzeville,
with people seated around tables and at the bar. The clock reads one o'clock, and the
place is still hopping with drinkers and dancers. Two bartenders serve customers and
restock the well-lit display of liquor, and couples dance furiously in the background
to music provided by the jukebox at the right. The strange head atop the jukebox may
be a peanut-vending machine known as "Smilin' Sam from Alabam'"; when a coin
was inserted into the head and the tongue was pulled, the machine would dispense
peanuts. Motley unified the composition through his use of repeated forms and a
pervasive burgundy tone that bathes the entire scene in intense, unnatural light. (The
artist had seen Edward Hopper's *Nighthawks* at the Art Institute the year before and
was intrigued by his use of artificial light.) The stylized figures are tightly intercon-
nected; they are arranged along a sharp diagonal that compresses the space into a
stagelike setting. The dynamic composition and heightened colors vividly express the
liveliness of the scene, making *Nightlife* one of Motley's most celebrated paintings.

PETER BLUME American, born Russia (now Belarus), 1906–1992
The Rock, 1944/48
Oil on canvas; 146.4 × 188.9 cm (57 ⅝ × 74 ¾ in.)
Gift of Edgar Kaufmann, Jr., 1956.338

When it was exhibited at the Carnegie International in Pittsburgh in 1950, *The Rock* was voted the show's most popular painting. Peter Blume's dramatic image of a shattered but enduring rock must have struck a responsive chord with many post–World War II viewers. Displaying a startling juxtaposition of images, the work evokes Surrealist dreamscapes made even more vivid by meticulous brushwork inspired by fifteenth- and sixteenth-century northern European painting. Although Blume's imagery resists easy interpretation, the work suggests a parable of destruction and reconstruction. The jagged rock looms at the center of the composition, still upright despite the removal of its base by workers below. On the right, smoke billows around the charred timbers of a house, an image that might allude to the bombing of London during World War II. On the left, a new building, encased in scaffolding, rises as laborers in the foreground cart slabs of stone toward it. The new structure recalls Frank Lloyd Wright's famous Fallingwater (1935–37) in southwestern Pennsylvania, the residence for which Liliane and Edgar Kaufmann commissioned the painting. Their son Edgar Kaufmann Jr. donated *The Rock* to the Art Institute in 1956.

GEORGIA O'KEEFFE American, 1887–1986
Sky above Clouds IV, 1965
Oil on canvas; 243.8 × 731.5 cm (96 × 288 in.)
Restricted gift of the Paul and Gabriella Rosenbaum Foundation; gift of Georgia O'Keeffe, 1983.821

In her seventies, Georgia O'Keeffe traveled in an airplane for the first time and was fascinated at the view looking down on the earth and the clouds. Around 1963, working in Abiquiu, New Mexico, she began a series featuring endless expanses of clouds. Starting with a relatively realistic depiction of small white clouds on a three-by-four-foot canvas, she progressed to more stylized images of the motif on larger surfaces, ultimately extending her idea across a canvas that spanned the entire twenty-four-foot width of her garage in *Sky above Clouds IV*, the culmination of the series. The painting was scheduled for installation in a 1970 retrospective of O'Keeffe's work at the Whitney Museum of American Art, New York, the Art Institute of Chicago, and the San Francisco Museum of Art. *Sky above Clouds IV* was never shown in San Francisco, however, because it could not fit through any door of the museum. The painting remained on loan to the Art Institute for more than a decade while the artist and public-minded collectors of her art arranged for it to become part of the permanent collection. This continued the special relationship between O'Keeffe and the Art Institute, which dates to 1905, when she was briefly a student at the School of the Art Institute; in 1943 her first museum retrospective was organized at the Art Institute. O'Keeffe presented the museum with an important group of modernist works, including a number of her own, in 1949, and she continued to make significant additions to this bequest until her death in 1986.

KOHL CONTAINER IN THE SHAPE OF A PALM COLUMN
Egyptian, New Kingdom, mid-Dynasty 18 or 19 (1352–1213 BC)

Glass; 8.2 × 3 × 3 cm (3 ¼ × 1 ⅛ × 1 ⅛ in.)

Gift of Theodore W. and Frances S. Robinson, 1941.1084

Glassworking in Egypt appeared suddenly as a fully developed industry under the pharaohs of the Eighteenth Dynasty (1550–1295 BC) and was probably imported from the older glass centers of the Eastern Mediterranean. During this time glass production was restricted to a handful of workshops producing vessels and objects intended only for the pharaoh and his court. In addition to small glass objects such as beads, amulets, and inlays, the new industry produced a wide variety of glass vessels for unguents, incense, and cosmetics. Particularly popular were vessels like this example made to contain kohl, a black pigment used by both men and women to outline their eyes. The kohl was applied with a thin rod, and the containers were sealed with stoppers made of linen and wax. The shape of this object recalls a palm column, a traditional element of Egyptian architecture. The bright, opaque colors of these early core-formed glass vessels—dark blue, turquoise blue, red, yellow, and white—seem to emulate semiprecious stones such as lapis lazuli, turquoise, and jasper. The rarity of these glass works (only some five hundred complete examples are known) indicates that they were precious commodities.

COFFIN AND MUMMY OF PAANKHENAMUN

Egyptian, Third Intermediate
Period, Dynasty 22 (945–715 BC)

Cartonnage, gold leaf, and pigment, and human
remains; 170.2 × 43.2 × 31.7 cm (67 × 17 ×
12 ½ in.)

W. Moses Willner Fund, 1910.238

Mummification is the ancient Egyptian
funerary practice of drying out a corpse
for preservation. Anointed with oils
and spices and protected with amulets,
this linen-wrapped body was placed in
a series of nesting coffins; the vividly
painted cartonnage was the innermost
shell. Across the surface of the mummy
case, inscriptions and painted scenes
and symbols identify the deceased—
Paankhenamun (The One Who Lives for
Amun)—and proclaim his wish to live
well in the afterlife. Another inscription
records that he was the doorkeeper of
the temple of Amun. The names and
titles on the coffin suggest that he lived
at Thebes. The central scene depicts
the presentation of the deceased by the
falcon-headed deity Horus to Osiris, the
ruler of eternity (shown, as was common,
as a mummy). Other divinities help the
deceased in his journey to the afterlife.
Despite the youthful features of the gilt
face, X-rays reveal that Paankhenamun
was middle-aged.

STATUE OF PTAH-SOKAR-OSIRIS

Egyptian, Ptolemaic Period
(305–30 BC)

Wood, preparation layer, pigment, gold, and
textile; 62.9 × 27.3 × 12.7 cm (24 $^3/_4$ × 10 $^3/_4$ × 5 in.)

Gift of Phoenix Ancient Art, S.A., 2002.542

This beguiling statue represents the
funerary god Ptah-Sokar-Osiris. He is
shown here in the form of a mummy,
recalling the pivotal story in Egyptian
mythology when Osiris's body was reas-
sembled with bandages by Isis, his wife
and sister, after he had been murdered
and thrown into the Nile River by his
brother, Seth. Exceptionally well preserved, the statue was assembled from
three pieces of wood, coated with a
preparation layer, and then decorated
with brilliant gold leaf and vivid polychromy. Ptah-Sokar-Osiris wears a headdress of feathers and horns, and a false
beard is attached to his face, which is
gilded, reflecting the belief that gods
had skin of gold.

Equally striking are the hieroglyphs
on the front and back of the statue indicating that it was made for a woman
named Ese-ir-dies (Isis Is the One Who
Made Her). The text also asks the king
to make offerings to Osiris, so that in
return the god will provide the dead
woman with "beer, bread, and every
good and pure thing on which the god
lives" to sustain her in the afterlife.
Osirid figurines were often included
among tomb furnishings to assist the
dead on their journey into the afterlife.

PAIR OF PROTOMES DEPICTING THE FOREPART OF A GRIFFIN
Greek; probably Samos, 625/575 BC

Bronze and bone or ivory; left: 20.3 × 7.6 × 7.6 cm (8 × 3 × 3 in.); right: 21.6 × 8.3 × 7 cm (8 ½ × 3 ¼ × 2 ¾ in.)

Katherine K. Adler Memorial Fund, 1994.38.1–2

The great holy sites of ancient Greece, such as the sanctuary of Zeus at Olympia and the Heraion of Samos, functioned as repositories for gifts brought by believers seeking divine favor. The most impressive of these offerings were large bronze cauldrons, which were set on a conical stand or tripod base and embellished with cast-bronze attachments like these two griffins. These beasts, facing outward, would have been fastened to the vessel by means of the rivets still present on their collars. This hollow-cast pair is remarkable for the superb quality of their craftsmanship, their condition, and their partially preserved inlaid eyes.

A mythical creature revered for its protective powers, the griffin combined a feline body, an avian head, and tall, horse-like ears. It has been argued that the beaked Protoceratops that once roamed Central Asia were the iconographic inspiration for these ferocious beasts. Travelers may have seen the fantastic fossilized remains of the dinosaurs and then created stories to account for them. Meanwhile, local inhabitants may have spread tales about their ferocity as a way to discourage marauders from looting their wealth. These two griffins are highly agitated; their mouths are agape and their tongues curl up as they screech bloodcurdling warnings.

AMPHORA (STORAGE JAR)

Etruscan, 530/520 BC

Attributed to the Ivy Leaf Group

Terra-cotta, decorated in the black-figure technique; 38.7 × 27.9 cm (15 ¼ × 11 in.);

diam.: 19.4 cm (5 ⅝ in.)

Katherine K. Adler Memorial Fund, 2009.75

During the sixth and fifth centuries BC, the Etruscans, who lived north of Rome, increasingly imported Athenian ceramics decorated with scenes of Greek mythology, religion, and daily life. Made of fine, iron-rich clay that fired orange, decorated with a rich black gloss, and sometimes embellished with white and purple-red details, the ceramic vessels produced in Athens were the finest of Classical antiquity.

Etruscan artists, no doubt eager to capitalize on the high demand for Greek vases, and perhaps also hoping to attract customers unable to afford the imported wares, set up a workshop, probably at Vulci, to produce facsimiles of the Athenian vases. This vessel's attenuated proportions and symmetrical profile create an especially elegant shape that belies the somewhat coarse texture of the local Etruscan clay from which it is made. The clay's poor quality also stymied attempts to replicate the highly refined surface finishes of Athenian vases. Nevertheless, the painter of this vase skillfully composed his scenes within trapezoidal picture fields bounded above by a decorative pattern of interlacing lotus buds and dots and along its sides by a single line. On the front, a hound looks back at a horse and hunter, while a stag and hare flee for their lives on the back.

FOOT OF A CISTA (STORAGE BOX)

Etruscan; probably Vulci, early 5th century BC

Bronze; 15.6 × 10.4 × 5.4 cm (6 ¹/₈ × 4 ¹/₈ × 2 ¹/₈ in.)

Katherine K. Adler Memorial Fund, 1999.559

With a bent-knee pose that connotes rapid movement, the Etruscan sun god Usil dashes across breaking waves, borne aloft by wings on his back and boots. Except for his footgear, he is nude. His arms extend away from his muscular body, which twists at the waist to face forward. This splendid figure was cast in one piece together with its support, which comprises stylized waves above a beaded band and a flat Ionic capital that tapers down to the paw of a feline creature that has unusually thick, fleshy pads.

With locally abundant sources of copper and modest amounts of tin, Etruscan metalsmiths excelled in fashioning a variety of beautiful bronze objects, including lamp stands, incense burners, mirrors, vessels, and containers. This remarkable object was one of three identical feet supporting a cista, or lidded chest, typically used by women to store their cosmetics and toiletries. The body of the chest was fashioned from a sheet of hammered bronze, and it was probably incised with intricate illustrations of mythological or other scenes. That part is now lost; only the solid-cast feet that once supported it survive. Its now-missing lid likely had an equally exquisite figural handle that would also have been solid cast.

BELLY-AMPHORA (STORAGE JAR)
Greek; Athens, 550/540 BC
Attributed to the Painter of Berlin 1686 or the Painter of Tarquinia RC 3984
Terra-cotta, decorated in the black-figure technique; 28.2 × 21.1 cm (10 ³/₄ × 8 ¹/₄ in.)
Katherine K. Adler Memorial Fund, 1978.114

Ancient artists frequently depicted events from the life of the demigod Herakles, especially the Twelve Labors he had to complete to attain immortality. On this amphora (storage jar) the great hero completes his first assignment—to kill a lion with an invincible hide that was terrorizing the village of Nemea. Here the contest has been decided; Herakles strangles the lion, whose jaws he has pried open with his bare hands. To the right stand Athena and Hermes; on the other stand a nymph and Iolaos, Herakles's nephew and companion. In subsequent episodes, Herakles often wears the lion's pelt, either as a headdress or over his arm, as a protective cloak.

These vases were used for the transport and storage of items such as wine and olives, and they were given as prizes in athletic competitions. Many vases have been damaged, either in antiquity or in modern times, and repaired. However, this amphora remains intact, with only a few losses, such as the chips on the rim, and some surface abrasion. The vivid white gloss that highlights the women's skin and the shield is especially well preserved.

STAMNOS (MIXING JAR)

Greek; Athens, c. 450 BC
Attributed to the Chicago Painter

Terra-cotta, decorated in the red-figure technique; 37 × 41.9 cm (14 ⁵/₈ × 16 ¹/₂ in.)

Gift of Philip D. Armour and Charles L. Hutchinson, 1889.22a–b

This refined Athenian stamnos (*pl.* stamnoi) was used to mix water and wine. Also valued for its beauty, this red-figure vessel (so called because the figures remain the natural color of the clay) portrays either Greek women or maenads, female participants in rites celebrating Dionysos, the god of wine. But unlike the frenzied and whirling figures of other Greek vases, these women convey calm, even elegance. This tender serenity, coupled with a softer, somewhat freer form, is a hallmark of the artist (referred to as the Chicago Painter because of this vase) and has been used to identify other works by him, principally similar stamnoi. Working in the potters' quarter of mid-fifth-century BC Athens, the painter was active during the construction of the Parthenon, the stylistic influence of which can be seen here. He worked closely with a master potter whose vases were individually shaped in a prescribed range of configurations. With refined designs that are gracefully adapted to its shape, this stamnos is a fine example of red-figure painting during the Classical era. It retains its original lid, a rarity among ancient vases.

TETRADRACHM (COIN) PORTRAYING ALEXANDER THE GREAT

Greek; minted in Ephesus, Asia Minor, 306/281 BC

Silver; diam. 3.1 cm; 16.78 g

Gift of Martin A. Ryerson, 1922.4924

Following the premature death of Alexander the Great in 323 BC, his generals, friends, and heirs engaged in forty years of wars over his empire. Lysimachus (r. 323–281 BC), one of Alexander's companions and bodyguards, used the king's image on his own coins in order to cast himself in the role of successor and legitimize his claim to the kingdom of Thrace. Alexander, responsible for establishing the conventions of royal portraiture, is depicted in his preferred manner: youthful and clean-shaven, with long locks of hair rising above his forehead and eyes cast upward. Additionally, he is shown with horns curling around his ears. These "horns of Ammon" symbolize Alexander's claim that he was the son of the Egyptian god Ammon—a claim reportedly confirmed by the oracle at the sanctuary of Zeus-Ammon at Siwa, Egypt.

On the reverse of the coin, Lysimachus exerts his own royal autonomy by naming himself "king." The goddesses Athena and Nike (Greek for "victory") crown his name with laurels, which symbolized victory or honor. The lion on the shield at Athena's side references Lysimachus's famous exploit of killing a lion with his bare hands and reinforces his association with Alexander, who used the skin of the Nemean lion as a symbol of power and courage.

ATTACHMENTS DEPICTING BUSTS OF SILENOI
Roman, mid-1st century BC/mid-1st century AD

Bronze, silver, and copper; left: 17.8 × 14.6 × 8.6 cm (7 × 5 ³/₄ × 3 ³/₈ in.); right: 18.7 × 16.2 × 8.9 cm (7 ³/₈ × 6 ³/₈ × 4 ¹/₂ in.)

Katherine K. Adler Memorial Fund, 1997.554.1–2

The Greek imagination was populated with a number of strange creatures. When their thoughts turned to wine, Greeks pictured mischievous young satyrs, the half-human, half-horse creatures who frolicked, danced, and chased hapless maenads. Satyrs symbolized suppressed hedonistic desires that were unleashed by the intoxicating elixir of the wine god Dionysos, known to the Romans as Bacchus. These creatures are mature satyrs, or silenoi (*sing.* silenos), and they once served as decorative elements for a type of couch on which elite, well-to-do Romans reclined at lavish banquets. Because wine was served at these festive events, creatures from Dionysos's entourage were popular subjects for such furniture attachments.

Each object is made of two pieces that were cast separately and fastened together. The proper right arm of the left silenos is lost, but the right one retains his separately made left arm. It and the wineskin slung over the corresponding shoulder were cast as one piece. The sclerae, or whites of their eyes, are silver, as are their teeth; furthermore, their lips were once inlaid with copper. Their remarkably animated facial expressions, with their furrowed brows and slightly parted lips, can be read as conveying pathos, perplexity, or perhaps inebriated befuddlement.

CAMEO PORTRAYING EMPEROR CLAUDIUS AS JUPITER

Cameo: Roman; Italy, AD 41/54; mount: Italian, late 16th century

Cameo: sardonyx; mount: gold, enamel, and pearls; with mount: 7.6 × 5.7 × 0.8 cm (3 × 2 ¼ × ⁵⁄₁₆ in.)

Gift of Marilynn B. Alsdorf, 1991.375

This exquisite cameo is thought to combine a portrait of the fourth Roman emperor, Claudius (r. AD 41–54), and the powerfully muscled body of Rome's supreme deity, Jupiter. The figure is nude except for an aegis (protective garment) wrapped around his right thigh, modestly drawn across his body, and draped over his left arm. A laurel wreath is tied around his head. A long scepter rests against his left forearm, and he holds a thunderbolt in his right hand. An eagle watches him from the ground. The aegis, thunderbolt, and eagle are symbols of Jupiter; the scepter and laurel wreath are those of the imperial office. Conjoined, they identify the emperor as the father-god, Jupiter, the supreme deity of the Roman pantheon.

A virtuoso gem engraver delicately coaxed his design from a single piece of sard-onyx comprising three thin, horizontal layers of naturally occurring colors (golden brown, white, and a dark blue-gray, respectively). He painstakingly removed the extraneous stone in order to carve the low-relief figures of Claudius and the eagle against the dark background, retaining a sufficient amount of stone around the perimeter to create a beveled border from the opaque layers of white and brown.

PORTRAIT HEAD OF EMPEROR HADRIAN
Roman, AD 130/38

Marble; 36 × 27.5 × 27.3 cm (14 1/4 × 10 7/8 × 10 3/4 in.)

Katherine K. Adler Memorial Fund, 1979.350

Of all the Roman emperors, Hadrian (r. AD 117–38) is the one whose portrait is most frequently found, across the empire from Britain to Persia, from Asia Minor to Egypt. Furthermore, among all his portraits, few equal this likeness in conveying the complex character of the emperor who inherited the Roman world at its greatest extent from Trajan (r. AD 98–117). Hadrian traveled widely, spending more than half of his twenty-one-year reign outside of Italy visiting the provinces, and he commissioned buildings, aqueducts, and roads in many cities. Citizens responded to his generosity by erecting numerous statues in his honor, and after his death he was deified and revered as a god.

Hadrian greatly admired the Greeks. Unlike previous emperors, who were clean-shaven, he wore a beard, perhaps in emulation of the Greek philosophers whom he so revered. Here his closely cropped beard contrasts with the thick, luxurious curls that frame his face. The eyes were enlivened through the drilling of pupils and the incising of irises, innovative features that were introduced into portraiture during his reign, likely around AD 130.

PORTRAIT BUST OF A WOMAN
Roman, mid-2nd century AD

Marble; 64.8 × 47.6 × 27.3 cm (25 ½ × 18 ¾ × 10 ¾ in.)

Restricted gift of the Antiquarian Society in honor of Ian Wardropper, the Classical Art Society, Mr. and Mrs. Isak V. Gerson, James and Bonnie Pritchard, and Mrs. Hugo Sonnenschein; Mr. and Mrs. Kenneth Bro Fund; Katherine K. Adler, Mr. and Mrs. Walter Alexander in honor of Ian Wardropper, David Earle III, William A. and Renda H. Lederer Family, Chester D. Tripp, and Jane B. Tripp endowments, 2002.11

Carved by a sculptor of exceptional talent, this exquisite portrait bust depicts an elegant Roman woman of wealth and distinction. The subject bears a solemn expression as she looks to her left, which affords a tantalizing glimpse of her intricate hairstyle. The wavy locks that frame her face are combed to the back, where they are woven into numerous braids, nearly all of which are wound into a heavy, multitiered bun worn at the upper part of the back of the head. This coiffure emulates a type worn by Faustina the Elder (d. AD 141), wife of Emperor Antoninus Pius (r. AD 138–61), suggesting that she lived during this period. A gem-encrusted diadem encircles the subject's head, alluding to her elevated social standing. Her garments are similarly luxurious, including her crisply pleated, gap-sleeved tunic, which is so thinly carved that light passes through parts of the marble. Out of modesty she also wears an overgarment, its deep folds indicating a thick material, possibly wool. Draped low across her torso, the mantle reveals the gentle swell of her right breast, an unusual feature of Roman busts of this period.

RELIEF OF A FALLING WARRIOR
Roman, 2nd century AD

Marble; 53.3 × 81 × 17.5 cm (21 × 31 ¹⁵/₁₆ × 6 ⁷/₈ in.)

Gift of Alfred E. Hamill, 1928.257

Around 435 BC, the Greek sculptor Phidias adorned the front of the shield at the side
of his gold-and-ivory statue of Athena in the Parthenon with scenes of Greeks bat-
tling Amazons in the Trojan War. In Roman times, certain figures from this complex
struggle were lifted out of their original context and enlarged to become decorative
reliefs for the walls of a colonnade or courtyard.

Here a wounded Greek warrior collapses to the ground after being struck a mortal
blow from behind. The dying warrior's noble countenance, the fillet or ribbon tied
around his forehead, and his powerful, athletic body epitomize what Phidias and his
pupils sought to project as the ideal of mature male dignity in the decade when Athens
was at the height of its power in the eastern Mediterranean world. Some five centuries
later, collectors such as the Roman emperor Hadrian sought this Phidian style, translated from a circular golden shield to a rectangular marble relief, to decorate their
palaces and villas. Athenian sculptors of the Roman era made a good living creating
and exporting such memories of past glories. This relief and a number of others were
found near Athens in the harbor of Piraeus, where they had been lost in a disaster,
likely while awaiting shipment.

SOLIDUS (COIN) PORTRAYING EMPEROR CONSTANTINE I

Roman; minted in Antioch,
late AD 324/early AD 325

Gold; diam. 1.9 cm; 4.48 g

Gift of Martin A. Ryerson, 1922.4903

In AD 313, Constantine I (c. 272–337,
r. 306–37) and his coruler Licinius
(c. 265–325, r. 308–24) jointly issued
the Edict of Milan, which aimed to end
religious intolerance by granting legal
rights to Christians and ordering the return of their confiscated property. This
solidus, bearing a large profile portrait
of Constantine wearing a laurel crown,
was issued during the period in which
Constantine both defeated Licinius to
become sole emperor and sponsored
the First Council of Nicaea (325), whose
goal was to establish the nature of Jesus
and his relation to God the Father. Bap-
tized on his deathbed, Constantine is
honored as the first Christian emperor,
and his reign marks the beginning of
the Christianization of the empire. He
transferred the capital of the Roman
Empire to ancient Byzantium, which was
renamed Constantinople in his honor.

HISTAMENON (COIN) PORTRAY-ING ROMANOS III ARGYROS WITH CHRIST ENTHRONED

Byzantine; minted in Constantinople
(now Istanbul), AD 1028/34

Gold; diam. 2.5 cm; 4.4 g

Gift of Mrs. Emily Crane Chadbourne, 1940.25

Romanos III Argyros (c. AD 968–1034,
r. 1028–34) was marked for succes-
sion to the throne by his father-in-law,
Constantine VIII, whose reign lasted
only three years. Romanos managed a
six-year reign that was riddled with ill-
conceived and poorly executed policies,
including a disastrous attempt to reform
taxation that left the empire's finances
in disarray and drove the less fortunate
into enforced servitude. In an effort to
halt the growing threat posed by Arabs
along the eastern frontier, Romanos personally led the army to confront them,
only to be thoroughly routed in a sur-
prise attack. Later conquests and victo-
ries did little to improve his reputation,
and he died, possibly at the hands or
order of his entirely disillusioned wife,
Zoe. On the front of this histamenon,
the enthroned and haloed Jesus holds
the Gospel book in his right hand. The
inscription reads "Jesus Christ, King of
Kings." On the reverse, the Virgin Mary
crowns the richly bedecked Romanos,
who holds a *globus cruciger*, indicating
that the emperor wields earthly power
on behalf of the Christian God.

DANIEL HUDSON BURNHAM American, 1846–1912
EDWARD HERBERT BENNETT American, born England, 1874–1954
DELINEATED BY JULES GUÉRIN American, 1866–1946
View of the City from Jackson Park to Grant Park, Looking Towards the West
(detail), 1907, plate 49 from *Plan of Chicago*, 1909
Rendered by Jules Guérin (American, 1866–1946)
Watercolor and graphite on paper; 103.5 × 480 cm (41 × 189 in.)
On permanent loan to the Art Institute of Chicago from the City of Chicago, 2.148.1966

"Make no little plans," Daniel H. Burnham reputedly exclaimed around the time he unveiled his *Plan of Chicago*, the first comprehensive metropolitan plan in the United States. Providing the vocabulary for Chicago architecture through the 1920s, the project was the legacy of Burnham, whose renown in large-scale city planning began when he was chief of construction for Chicago's 1893 World's Columbian Exposition. Commissioned by the Commercial Club of Chicago, the plan was developed with the assistance of architect Edward H. Bennett, who elaborated parts of it after Burnham's death in 1912 and was responsible for executing many of its recommendations. Emulating the grand classical design of European cities, Chicago was to become "a Paris by the Lake." Features included the development of Chicago's lakefront and Lake Shore Drive, the construction of Grant Park, and the transformation of Michigan Avenue into a premier commercial boulevard following the completion of the Michigan Avenue bridge. Eleven of the seventeen perspective views were rendered by Burnham's frequent collaborator, the Beaux-Arts-trained Jules Guérin. The draftsman's stunning, impressionistic views, with their unusual perspectives and dramatic use of color, bring the *Plan of Chicago* to life, imbuing it, as Burnham stated about his own aims, with the "magic to stir men's blood."

WALTER BURLEY GRIFFIN American, 1876–1937
DELINEATED BY MARION MAHONY GRIFFIN American, 1871–1962
Rock Crest–Rock Glen: Perspective Rendering, c. 1912
Lithograph and gouache on green satin; 59 × 201 cm (23 ¼ × 79 ⅛ in.)
Gift of Marion Mahony Griffin through Eric Nicholls, 1988.182

Walter Burley and Marion Mahony Griffin were exceptional figures in the Prairie
School, for they not only designed individual buildings but also planned housing
developments, universities, and entire cities. In their partnership (formed in 1911 at
the time of their marriage), Walter Burley Griffin was chief designer, while Marion
Mahony, one of the nation's first women to distinguish herself in architecture, contrib-
uted to design and produced the spectacular renderings for which the firm was
noted. In this exquisite work, she delineated the pair's major domestic work and the
most important planning scheme of the Prairie School: the Iowa housing development Rock Crest–Rock Glen (begun in 1912). The vaguely Japanesque intertwining
of single-family dwellings within the eighteen-acre site is a perfect encapsulation of
the Prairie School's emphasis on the harmonious integration of suburban domesticity
and a tamed, almost pastoral, nature. Of the sixteen proposed houses, eight were
built, four by the Griffins. Just as construction began, the couple won the international competition to plan Canberra, the new capital of Australia; the commission
allowed them to bring their aesthetic to an international audience.

FRANK LLOYD WRIGHT American, 1867–1959
Avery Coonley Playhouse: Triptych Window, 1912

Clear and colored leaded glass in oak frames; center panel: 89.5 × 109.2 cm (35 ¼ × 43 in.); each side panel: 91.4 × 19.7 cm (36 × 7 ¾ in.)

Restricted gift of Dr. and Mrs. Edwin J. DeCosta and the Walter E. Heller Foundation, 1986.88

This colorful, whimsical triptych window is from the Avery Coonley Playhouse, a small structure that Frank Lloyd Wright designed as an addition to the Coonleys' suburban Chicago estate, which he had previously completed in 1908. Louis Sullivan's foremost student, Wright continued his teacher's search for an indigenous American architecture. Like Sullivan, Wright drew inspiration from nature and natural forms, and both men were pioneers of the Prairie Shool of architecture, characterized by low-slung, horizontal lines and rambling, open spaces that reflect the gently rolling landscape of the Midwest. Odes to the middle-class American family at the turn of the century, Wright's residences are organic, designed not only to adapt to a family's changing structure but also to contain the sense of a unified and harmonious whole. Every detail of the Coonley complex, like all of Wright's projects, bore his personal imprint, down to the creation and placement of the furniture and the design of this window. Referencing such Americana as the flag and colored balloons, Wright explored the use of glass both as a transparent screen uniting exterior and interior and as a decorative element, the colors and design of which anticipate the later abstractions of Piet Mondrian (see p. 212).

LOUIS H. SULLIVAN American, 1856–1924
Impromptu!, 1922, plate 16 from *A System of Architectural Ornament*, 1924
Graphite on Strathmore paper; 57.7 × 73.5 cm (22 ³/₄ × 29 in.)
Commissioned by the Art Institute of Chicago, 1988.15.16

In 1922 the Art Institute's recently opened Burnham Library of Architecture commissioned Louis Sullivan to make drawings illustrating his renowned theories of architectural ornament. These masterpieces were published together as *A System of Architectural Ornament, According with a Philosophy of Man's Powers* by the American Institute of Architects in 1924; this was Sullivan's final statement about the geometry underlying both natural and man-made forms. In his search for an original American architecture, Sullivan drew his inspiration from nature, not unlike the nineteenth-century American poets and writers whom he emulated. Like them, he intended ornament to function evocatively as well as to represent organic growth, evolving from closed geometric units to open, efflorescent forms. In *Impromptu!*, the sixteenth of the twenty delicate drawings in his treatise, Sullivan produced one of his most open, vibrant, and fluent compositions. Giving free rein to expansive whiplash appendages and spiral stalks, the architect combined nature's infinite creative variation and incessant change with an intense emotional expressionism. To convey these poetic nuances, Sullivan's correlating notation describes the design as entering "the domain of Virtuosity, Romance and Symbolism."

LUDWIG MIES VAN DER ROHE American, born Germany, 1886–1969
Court House Studies: Interior Views Showing Steel Columns, c. 1931–38
Ink on paper, mounted on archival board (one of two sheets); 21.4 × 29.9 cm (8 $^{7}/_{16}$ × 11 $^{3}/_{4}$ in.)
Gift of A. James Speyer, 1981.937

Ludwig Mies van der Rohe is widely recognized as one of the most influential figures in the development of modern architecture. Operating on the principle of "less is more," he utilized materials such as industrial steel and plate glass in his strikingly minimal designs, which are notably free of decorative forms. As director of the German Bauhaus during the early 1930s, Mies formalized his notion of unifying form with function. In 1937 he immigrated to Chicago, where he became director of the School of Architecture at the Armour Institute of Technology (later the Illinois Institute of Technology). His legacy is still felt in the school program's stress on the fundamentals, materials, and function of architectural design. This *Court House Study* depicts a vast, open interior in which two slender columns provide the only visible means of support. The wide-angle perspective emphasizes the building's strong horizontal character. A nearly seamless wall of glass fills living areas with light and dissolves the boundary between interior and exterior.

R. BUCKMINSTER FULLER American, 1895–1983
Dymaxion Car: Section, 1933
Ink on tracing paper; 34.3 × 91 cm (13 ½ × 35 ¹³⁄₁₆ in.)
Through prior gift of Three Oaks Wrecking Company, 1990.167.1

Trained in engineering, Buckminster Fuller made significant contributions to disciplines including architecture, industrial design, philosophy, and social science. Central to all his endeavors was a holistic understanding of the universe and a desire to use science and technology in a sustainable manner to better serve mankind and the planet. Fuller coined the term *dymaxion* to label his inventions that applied available technology to provide the greatest possible efficiency. In 1927 he began investigating designs that would revolutionize transportation. Fuller used existing automotive parts and boat and airplane technology to design the *Dymaxion Car*, which debuted to an awed public at the 1933 Century of Progress Exposition in Chicago. The aerodynamic bullet shape and lightweight aluminum chassis enabled the car to reach speeds of 120 miles per hour, and consumed thirty miles per gallon. The three-wheeled vehicle had exceptional maneuverability due to its rear-wheel drivetrain. Fuller refined the design in the 1940s, but a prototype proved prohibitively expensive to manufacture. Although considered too radical to mass-produce at the time, Fuller's *Dymaxion Car* presaged many features considered standard in today's automobiles.

BERTRAND GOLDBERG American, 1913–1997
River City: Aerial Perspective, 1979
Ink and pencil on tracing paper; 45.6 × 57.9 cm (18 × 22 ³/₄ in.)
The Archive of Bertrand Goldberg, gifted by his children through his estate, Rx23664/110.279

In 1932 eighteen-year-old Bertrand Goldberg left his native Chicago to study at the
Bauhaus in Germany, becoming one of the first Americans to work under the guid-
ance of Ludwig Mies van der Rohe. The next year, he returned home and worked at
various Chicago firms until he founded his own practice in 1937. He is best known
for Chicago's Marina Towers, America's first mixed-use urban-housing complex,
which he completed in 1967. Two decades later, Goldberg made plans for the even
more ambitious River City. Conceived as part of a huge marina along the south
branch of the Chicago River, the development was to consist of a vast complex of
linked towers housing thousands of residents. Believing that architecture should
address the needs of the many, Goldberg envisioned River City as a self-sufficient
environment that would foster a sense of community. Six clusters of seventy-two-
story buildings, featuring the architect's now trademark curvilinear concrete shell
construction and cantilevered balconies, would wind a serpentine path along the
river's edge. Although the full scope of River City was never realized, a scaled-back
version was built in 1987. Despite its diminished proportions, River City drew high
praise and was hailed by the *New York Times* as "a remarkable space, unusually
lyrical and soft in feeling for a structure finished in harsh concrete."

STANLEY TIGERMAN American, born 1930
The Titanic, 1978
Photomontage on paper; approx. 28 × 35.7 cm (11 ¹⁄₁₆ × 14 in.)
Gift of Stanley Tigerman, 1984.802

The groundbreaking innovations of Ludwig Mies van der Rohe left a lasting impact
on both the practice and teaching of architecture in the United States, especially in
Chicago. As director of the School of Architecture at the Illinois Institute of Technology, Mies stressed the importance of bold, clean designs based on structure,
materials, and function. Stanley Tigerman was among the many architects schooled
in the Miesian tradition, and he based much of his work in the 1960s and 1970s
on the designs of the famed architect. Tigerman's restless curiosity and iconoclastic
spirit, however, led him to question the authority and durability of Mies's program.
The Titanic is a conceptual project that was meant to provoke architects to contend
with the Mies legacy, challenging them to choose sides: move beyond Mies or remain
cemented to the past. The photocollage pitches Mies's Crown Hall (1950–56), one of
the architect's most iconic and revered designs, into the deep. Tigerman mailed
copies of the work to members of the architectural establishment, including an offer
of a one-way ticket on the *Titanic*. Although the title of the work portends the end
of Mies's dominance, Tigerman acknowledged that many would see the building as
rising back to the surface, ever triumphant.

GAROFALO ARCHITECTS American, 1993–2010
Markow House: Design Drawings, 1997–98
Color computer print on paper; 91.4 × 61.7 cm (36 × 24 ⁵⁄₈ in.)
Gift of Douglas Garofalo, 2000.471.2

The Chicago firm Garofalo Architects was an early leader in digital architecture. The firm's Markow House represents the studio's initial foray into digital production methods, and it is one of the first realized residences created through this new technology. Using animation software, principal Douglas Garofalo conceived a 2,000-square-foot addition that radically reworked the Markows' 1960s split-level home in suburban Chicago, allowing interior and exterior spaces to break free of compartmentalized conformity. This digital rendering, called an exploded axonometric diagram, shows the layers of forms and shapes that constitute the building. Rather than conceal the existing structure, Garofalo chose to maintain the twin-gabled rear and create a dramatically different front facade that emphasizes the home's hybrid nature. The angular, folding roof planes are visible from all sides, and the exterior walls are boldly painted purple, blue, gray, and yellow. In the interior, a network of glass walkways and ramps weaves in and out of the structure. Garofalo transformed this typical suburban Chicago residence into a spatially complex, dynamic structure that stands apart from the surrounding architecture.

TOKUJIN YOSHIOKA Japanese, born 1967
Honey-Pop Armchair, 2001
Honeycomb-paper construction; unfolded, 79.4 × 81.3 × 81.3 cm (31 × 32 × 32 in.)
Restricted gift of the Architecture & Design Society, 2007.111

Tokujin Yoshioka's unfettered creativity was greatly nurtured by fashion designer Issey Miyake, who hired the young designer in 1988. Yoshioka's lack of specific fashion training left him free to experiment with unexpected materials. The designer's *Honey-Pop Armchair* defies the notion of furniture as merely functional. Both sculptural and ethereal, the chair, made entirely of paper, plays upon the intangible idea of an object and the materiality of its being. Without an underlying frame, the chair is supported entirely by a complex of hexagons made out of 120 layers of paper glued together. The name *Honey-Pop* refers not only to its appearance as a giant honeycomb but also to the legacy of Pop Art, which championed commonplace yet unorthodox materials. The *Honey-Pop Armchair* debuted at the 2002 Milan International Furniture Fair. In assembly-line fashion, Yoshioka laid out a thick roll of the layered paper, cutting out seat shapes, which he opened up like a book to create the chair and reveal its seemingly insubstantial honeycomb structure. To show its tensile strength, the artist sat on the chair, demonstrating how the weight of his body actually fixed the paper folds into place.

HELLA JONGERIUS Dutch, born 1963
Repeat Dot Textile (detail), 2002
Manufactured by Maharam
Cotton, polyester, and rayon upholstery; unfolded, 79.4 × 81.3 × 81.3 cm
(31 × 32 × 32 in.)
Gift of Maharam, 2007.114.4

Collaboration with designers has become a hallmark of the New York–based textile firm Maharam, adding dynamic partnerships with renowned contemporary designers to their important archive of midcentury reissues. Maharam often commissions designs from practitioners whose primary work lies outside textile design—an approach that results in a wide range of critical artistic engagements with the medium. Hella Jongerius's 2002 *Repeat Dot* takes inspiration from her close observation of the manufacturing process in textile mills producing Maharam designs. Focusing on the technology and by-products used to create woven fabrics, this work recalls the perforations of punch cards used to program Jacquard looms, overlaid with white screen-printing that mimics the codes and handwritten notes used to make changes to fabric samples. Her *Repeat* series also has a unique means of application as the repeats of different patterns of the design occur at wide intervals, offering users a level of customization by choosing to use one or more of the patterns in a single piece of fabric.

HERNÁN DÍAZ ALONSO American, born Argentina 1969
XERFIROTARCH American, founded 2001
Sur, Long Island City, New York, 2005
Acrylic and nylon; 7.6 × 61 × 33 cm (3 × 24 × 13 in.)
Department of Architecture and Design Purchase Fund, 2006.311

Since its inception in the early 1990s, digital architecture has moved into widening
frontiers, fusing with other disciplines to enable unexpected formal explorations
and generate new typologies that are changing the way in which structures are aes-
theticized and fabricated. As the field has matured, Hernan Díaz Alonso, principal
architect of the Los Angeles firm Xefirotarch, has emerged as a significant figure;
his studio's grotesque, animal-like forms exemplify just how far digital practice has
evolved. Shown here is the model for *Sur,* the firm's winning entry for the Museum of
Modern Art/P.S.1 Young Architects Program. The piece is composed of an acrylic
surface that supports three-dimensional forms printed from nylon composite. The
actual pavilion was constructed of bent aluminum tubing clad with reflective fabric
sheathing and fiberglass benches and platforms painted Ferrari red. The title *Sur,*
taken from a popular Argentine tango, refers to the rhythmic forms of the work. While
Díaz Alonso draws freely from a wide range of visual-arts disciplines—especially film
and video—he combines these influences with digital manipulation and distortion to
explore the limits of beauty and scale. His constructions reintroduce an experimental
notion of figuration to the pedagogy and practice of digital architecture.

STUDIO GANG ARCHITECTS American, founded 1997
JEANNE GANG American, born 1964
Aqua Tower: Presentation Model, 2005
Acrylic; 106.7 × 40.6 × 40.6 cm (42 × 16 × 16 in.)
Restricted gift of the Architecture & Design Society, 2011.115

Studio Gang's 82-story Aqua Tower is among Chicago's most important tall buildings of the 2000s. The tower's urban context helped determine its undulating exterior, resulting in unique concrete balconies designed to give residents views of specific Chicago landmarks, control solar exposure, and create sight lines between neighbors that can encourage socializing and a sense of community. Evoking the flow of wind, water, and topography, the building was designed and constructed with a combination of digital and analogue techniques to create mass-produced, yet custom-made, forms. Aqua Tower fuses Studio Gang's rigorous research process with a dedication to strong architectural expression.

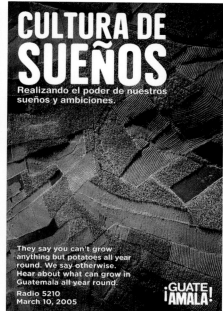

BRUCE MAU Canadian, born 1959
¡GuateAmala! Posters, 2006
Paper; 91.4 × 61.7 cm (36 × 24 ⅝ in.)
Gift of Bruce Mau, 2009.62.1–2

Working across all fields of visual communications, Bruce Mau strives to make works of social significance and meaning. Invited by the Fundación Proyecto de Vida, a collective of Guatemalan leaders, to create a campaign that would encourage Guatemalans to think positively about their country's future, Mau's studio created ¡GuateAmala!, which translated from Spanish means "To love Guatemala." This attention-grabbing slogan began as the centerpiece of a series of projects launched in 2006 that included the posters shown here. Installed across the country, these vibrant works—featuring local inhabitants and portraying the rich culture and heritage of Guatemala—became a provocative communication tool.

GREG LYNN American, born 1964
Flatware, 2007
Sterling silver; dimensions variable; length of knife: 23 cm (9 ⅛ in.)
Celia and David Hilliard Fund; restricted gift of the Architecture & Design Society, 2007.646.1–5

The flatware that architect and designer Greg Lynn created for Alessi is a brilliant re-interpretation of the figurative tradition in tableware design. With its sinuous lines, the set formally reflects Lynn's ongoing interest in Art Nouveau and the late nineteenth-century designs of architect and designer Victor Horta. Beginning with the premise that the design of all utensils originates with the spoon, Lynn conceived of the cutlery as a kind of genetic system made up of stem, leaf, and flower and capable of endless variations. Lynn produced the flatware out of layers of liquid metal using a three-dimensional digital-printing method. The result is that each piece is figuratively articulated and differentiated from the others by subtle mutations, as in the basin and tines of the fork, which blend in surprising combinations.

HULGER British, founded 2005
SAMUEL WILKINSON DESIGN British, founded 2007
Plumen 001 (set of 15) (detail), 2010
Glass, ABS plastic, wires, and electronic fillings; 7.6 × 61 × 33 cm (3 × 24 × 13 in.)
Gift of Hulger, 2011.784

Challenging the sterile functionalism of compact fluorescent lightbulbs, London design company Hulger and British product designer Samuel Wilkinson reimagined these devices as aesthetic objects in their own right. Wilkinson drew on the raw qualities of the glass tubing used in low-energy bulbs to create a dynamic sculptural form that is revealed through movement. Like the best high-tech retoolings of traditional designs, the *Plumen* lightbulb pays homage to history with references to the arching shape of the filaments in early incandescent bulbs while promoting the cause of energy conservation for the future.

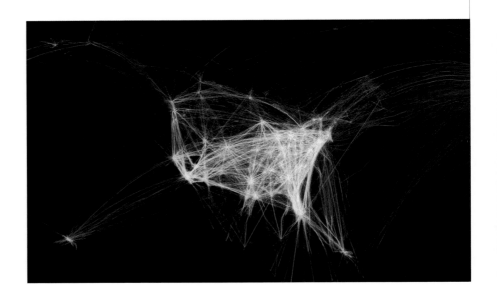

AARON KOBLIN American, born 1982
Flight Patterns, 2011
Animation
Funds provided by the Architecture & Design Society, 2011.275

Flight Patterns is a time-lapse animation that employs data visualization and pro-
cessing, an open-source computer programming environment, in order to display
American air-traffic patterns and densities over a twenty-four-hour period. Begun
as a larger project at UCLA with designers Scott Hessels and Gabriel Dunne, Aaron
Koblin's animations follow the routes of 140,000 airplanes crossing the United States
beginning at 5:00 p.m. Eastern time. Koblin uses variations of color and pattern
to illustrate a wide range of data and events, including aircraft type, alterations to
routes, changes in flight traffic over certain geographical areas, weather systems, and
no-fly zones. As the animation reveals multiple iterations of flight patterns during
the cycle, the viewer experiences a changing, phantom geography of the country with
airline hubs appearing as bright points of diffusion within a complex web.

CONTAINER WITH LID
Northern Nguni, possibly Zulu; KwaZulu-Natal, South Africa,
mid-/late 19th century
Wood; 46 × 27.9 cm (18 ⅛ × 11 in.)
Ada Turnbull Hertle Fund, 1979.539

The graceful ovoid form of this container and the precisely aligned and executed fluted lines that embellish it, articulating alternating triangles, display great artistry. A closely related work acquired by the British Museum in the 1860s, during a period of growing pressure from the British on the Zulu Kingdom, helps to pinpoint a date for the Art Institute's container. They are part of a small group of highly decorative vessels, made in the mid- to late nineteenth century, that are widely admired but not well understood. Also tied to this group are several neck rests that have similarly shaped legs and various miniature containers. While scholars have speculated on their possible uses, the virtuoso sculptural quality of this container and its related works indicates that they were held in high esteem. Deeply incised fluting also embellishes more familiar status objects from the region, including meat platters, neck rests, snuff containers, and staffs. It is possible that these were all prestige objects intended for high-ranking members of society. Another intriguing possibility is that artists within the Zulu Kingdom made these extraordinary works of art for sale to a growing foreign clientele that included European merchants, military personnel, missionaries, settlers, and travelers.

TRIPTYCH ICON WITH CENTRAL IMAGE OF THE VIRGIN AND CHILD

Central Ethiopia, late 17th century, reign of Iyyasu I (1682–1706)

Tempera on linen, mounted on wood and bound with cord; 67 × 74 cm (26 ³/₈ × 29 ¹/₈ in.)

Director's Fund, 2006.11

In the highlands of Ethiopia, Orthodox Christianity stretches in an unbroken line of practice from the fourth century to the present day. Although painted icons are known from the late fourteenth century, demand for them increased greatly in the mid-fifteenth century, when the worship of the Virgin Mary was formalized in the Ethiopian Orthodox liturgy. Considered sacred, icons were venerated in weekly services and on feast days.

The central image of this finely rendered triptych presents Mary with the young Jesus on her lap. She grasps a handkerchief in her left hand, while her son blesses her with his right hand and holds a book in his left. This depiction derives from a painting long held in the Basilica of Santa Maria Maggiore in Rome. The image was reproduced and disseminated by missionaries beginning in the early seventeenth century. Upon its arrival in Ethiopia by the mid-seventeenth century, it revolutionized the representation of the Virgin and Child. Here Christ is portrayed wearing a checkered robe and a beautifully detailed cowrie-shell necklace. The two sit enthroned on an Ethiopian-style bed, flanked by the archangels Gabriel and Michael. This image is surrounded by secondary themes, including the Crucifixion at right and the Ascension and Saint George slaying the dragon at left.

MASK (*MUKENGA*)

Kuba; Western Kasai region, Democratic Republic of the Congo, late 19th/
mid-20th century

Wood, glass beads, cowrie shells, feathers, raffia, fur, fabric, thread, and bells; 57.5 × 24.1 × 20.3 cm
(22 ⅝ × 9 ½ × 8 in.)

Laura T. Magnuson Fund, 1982.1504

Formed in the seventeenth century, the Kuba Kingdom unites an ethnically diverse
population across the Western Kasai region of today's Democratic Republic of the
Congo. This mask, *mukenga*, is a regional variant of a Kuba royal mask that is made
only in the northern part of the kingdom. The mask's form and lavish embellishment
are associated with wealth and status. Cowrie shells and glass beads, once highly valued
imports, cover much of its surface. A stylized elephant trunk and tusks rise from the
top, evoking the powerful animal and the wealth accrued by the Kuba in the nineteenth
century through control of the ivory trade. The tuft of red parrot feathers that is suspended from the tip of the trunk and the fur of a spotted feline on the mask's face are
insignias of rank.

 During the funerals of titled aristocrats, a member of the men's initiation society
may dance wearing the *mukenga* mask and an elaborate costume that includes many
layers of woven raffia skirts and cowrie- and bead-laden belts, gloves, bracelets, and
anklets. The deceased is laid out in identical attire, underscoring the association
between the spirit, which is manifested through the performance of the mask, and
the realm of the ancestors.

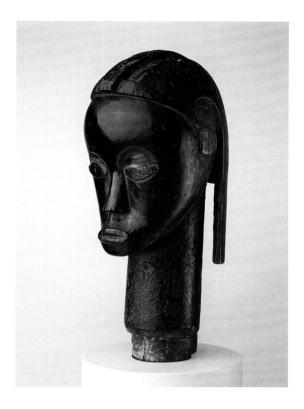

RELIQUARY HEAD
Fang; Gabon, mid-/late 19th century

Wood and copper; h. 39.4 cm (15 ½ in.)

Frederick W. Renshaw Acquisition Fund; Robert Allerton and Ada Turnbull Hertle endowments; Robert Allerton Income Fund; Gladys N. Anderson Endowment, 2006.127

Communion with the ancestral dead is an important focus of art and ritual for the Fang people of southern Cameroon and northern Gabon. This large, beautiful head was made to sit with its neck inserted into the lid of a bark reliquary box that held the selected remains, most often skull fragments, of an honored ancestor. Kept in a dark corner of a man's sleeping room, the head and box protected the remains and embodied the deceased, keeping his or her force available to the living. This reliquary head's almond-shaped eyes were embellished with copper-alloy inserts, one now missing, that would have reflected light in a startling manner, adding to the work's mysterious aura. The wide-eyed stare also lends a childlike quality to the ancestral likeness that would have been appreciated by the Fang. Within their worldview, the balance of opposing elements—infant and ancestor, birth and death—is considered a fundamental aspect of human existence. The sleek and refined features of this sculpture, including a high domed forehead, a jutting chin, and an elongated nose that is visually balanced by a plaited coiffure, highlight classic qualities of Fang abstraction that likewise embody opposition. These stylistic elements had a strong influence on the work of early twentieth-century artists such as Paul Klee, Henri Matisse, and Pablo Picasso.

VERANDA POST OF ENTHRONED KING AND SENIOR WIFE (*OPO OGOGA*)

Olowe of Ise (died 1938)

Yoruba; Ikere, Ekiti region, Nigeria, 1910/14

Wood and pigment; 152.5 × 31.75 × 40.6 cm (60 × 12 1/2 × 16 in.)

Major Acquisitions Centennial Fund, 1984.550

This veranda post is one of four that were sculpted for the palace at Ikere by the renowned early twentieth-century Yoruba artist Olowe of Ise. It is considered among the artist's masterpieces for the way it embodies his unique style, including the interrelationship of figures, their exaggerated proportions, and the open space around them. The composition and iconography of the work also masterfully reflect Yoruba concepts of divine kingship. Although the king is the focal point of the sculpture, his portrayal suggests a ruler's dependence on others. He sits with a lowered gaze and dangling legs and is weighed down by his beaded crown, the ultimate source of his authority. Such crowns are spiritually charged accessories that confer power to a ruler. The stately female figure behind the king represents his senior wife. Her large scale and pose, with hands on the king's throne, underscore her importance; she had the critical role of placing the power-invested crown on the king's head during his coronation. Moreover, the senior wife used political acumen and spiritual knowledge to protect the king's interests during his reign. The small figures at the king's feet represent a kneeling woman, the flute-playing trickster god Esu, and a fan bearer, now missing.

CEREMONIAL DRUM (*PINGE*)

Senufo; Côte d'Ivoire, 1930/50

Wood, hide, and applied color; 122.9 × 49.2 cm
(48 ³/₈ × 19 ³/₈ in.)

Robert J. Hall, Herbert R. Molner Discretionary,
Curator's Discretionary, and African and
Amerindian Art Purchase funds; Arnold Crane,
Mrs. Leonard Florsheim, O. Renard Goltra,
Holly and David Ross, Departmental Acquisi-
tions, Ada Turnbull Hertle, and Marion and
Samuel Klasstorner endowments; through prior
gifts of various donors, 1990.137

This elaborate ceremonial drum takes
the form of a seated woman gracefully
balancing a load on her head. The figure's
stylized features are characteristic of
Senufo figural art, in particular that of
the hereditary *kulebele* woodcarvers, a
group of artists who have historically
traveled widely to work on location for
patrons who commission their work.
The strong and dignified female figure
that holds this drum aloft evokes the
Senufo ideal of women as family found-
ers and spiritual mediators and guardians.
Her composed expression projects a
sense of inner calm that belies the great
weight she carries, while her seated pose
reflects a position of honor within the
community. The drum's hide-covered
resonating chamber is embellished with
motifs that allude to conflict and competition, including warriors, a snake devou-
ring a fish, and a crocodile biting into
the decorative edge of the drum itself.
These motifs emphasize the importance
of knowledge and power in a world of
competing spiritual and temporal forces.

In some Senufo communities, men
play ceremonial drums during agricultural competitions or initiation rituals.
Women may also play them during commemorative funerals for women of status.

PAIR OF HEADDRESSES (*CI WARA KUNW*)
Bamana; Baninko region, Mali, mid-19th/early 20th century

Wood, metal, brass tacks, and grasses; left: 98.4 × 40.9 × 10.8 cm (38 ³/₄ × 16 ¹/₈ × 4 ¹/₄ in.), right: 79.4 × 31.8 × 7.6 cm (31 ¹/₄ × 12 ¹/₂ × 3 in.)

Ada Turnbull Hertle Endowment, 1965.6–7

Among the Bamana of central Mali, farming is an ancient and noble profession that is entwined with religious beliefs and ritual practices. The invention of agriculture is credited to a mythical hero named Ci Wara, literally "farming animal," who was half human and half beast. A Bamana men's association named for Ci Wara is dedicated to the practical aspects of farming and the social and ritual structures that support it. Among its activities, the association sponsors masquerade performances that take place as farmers work together in communal fields. The performances encourage them to work even harder while also celebrating their agrarian heritage. These Ci Wara headdresses combine the graceful head, neck, and horns of the antelope with the short legs, compact body, and tough, pointed nose (used to dig into hard, dry ground) of the pangolin, or scaly anteater. Viewed from the side, the figures' silhouettes are enlivened by the articulation of positive and negative space. Such headdresses, in male and female pairs, are worn in ceremonial performances, though few pairs remain united in museum collections today, making this outstanding twosome all the more remarkable. The female carries a spry young male on her back, suggesting the fertile union of men and women and of earth, water, seeds, and sun.

ARTS OF THE AMERICAS

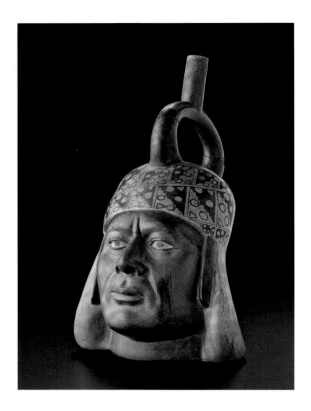

PORTRAIT VESSEL OF A RULER
Moche; north coast, Peru, 100 BC/AD 500

Ceramic and pigment; 35.6 × 24.1 cm (14 × 9 ½ in.)

Kate S. Buckingham Endowment, 1955.2338

Among the most distinctive art objects of the ancient Peruvians were ceramic vessels produced by the artists of the Moche culture, which flourished on the north coast between about 100 BC and AD 500. Remarkable for their sculptural naturalism, these stirrup-spout bottles were molded without the aid of a potter's wheel and painted in earth tones. Moche potters represented everything about their world, from domestic scenes to architecture, ritual events and royal personages, and animals and plants. This portrait vessel portrays individual characteristics—the furrowed brow and full, slightly protruding upper lip—as well as general features recognizable among Peruvian Indians today. With his commanding expression and proud bearing, the depicted ruler conveys an indelible sense of the power of Moche leaders. His elite status is further indicated by his fine headdress, decorated with the geometric motifs of Moche textiles, and by his elongated ear ornaments and the traces of facial paint on his forehead and cheeks. Vessels such as this were placed in burials as funerary offerings, but before they accompanied an individual to the grave, they may also have been sent as emblems of royal authority from a center of power to neighboring districts along with gifts of textiles and other ceremonial presents.

CEREMONIAL KNIFE (*TUMI*)

Chimú; north coast, Peru, 1100/1450

Gold with turquoise inlay; 34 × 12.7 cm
(13 ³/₈ × 5 in.)

Ada Turnbull Hertle Endowment, 1963.841

Naymlap, the heroic founder-colonizer of the Lambayque Valley on the north coast of Peru, is thought to be the legendary figure represented on the top of this striking gold *tumi* (ceremonial knife). It would have been carried by dynastic rulers during state ceremonies to represent, in a more precious form, the copper knives used for animal sacrifices. Here Naymlap stands with his arms to his abdomen and his feet splayed outward. His gold headdress has an elaborate open filigree design. Turquoise—for the peoples of ancient Peru, a precious gem related to the worship of water and sky—is inlaid around the headdress cap and in the ear ornaments. The tumi was made with diverse metalworking techniques. Solid casting was used to produce the blade. The face and body were created with annealing (heating, shaping, and then cooling) and repoussé, in which the relief design is hammered into a mold from the reverse side. Finally, the small ornaments around the top of the headdress were separately hammered or cast, then soldered into place. This tumi and many other gold, silver, and textile objects were made in royal workshops and ceremonially presented to high officials as emblems of rank and authority.

POLYCHROME BOWL

Probably We'wah (c. 1848–1896), Zuñi; Zuñi Pueblo, New Mexico, United States, c. 1890

Ceramic and pigment; 16.5 × 42 cm (6 ½ × 16 ½ in.)

Gift of Charles and Marjorie Benton, 2010.550

Toward the end of the nineteenth century, an artistic renewal occurred throughout the Southwest as centuries-old styles and techniques were recast in response to increasing public interest in Native American art and culture. Potters from several pueblos, or towns, developed innovative vessel shapes and designs by adapting and adding to the achievements of their ancestors. The styles and symbolic forms expressed each community's particular historical identity and sense of place. The interior of this bowl is filled with a large, X-shaped symbol with arms emerging from a crosshatched diamond— a reference to the four sacred directions of the Zuñi world. The red, hooked motifs between the arms represent *pahos*, prayer sticks with attached feathers that were placed at sacred locations to petition for rain. On the exterior, zigzag lines flanked by red and black triangles signify lightning and rainfall. Many features of this vessel are characteristic of ceramics made by We'wah, one of the most renowned Zuñi artists, who held a special status within his community as one of their *lhamanas*. These highly respected individuals typically were born male but followed traditional female gender roles, including pottery making and weaving, and served as mediators with special ceremonial and spiritual responsibilities.

RITUAL CACHE

Salado branch of the Mogollon; southeastern Arizona, United States, 1300/1400

Wood, stone, plant fibers, cotton, feathers, hide, and pigment; male figure: h. 64 cm (25 ¼ in.); female figure: h. 36 cm (14 ³⁄₁₆ in.)

Major Acquisitions Centennial Endowment, 1979.17.1–11

Discovered wrapped and hidden in a remote, dry cave, this cache of ritual figures comes from the Salado culture, which flourished in the mountains of southwestern New Mexico and southeastern Arizona between the fourteenth and fifteenth centuries. Brilliantly colored and adorned with flicker feathers and dyed cotton string, these effigies once formed an altar as agents for communion with the life-giving spirits of the earth and sky. The large male figure, with his feather necklace and bold black-and-turquoise zigzag pattern, features sky symbolism. The smaller, female figure is a more self-contained form, probably corresponding to the earth. Her ocher color likely refers to maize and pollen, symbols of sustenance and fertility. The accompanying figures are a mountain lion (the chief predator in the region) and two serpents (carved from cottonwood roots), representing agents of communication with the earth and the seasonal cycle of fertility. Curved wooden throwing sticks for rabbit hunting complete the ensemble. Testimony to the antiquity and endurance of the worship of earth and sky and to the spiritual bonds between people and animals, these objects bear close resemblance to ritual figures and implements still used today among the diverse Pueblo peoples.

SHELL MOSAIC RITUAL MASK
Teotihuacan; Teotihuacan, Mexico, 300/600

Stone and spondylus (spiny oyster) shell with stucco; 18 × 21 × 11 cm (7 ¹/₈ × 8 ¹/₄ × 4 ⁵/₁₆ in.)
Through prior gifts of Mr. and Mrs. Arthur M. Wood and Mr. and Mrs. William E. Hartmann; Robert
Allerton Trust; through prior gifts of Ethel and Julian R. Goldsmith and Mr. and Mrs. Samuel A. Marx;
Morris L. Parker Fund; restricted gifts of Cynthia and Terry Perucca and Bill and Stephanie Sick;
Wirt D. Walker Trust, Bessie Bennett, and Elizabeth R. Vaughn funds; restricted gifts of Rita and Jim
Knox and Susan and Stuart Handler; Edward E. Ayer Fund in memory of Charles L. Hutchinson and
Gladys N. Anderson Fund; restricted gift of Terry McGuire; Samuel P. Avery and Charles U. Harris
Endowed Acquisition funds, 2012.2

Teotihuacan, the ruins of which are located near Mexico City, was one of the largest
and most complex cities in the world during the first millennium AD. Although this
mask shares features common to others from the city—a broad forehead, prominent
nose, receding chin, and widely spaced cheekbones—it is subtly unique, indicating that
it may represent a stylized portrait. Tied to wooden armatures adorned with feathers,
jewelry, and garments, such masks were displayed in residential compounds and temples
where they were the focus of rituals commemorating ancestors who acted as intermediar-
ies between the living and the deified forces of nature. An older, recut stone mask was
covered with mosaic tiles made from the inner layer of spondylus shell imported from
the Pacific coast. The use of this exotic material suggests the far-reaching power, authority, and wealth of Teotihuacan. Spondylus was also considered sacred, associating this
mask and the individual it honors with the generative power of lakes, rivers, and the sea.

VESSEL OF THE DANCING LORDS

Ah Maxam (active mid-/late 8th century), Late Classic Maya; vicinity of Naranjo, Petén region, Guatemala, 750/800

Ceramic and pigment; 24 × 15.8 cm (9 ½ × 6 ¼ in.)

Ethel T. Scarborough Fund, 1986.1081

According to ancient Maya belief, after several failed attempts the gods succeeded in populating the earth when they created humanity out of maize, the staff of life. In the *Popol Vuh*, a sixteenth-century epic of the K'iche' Maya, the death and resurrection of the maize god was likened to seed corn that sprouted and produced new life. This vessel from the Late Classic period (600–800) depicts a Maya ruler attired as the maize god in three almost-identical panels. On his back, the ruler wears an enormous rack containing brilliant feathers, heraldic beasts, and related emblems. Just as maize plants sway to and fro, the maize god dances to the rhythm of life—often, as seen here, in the company of a dwarf. Among the Maya, dwarfs were seen as special beings with powerful spiritual connections to the earth and the interior world below. This vase refers to a rite of passage in which dwarfs assist the soul of the deceased into the domain of the dead, from which it would eventually be reborn in the royal lineage, just as maize sprouts again in the cycle of nature's renewal. This vase of the Dancing Lords may have been painted as a funerary offering for a noblewoman with dynastic connections in the city of Naranjo, where it was made.

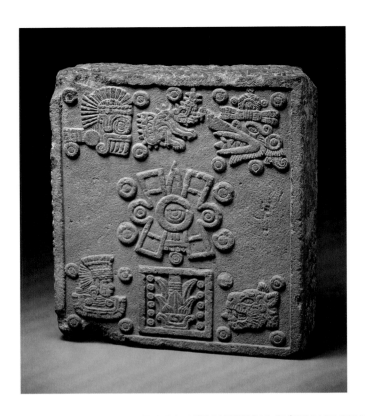

CORONATION STONE OF MOTECUHZOMA II (STONE OF THE FIVE SUNS)

Aztec (Mexica); Tenochtitlan, Mexico, 1503

Basalt; 55.9 × 66 × 22.9 cm (22 × 26 × 9 in.)

Major Acquisitions Fund, 1990.21

This stone, commemorating the beginning of the reign of Emperor Motecuhzoma II, was originally located within the ritual center of Tenochtitlan, the capital of the extensive empire conquered by the Aztecs between 1428 and 1519. The ruins of the city lie beneath downtown Mexico City. Known as the *Stone of the Five Suns*, this monument draws connections between Aztec history and the cosmic scheme. The quadrangular block is carved with the hieroglyphic signs of five successive cosmic eras, called "suns" in the language of the Aztecs. These eras were mythic cycles of creation and destruction that began in the time of genesis and continued with the birth of humankind and the period of Aztec rule. From "4 Jaguar-sun" in the lower-right corner, the eras proceed counterclockwise through "4 Wind-sun," "4 Rain-sun," and "4 Water-sun." The X carved in the center represents "4 Movement-sun," the sign of the present era for the Aztecs. The year "11 Reed" in the square cartouche refers to 1503, the year of Motecuhzoma's coronation, while the day listed above it—"1 Crocodile"—corresponds to July 15, when the ceremony probably occurred. On the underside, the hieroglyphic date "1 Rabbit" denotes the beginning of things in the distant mythological past. The sculpture thus legitimizes Motecuhzoma's rule as part of the cycle of birth, death, and renewal and presents him as heir to the world in the present era of creation.

KNEELING FIGURE
Chinese, probably Sichuan Province, late 2nd millennium BC
Chlorite; 19.6 × 7 × 9.8 cm (7 $^5/_8$ × 2 $^3/_4$ × 3 $^7/_8$ in.)
Edward and Louise B. Sonnenschein Collection, 1950.671

This starkly poignant figure, probably a male, kneels with his hands bound behind
him with two rounds of thick rope. Parted down the middle, his hair resembles an
open book; finely incised parallel lines suggest that it has been meticulously combed,
and a long double braid hangs down his back. His facial features are defined by
raised eyebrows, high cheekbones, a tight mouth that curves slightly downward, and
large pierced ears that project perpendicularly from his head. Evoking fierceness and
shock, the man stares blankly ahead—like a subdued victim anticipating a terrifying,
painful punishment. Figures with proportions and features similar to this sculpture
have recently been unearthed at sites in southwestern Sichuan Province that date to
the second millennium BC. Whereas those images were carved from more roughly
textured stones and sometimes preserve traces of pigment, this example's smooth,
blackish-green surface appears unique. Scientific analyses indicate that the sculpture
was probably darkened by burning before burial and, upon rediscovery, was polished
and saturated with wax.

CAULDRON (*DING*)

Chinese, Western Zhou dynasty (1046–771 BC), early 9th century BC

Bronze; 49 × 43 cm (19 3/8 × 16 15/16 in.)

Major Acquisitions Centennial Fund, 2005.426

As this monumental cauldron demonstrates, the most distinctive bronze vessels of early China represent important historical documents as well as stunningly powerful works of art. Designed to contain offerings of meat in ritual ceremonies, this vessel was cast with a lengthy inscription on its interior bowl. The text commemorates a solemn ritual ceremony at the imperial court of the Zhou, the second dynasty recorded in Chinese texts, and explains that Captain Wang, a noble official who had been rewarded for his loyal service to the Zhou king, commissioned this vessel to honor his deceased father and record the occasion for succeeding generations. Together with the inscription, the vessel's shallow profile and austere surface decor date it to the early ninth century BC. Although the monsterlike masks that project from each leg display animal imagery common on older bronzes, the two registers of hooked, ribbonlike bands that encircle the bowl preserve only traces of early dragon or bird patterns. The transition from zoomorphic to abstract surface designs marks a significant turning point in the art of early Chinese bronzes. Recent archaeological discoveries of similar bronze vessels in China indicate that this cauldron was most likely buried as part of a large hoard.

PAIR OF DRAGON PENDANTS

Chinese, Eastern Zhou dynasty, Warring States period (c. 480–221 BC),
4th/3rd century BC

Jade; left: 9.2 × 16.8 × 0.7 cm (3 ³/₅ × 6 ³/₅ × ³/₁₀ in.); right: 8.6 × 16.5 × 0.6 cm (6 ¹/₂ × 3 ³/₈ × ¹/₄ in.)

Edward and Louise B. Sonnenschein Collection, 1950.640–41

These matching pendants were designed as serpentine dragons with backturned heads, coiled tails, and small fins that project above and below their undulating trunks. The rhythmic fluency of these creatures belies the unyielding quality of jade—a compact, fine-grained stone that cannot be carved and must be worn away with abrasive paste applied to its surface with saws, grinders, and drills. The craftsman's remarkable dexterity with this intractable material is displayed in smoothly rounded, heart-shaped units and delicately incised spirals, striations, and cross-hatching that thoroughly enliven both the front and back surfaces. Their substantial size and thickness, technical refinement, and glossy polish point to aristocratic patronage. That these pendants were likely designed to drape down the owner's shoulders or from a waistband is indicated by holes pierced for suspension through the creatures' hindquarters. Toward the end of the Bronze Age when these pendants were created, sinuously curved dragons had become prominent motifs in many luxurious materials. Contemporary literature suggests that such dynamic creatures were not merely decorative but also envisioned as supernatural beings. When buried with the deceased, jade pendants like these may have reflected widely held beliefs in the dragon as a vehicle that could transport the human soul on its journey to the netherworld.

EQUESTRIENNE

Chinese, Tang dynasty (618–907), 725/50

Earthenware with polychrome pigments; 56.2 × 48.2 × 39 cm (22 ⅛ × 19 × 15 ⅜ in.)

Gift of Mrs. Potter Palmer Wood, 1970.1073

Chinese ceramic figures made exclusively for burial often vividly evoke the fashions and recreational activities of their aristocratic owners. This figure sensitively captures a quiet moment in the life of a matronly equestrienne, who gently guides her horse. The animal's powerful neck and flanks, long legs, trimmed mane, and decoratively tied tail are features distinctive to the handsome breeds that were brought to China from the empire's northwestern frontiers as well as from sites as far west as the Aral Sea. Carefully twisted strands of clay realistically depict the fur-like texture of the animal's saddle blanket. The woman's full proportions—evident in the folds of her flowing, wide-sleeved robe, as well as in her plump cheeks and double chin—are enhanced by her loosely gathered coiffure, which is topped with a dangling forehead bun. Her weight, costume, and hairstyle reflect early-to-mid-eighth-century ideals of feminine beauty. Stylistically, the woman closely resembles figures that archeologists have recently unearthed from the tombs of high-status individuals that are datable to about 740.

HEAD OF A *LUOHAN*
Chinese, Northern Song, Liao, or Jin dynasty, c. 11th century

Hollow dry lacquer; 28.6 × 18 × 20 cm (11 ¹/₄ × 7 ¹/₁₆ × 7 ⁷/₈ in.)

Gift of the Orientals, 1928.259

In traditional Buddhist belief, the *luohan* is a disciple who has attained enlightenment through intense personal effort. Beginning in the ninth century, the worship of luohan and their depiction in art evolved primarily in the context of the Chan (Zen), or "meditation," sect of Buddhism. This head was created in the delicate technique of hollow dry lacquer. The artisan first soaked layers of coarse cloth in lacquer (a thick sap tapped from a sumac tree) and applied these to a clay core formed over an arma-ture of wood or other material. After allowing the work to dry, he applied a thick layer of lacquer paste to create the basic shape of the sculpture and a thinner coat into which he care-fully modeled the eyes, high cheekbones, and other facial features. After removing the core and supporting armature, he set colored beads behind the eyes to represent irises and pupils. Finally, he painted the surface and perhaps applied gilding. Although these surface finishes have disintegrated over the centuries, the sensitively executed facial features preserve the insightful expression of the luohan.

PAIR OF CUPS

Chinese, Qing dynasty (1644–1911), Yongzheng reign mark and period (1723–35)

Porcelain painted with underglaze blue and overglaze *doucai* enamels; each: 5.7 × 10.2 cm (2 ¼ × 4 in.)

Bequest of Henry C. Schwab, 1941.701a–b

The emperors of China's last dynasty, the Qing, were enamored of exquisitely decorative objects and recruited remarkable craftsmen to serve their court. During his brief reign, the Yongzheng emperor, himself an artist and astute connoisseur, took a personal role in overseeing the imperial kilns. In their elegance and technical sophistication, these extraordinarily thin cups exemplify his exacting standards. Their floral medallions were delicately outlined in pale cobalt blue and, after glazing and firing, filled with soft, translucent enamels. So perfectly do these enamels fill the outlines that this technique is known as *doucai* (joined or dovetailed colors). Although quite different from the naturalistic floral motifs that characterize many Qing imperial porcelains, these medallions are also seen in rare examples of exquisite Yongzheng ware in the Palace Museum in Beijing. Their style may reflect the influence of Japanese lacquers, which were imported into China in the sixteenth and seventeenth centuries and subsequently inspired creative copies by Chinese palace craftsmen. The Yongzheng emperor was renowned for having encouraged innovative and sometimes foreign-inspired design in ceramics as well as other decorative arts.

YANG PU MOVING HIS FAMILY (DETAIL)
Chinese, Yuan dynasty (1279–1368), late 13th century

Handscroll; ink and light color on paper; 52.7 × 231.1 cm (20 3/4 × 91 in.)

Kate S. Buckingham Endowment, 1952.9

With a lively combination of realism and caricature, this detail of the painting *Yang Pu Moving His Family* depicts a group of peasants transporting a rustic scholar and his family across a stream. Distinguished by his official government cap, with its long streamers, the otherwise disheveled, bare-legged scholar bids farewell to his neighbors on the shore. Servants valiantly attempt to carry children and the family's belongings—scrolls, furniture, and dishes—through the water. The scholar depicted here may represent Yang Pu, a character described in stories of the Southern Song dynasty (1127–1279). According to folklore, Yang Pu initially declined, and then reluctantly accepted, his appointment to a government position in the capital city. Chinese law forbade civil officials from working in their native districts, and as a result, many were required to relocate to distant cities. Painters and poets frequently depicted the theme of farewell, or "noble parting," exemplified by the story of Yang Pu. The twigs that protrude from the official caps of the men depicted here may allude to the ancient Chinese custom of presenting departing friends with small branches from a willow tree.

LI HUAYI
American, born China 1948
Landscape, 2002
Ink and color on paper; 182 × 98.3 cm
(71 ¹¹/₁₆ × 38 ¹¹/₁₆ in.)
Comer Foundation Fund, 2004.450

Impressive in scale and refinement, this depiction of a dramatic ravine evokes the monumental landscapes attributed to China's foremost painters of the tenth and eleventh centuries. Like those early masters, Li Huayi captured the continuous momentum and flux of nature. Steeply curving banks edged by windswept trees tower precariously over the water, whose receding flow is echoed by the cloud-like mist hovering above. This dynamic image is rendered by the artist's distinctively expressive method of painting. After defining the composition with large areas of ink spilled onto the paper or worked with a broad brush, Li gradually rendered mass and solidity with denser layers and then allowed the paper to dry before adding details with a small, finely tapered brush. By the artist's own account, such powerfully fresh landscapes exist only in his mind and do not reflect direct observation of nature.

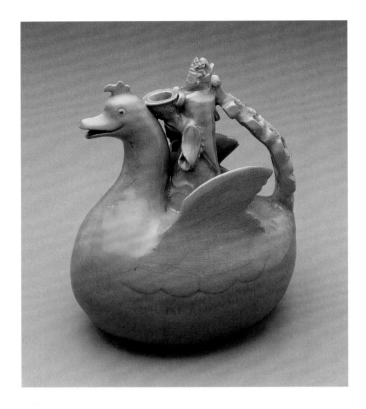

BIRD-SHAPED EWER WITH CROWNED RIDER HOLDING A BOWL

Korean, Goryeo dynasty (918–1392), 12th century

Stoneware with celadon glaze and underglaze incised decoration; 21.4 × 17.7 × 13.2 cm
(8 ¹/₂ × 7 × 5 ¹/₂ in.)

Bequest of Russell Tyson, 1964.1213

The prosperous Goryeo dynasty that gave its name to modern-day Korea produced some of the world's most esteemed ceramics. Preeminent among these are celadons, whose iron-rich glazes had been refined by Chinese potters to create a subtle range of gray and bluish-green hues. Under the Goryeo court, Korean craftsmen drew upon the Chinese celadon tradition to create wares of unprecedented beauty and ingenuity. The technical refinement and stylistic naiveté of this intricately constructed bird-shaped ewer exemplify a distinctively Korean aesthetic. Whereas the creature's plump body resembles a duck's, its head is crowned with a cockscomb. Disproportionately small wings project out as if in flight, while the tail swoops upward to form a reticulated handle that supports a man who stands atop the bird's back, holding a bowl. His elaborate headdress and long, flowing robe suggest that he represents an immortal. Details of his garments, as well as of the bird's overlapping scales and layered feathers, were finely carved and incised into the clay body before glazing and firing; areas where the glaze naturally pooled appear a slightly deeper green. As a final touch, dots of underglaze iron brown accent the eyes. Although wine or other liquids could be poured into the figure's bowl and out through the bird's smiling beak, this vessel may have been designed purely as an ingeniously whimsical work of art.

CHAEKGEORI

Korean, Joseon dynasty (1392–1910),
19th century

One panel of an eight-panel screen; ink and
color on paper, mounted on silk brocade with a
wood frame; 162.5 × 415.2 cm (63 ¹⁵/₁₆ × 163 ⁵/₈ in.)
Wirt D. Walker Fund, 2006.3

Chaekgeori are Korean still-life paintings
that were popular during the latter part of
the Joseon dynasty. Three-dimensional
effects were commonly used in chaekgeori,
as was reversed perspective, in which
distant objects are shown larger than
those nearby, thus flattening the pictorial surface. These different treatments
of spatial illusion resulted in compositions with a highly graphic feel that is
enhanced by the decorative patterning on the depicted objects. It is clear
that such still-life images did not have
realism as a goal. Instead, chaekgeori
(defined as "painting[s] of books and associated things") were seen as conveyers
of cultural values. They were most often
displayed within studios or schools and
reflected reverence for scholarship and
learning. In this screen, scholarly tools
are depicted along with flowers, plants,
food, rare imported objects, and religious implements. These motifs express
varied meanings; for example, eggplant
represents the promise of a long life,
while musical instruments symbolize harmony among people. Such a profusion
of auspicious meanings indicates that
chaekgeori may not have been restricted
to the scholarly environment; they may
also have served as talismans ensuring
harmony within the home and beyond.

BISHAMON
Japanese, Heian period (794–1185), 11th century
Wood with traces of polychromy; h. approx. 135 cm (52 ³/₄ in.)
Robert Allerton Endowment, 1968.145

This is one of the Art Institute's most prized works of Japanese Buddhist sculpture. Bishamon (also known as Tamonten or Vaisravana) is the chief of the four guardian devas (or *shitennō*) who protect the four cardinal directions in a Buddhist sanctuary. Together, they defend the entire world against evil and promote the seeking of enlightenment. Originally an Indian folk deity who was later adopted by Buddhism, Bishamon wards off harmful influences to the north.

Glaring at those who pose danger to the Buddhist law, Bishamon is clothed in full armor, ready to take on the Buddha's enemies. The figure is carved from wood in an intricate style that conveys action while also paying attention to the smallest details of his costume. The dynamic representation of Bishamon's figure—the sway of his hips and the opposing movements of his arms, with his sleeves swinging as if caught in a divine breeze—effectively expresses the guardian's strength and determination. His elaborate helmet is actually carved from the same piece of wood as the head. The plated armor was elaborately decorated with dragons, flowers, and other patterns depicted in gold and bright colors, ample traces of which remain. Bishamon once held a miniature reliquary in the upturned palm of his left hand and a sword in the right, symbolizing his duty to defend the Buddhist law.

LEGENDS OF THE YUZŪ NEMBUTSU SECT (detail)

Japanese, Kamakura period (1185–1333), mid-14th century

Handscroll; ink, color, and gold on paper; 30.5 × 1176.9 cm (12 × 463 ³⁄₈ in.)

Kate S. Buckingham Endowment, 1956.1256

One of the most important and beautiful records of Amidism, a Buddhist salvation theology, is this rare narrative handscroll. It recounts details from the life of Ryōnin (1073–1132), a charismatic Tendai monk who founded the Yuzū sect. The Buddhist concept of *yuzū* refers to the interrelationship or initial oneness of all things. The dynamically new approach to salvation that Ryōnin developed from yuzū reasoned that if all things are interrelated, the meritorious action of one individual benefits many. Followers of Amidism registered their names in a tally book, pledging to recite the brief *nembutsu* prayer, an invocation of the Amida Buddha, at specific times during the day. Contrasted with the dense and elite ritual of Buddhist teachings of the Heian period (794–1185), this simple, more populist approach to Buddhism had enormous appeal. Commissioned and executed in the mid-fourteenth century, during the revival of the Yuzū sect, this lengthy horizontal scroll is unrolled from right to left and intended to be studied in successive sections each approximately the width of the viewer's shoulders.

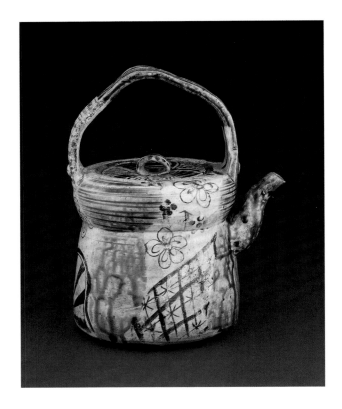

ORIBE-TYPE EWER
Japanese, Momoyama period (1573–1615), early 17th century

Stoneware with copper-green and white glaze and underglaze iron-wash decoration; 26.7 × 21.6 cm (10 ½ × 8 ½ in.)

Gift of Robert Allerton, 1959.5

Furuta Oribe (1544–1615) was a military general–turned–tea aesthete whose style of presentation at tea gatherings catered to the samurai class and rulers of seventeenth-century Japan. In contrast to his predecessors, Oribe preferred tea wares that were bold and eccentric rather than subtle and rustic. He was the first to recognize the beauty of artfully misshapen ceramics for use in tea gatherings. Ewers such as this were employed as water containers during the meal that preceded the tea service. Their distinctive glaze contains copper, which turned green in the firing process. This glaze, along with slightly off-kilter or distorted shapes, became trademarks of Oribe ware produced in the Mino region (now Gifu Prefecture) of Japan.

This vessel features drawings of plum blossoms, wheels, a hexagonal tortoise-shell pattern, and a lattice, all done in an underglaze iron wash. This is typical of such wares, which most often do not have a single decorative theme, but rather depict a mélange of almost abstract motifs akin to the popular patterning on textiles of the period.

SESSON SHUKEI Japanese, c. 1490–after 1577
Landscape of the Four Seasons, c. 1560
Pair of six-panel screens; ink and light color on paper; each: 174.2 × 357.2 cm (68 ⅝ × 140 ⅝ in.)
Gift of the Joseph and Helen Regenstein Foundation, 1958.167–68

Sesson Shukei was a Zen Buddhist monk and painter who achieved his idiosyncratic painterly style during an itinerant career in eastern Japan, seemingly without ever traveling to Kyoto, Japan's cultural and political capital at the time. Sesson's dream-like Chinese landscape expands before our eyes in understandable spatial depth, an effect that is enhanced by the folds of the screen. Reading the composition in the same manner as the Japanese language, from right to left, the seasons flow from the first red plum blossoms of the year, depicted on the right side of the right screen (top), all the way across to the snow-covered mountains on the far left side of the left screen (bottom). A mountain temple on the right and a village on the left enclose an inlet upon which boats come and go. People bustle about in activity, geologically impossible rock formations twist and turn, and water splashes out from the bottom of a waterfall like reaching fingers.

For adherents of Zen Buddhism, a sect with origins in China, idealized landscapes described a world akin to paradise, in which intellectual and religious activities could be pursued unhindered and the cycle of the seasons symbolized the harmony and rebirth inherent in the natural world.

TOSA MITSUOKI Japanese, 1617–1691
Flowering Cherry and Autumn Maples with Poem Slips, 1654/81
Pair of six-panel screens; front: ink, color, gold, and silver on silk; each: 144 × 286 cm (51 9/16 × 100 13/16 in.)
Kate S. Buckingham Endowment, 1977.156–57

Japanese aristocrats engaged in the elegant custom of recollecting classical poetry while viewing spring and autumn foliage. In these delicate screens, premier court painter Tosa Mitsuoki meditated on the inevitable passage of beauty by depicting the melancholy hours after the departure of reveling courtiers. A cherry tree bursts into bloom on the right screen (seen here at top), while its mate displays the brilliant red and gold foliage of maples in autumn. Slips of poetry, called *tanzaku*, waft from the blossoming limbs, the lingering signs of a human presence. Courtiers (whose names are recorded in a seventeenth-century document) assisted Mitsuoki by inscribing the narrow strips with quotations of appropriate seasonal poetry from twelfth- and thirteenth-century anthologies. The screens were either commissioned by or given to Tōfukumon'in (1607–1678), a daughter of the Tokugawa shogun who married the emperor Gomizunoo (1596–1680). In an era otherwise marked by increasing control of the feudal shogunate over imperial prerogatives, this royal couple encouraged a renaissance of courtly taste that nostalgically evoked the past glories of early medieval aristocratic life.

IKE TAIGA Japanese, 1723–1776
Group Pilgrimage to the Jizō Nun, 1755/65
Hanging scroll; ink on paper; 54.9 × 123.2 cm (21 ⅝ × 48 ½ in.)
Kate S. Buckingham Endowment; Margaret Gentles Fund; restricted gift of Roger L. Weston,
George and Roberta Mann, Harlow and Susan Higinbotham, Charles C. Haffner III, and James M.
and Carol D. Trapp, 2005.168

Ike Taiga was a revolutionary known for revitalizing Japanese painting traditions in
the eighteenth century. He infused the Chinese-inspired ink painting (*nanga*) that
was gaining favor among intellectuals in Kyoto with a purely Japanese aesthetic and
humor. *Group Pilgrimage to the Jizō Nun* is a snapshot of contemporary life in Japan
presented from Taiga's unique perspective. The print depicts pilgrims making offerings
to the Jizō nun, a holy woman believed to be able to communicate with the bodhisattva
Jizō, who had the power to save souls in the afterlife.

   Group Pilgrimage contains an inscription relating the story of the Jizō nun. Taiga
was a master calligrapher, poet, and seal carver and was well versed in all forms of
writing, from ancient seal script to cursive kana. Here he rendered the inscription in
a cursive, informal style very much in keeping with the spontaneity of the painting
itself. Taiga was also renowned for his use of finger painting and other odd techniques.
Although opinions vary as to whether or not this work is a finger painting, it is clear
that Taiga did not use a traditional brush. It seems likely that this could be a "paper
twist painting," in which the artist worked with scraps of twisted paper charged
with ink.

SUZUKI HARUNOBU Japanese, 1725–1770
Evening Snow on a Floss Shaper, from the series *Eight Views of the Parlor*
(*Zashiki hakkei*), 1766
Color woodblock print; *chūban*; 28.7 × 21.6 cm (11 5/16 × 8 1/2 in.)
Clarence Buckingham Collection, 1928.903

The famous series *Eight Views of the Parlor* was produced in 1766, around the time of the emergence of full-color prints in Japan. The series contains eight prints that were housed together in a fanciful wrapper, all of which are now in the Art Institute's collection. These scenes present visual puns based on well-known themes of the Xiao and Xiang Rivers in China, each of which has its own poetic title. For *Evening Snow,* Suzuki Harunobu depicted silk floss as snow and the floss shaper as the mountain rather than showing snow-covered hills.

Such witty visual riddles would have been appreciated by the audience of these prints—wealthy, well-educated townsmen who participated in poetry circles. One such figure was Ōkubo Jinshirō Tadanobu, whose pseudonym was Kyosen. It is thought that he produced this set, engaging Harunobu's services as well as those of the printer. In fact, this image contains Kyosen's handwritten signature, leading scholars to believe that the Art Institute's set is the first edition. Sets with Harunobu's signature exist in other collections.

TŌSHŪSAI SHARAKU Japanese, active 1794–95
The Actor Bandō Mitsugorō as Ishii Genzō, 1794/95
Color woodblock print; *ōban*; 37.5 × 24.7 cm (14 ³/₄ × 9 ³/₄ in.)
Clarence Buckingham Collection, 1940.1086

Almost nothing is known of the life of Tōshūsai Sharaku, whose entire oeuvre of
bold portraits of Kabuki actors was produced during a ten-month period in 1794–95.
Sharaku's prints are frank and piercing, combining satire with decorative power. His
aggressive style is made all the more dramatic by his use of a dark mica background,
which throws the silhouette of the posturing actor into strong relief. Depicted here is
the actor Bandō Mitsugorō portraying the character Ishii Genzō at the peak dramatic
moment of the play *The Iris Sōga of the Bunroku Era (Hanaayame Bunroku Sōga)*.
With a look of intense fury, Genzō draws his sword to aid his two brothers-in-law in
avenging their father's murder. The play is based on an event that occurred in 1701
that disrupted the civil order of the Tokugawa shogunate and scandalized the population of Edo. Commentary on contemporary issues was discouraged by the Japanese
government, however, so the play was disguised as a literary recounting of a famous
twelfth-century act of filial revenge that occurred in the Sōga family. Unlike the elite
and highly stylized Noh theater, Kabuki was a popular form of drama that reflected
and catered to the tastes and pleasures of the emerging merchant class.

KATSUSHIKA HOKUSAI Japanese, 1760–1849

The Great Wave off Kanagawa, from the series *Thirty-Six Views of Mount Fuji*, 1830/31

Color woodblock print; *ōban*; 25.4 × 37.6 cm (10 ⅛ × 14 ¾ in.)

Clarence Buckingham Collection, 1925.3245

In the early nineteenth century, the pigment known as Berlin or Prussian blue (*bero*) became more widely available and affordable, inspiring a new flourishing of landscape imagery in print design that could make the most of the strong color. Produced between the late 1820s and early 1830s, Hokusai's series of prints studying the ancient pilgrimage site of Mount Fuji is among the most celebrated and majestic art of the nineteenth century. Whether the volcano is visually dominant, as in many of the prints, or reduced in scale, as it is here, the series is a virtuoso display of Hokusai's compositional skill. With its bold linear design, striking juxtapositions, and careful use of color, *The Great Wave* is a compelling image of the mountain. Not only do the surging breakers seem to swamp the boaters, but—to the Japanese eye, accustomed to reading from right to left—the great claw of a wave appears almost to tumble into the viewer's face. Even Mount Fuji appears fragile, about to be engulfed by the uncontrollable energy of the water. This iconic image has been used widely in contemporary designs, ranging from comics and advertisements to book jackets and record covers.

COW SUCKLING A CALF

Madhya or Uttar Pradesh, India, c. 9th century

Buff sandstone; 55.3 × 73.7 × 9.6 cm (22 ³/₄ × 29 × 3 ³/₄ in.)

Gifit of Marilynn B. Alsdorf, 2006.180

This naturalistic relief panel depicts a calf sucking milk from his mother while she stands patiently looking out at the viewer. Her placid eyes; floppy ears; undulating dewlap; small, upwardly curving horns; and hump help identify her as belonging to the distinctive breed of Brahman cattle originally bred in India. Cows enjoy a respected status in India: they are regarded as the nourishing mother, as portrayed in this frieze, and even their waste is used in purification rituals and for fuel.

In the medieval period in India, the cow came to be particularly associated with Krishna, an incarnation of the Hindu god Vishnu, who grew up in Vrindavan (near Mathura) among cowherds, a theme much celebrated in art. Less common are individual portrayals of a cow and calf, like this relief, which most likely came from the walls of a Hindu temple, possibly from central India, and can be dated to around the ninth century. It is possible that this relief was once part of a larger narrative scene on a temple wall, perhaps depicting Krishna among cows and cowherds.

SHIVA AS LORD OF THE DANCE (*NATARAJA*)
Tamil Nadu, India, Chola period, 10th/11th century

Bronze; 69.3 × 61.8 × 24.1 cm (27 ¼ × 24 ¼ × 9 ½ in.)

Kate S. Buckingham Fund, 1965.1130

Shiva, one of the most important Hindu divinities, is here depicted as the Lord of the Dance (*Nataraja*), an iconic image in Indian art. Shiva's cosmic dance sets in motion the rhythm of life and death; it pervades the universe, as symbolized by the ring of fire that is filled with the loose, snakelike locks of the god's hair. One pair of his arms balances the flame of destruction and the hand drum (*damaru*) that beats the rhythm of life while another performs symbolic gestures: the raised right hand means "fear not," and the left hand (*gajahasta*) pointing down toward his raised left foot signifies release from the ignorance that hinders realization of the ultimate reality. Shiva is shown perfectly balanced, with his right leg planted on the demon of darkness (*Apasmara*), stamping out ignorance. The tiny figure of the personified river goddess, Ganga, is caught up in his matted, flowing locks. Shiva was believed to break the fall of the great Ganges River as it descends from the Himalayas by standing beneath the waters, which divide over his hair, becoming the seven holy rivers of India. This classic bronze comes from the Chola period in the south of India. Icons such as this were carried in procession during religious ceremonies.

BUDDHA (*SHAKYAMUNI*) SEATED IN MEDITATION (*DHYANAMUDRA*)

Nagapattinam, Tamil Nadu, India, Chola period, c. 12th century

Granite; 160 × 120.2 × 56.3 cm (63 × 47 ⁵/₁₆ × 22 ³/₁₆ in.)

Restricted gift of Mr. and Mrs. Robert Andrew Brown, 1964.556

This meditating Buddha comes from the coastal town of Nagapattinam in southern India, which was, as a result of settlers from Srivijaya (Indonesia), one of the few places where Buddhism was still flourishing in the twelfth century. The Buddha—with his elongated earlobes, the wheel marks on his palms, the *urna* between his brows, and the cranial protuberance covered with snail-shell curls—is seated in the posture of meditation, with his hands resting on his lap (*dhyanamudra*), wearing a seemingly diaphanous monastic garment. As in other images from Nagapattinam, a flame emerges out of the Buddha's cranial protuberance, probably signifying wisdom. This monumental granite sculpture originally would have graced a monastic site at Nagapattinam, which is also well known for its Buddhist bronzes. The Tamil inscription covering its back is no longer legible.

KARTTIKEYA, GOD OF WAR, SEATED ON A PEACOCK
Madanapalle, Andhra Pradesh, India, Ganga period, c. 12th century

Basalt; 150.5 × 121 × 39 cm (59 $^1/_{16}$ × 47 $^5/_8$ × 15 $^3/_8$ in.)

Restricted gift of Mr. and Mrs. Sylvain S. Wyler, 1962.203

Karttikeya, the god of war, is known by various names, including Skanda, Kumara, and Shanmukha, as well as Murugan in southern India, where he is very popular. This monumental basalt sculpture is probably from the Madanapalle region of Andhra Pradesh. Carved in the round and riding a peacock, the commander of the gods is shown with six heads (*shanmukha*) and twelve arms, ten of which hold weapons aloft. Multiple arms and heads of Hindu deities usually denote their super-human power. According to legend, Karttikeya was born from the spilt seed of the Hindu divinity Shiva. He developed his six heads in order to nurse from his six mothers, the Pleiades (or Krittikas—hence his name, Karttikeya), a constellation of stars. The complex accounts of his miraculous birth and heroic exploits indicate that his character combines several streams of folk belief.

MIRROR FRAME WITH TREE OF LIFE MOTIF

India, Mughal period, 17th/18th century

Nephrite jade, gold, rubies, emeralds, and diamonds inset in the *kundan* technique; 16.4 × 10.2 × 1 cm
(6 7/16 × 4 × 3/8 in.)

Gift of Mr. and Mrs. Chester D. Tripp, 1970.474

This exquisite Mughal mirror frame of pale-green nephrite jade is inlaid with gems in the *kundan* technique, a quintessentially Indian method of gem setting. The motif of this luxury item designed for the Mughal court is a tree of life with inlaid gold stems and leaves and buds of rubies, diamonds, and emeralds. Above the naturalistically depicted plant are two abstracted Chinese-style clouds in gold. Acanthus-leaf motifs adorn the top and bottom of the frame, while the mirror handle is in the shape of an unopened flower bud.

Jade was imported into India from the Khotan region of China. The owner of the jade concession there, the merchant Khwaja Mu'in, visited the court of Mughal emperor Akbar in 1563 and presented him with jade pieces. The earliest Mughal jades reflect Timurid, Ottoman, Safavid, and Chinese influences, and the finest jade objects were produced during the Jahangir and Shah Jahan periods in the seventeenth century. Jade was used for eating and drinking vessels, jewelry, sword hilts and scabbards, belt buckles, mirrors, and hookah parts. Inlaying jade with gold and setting it with gems was a popular Mughal technique derived from earlier Timurid traditions in Iran and Central Asia. This frame is a fine example of the union of various cultural motifs in a single object—a hallmark of Mughal art.

MONUMENTAL PORTRAIT OF A MONKEY

Mewar, Udaipur, Rajasthan, India, 1705/10
Attributed to the Stipple Master (Indian, active c. 1692–c. 1715)

Opaque watercolor and gold on paper; image: 45 × 56 cm (17 ¹¹/₁₆ × 22 in.)
Lacy Armour Fund, James and Marilynn Alsdorf Acquisition Fund, 2011.248

Except for depictions of the monkey-god Hanuman, monkeys are rarely the subject of portraits in India. In this monumental portrait, therefore, we are looking not only at an unusual subject matter but also at a study of an extraordinary simian: one with human features complete with a beard, pale eyes, and long, slender hands. The inscription on the back of this work, written in Devanagari, states that the monkey is named Husaini and "comes from" Nawab Davad (or Daud) Khan. This name most likely refers to Daud Khan Panni, a powerful nobleman and a *faujdar* (a military commander and territorial administrator) who served the Mughal emperors from Aurangzeb (r. 1658–1707) through Farrukhsiyar (r. 1713–19), in various parts of India. The painting has been dated to 1705/10 and is attributed to the anonymous artist now called the Stipple Master. Working in tandem with his patron Maharana Amar Singh II of Mewar (r. 1698–1710), this artist was the initiator of a new painting style in Mewar in the late seventeenth and early eighteenth centuries. A group of about forty-six paintings, including the present work, has now been attributed to this artist-patron duo.

GOD SHIVA AS A DEIFIED KING

Southern Vietnam or Cambodia,
Angkor period, 13th century

Bronze; 65.8 × 21.3 × 20.3 cm (25 7/8 × 8 3/8 × 8 in.)

Gift of Marilynn B. Alsdorf, 1998.752

This bronze icon of the Hindu god Shiva comes from Vietnam or Cambodia and differs in several aspects from his original renditions in India. Here, for example, Shiva is identifiable by his snake armband and the presence of his third eye, with his long hair tied up in a topknot like that of an ascetic. In India, on the other hand, he is usually shown as a smooth-faced youth in one of his several guises: a wild yogi; a young husband and family man accompanied by his bull, Nandi; Lord of the Dance; or an abstract symbol of creation. Here he appears with all the weight and importance of a mature, distinguished royal personage. Around the neck and shoulders he bears a multistrand necklace; in his ears are massive, pendant earrings; and around the hips he wears a patterned sampot with a long ornamental panel falling in a point over his thigh.

This sculpture was discovered in Vietnam, although it may have been moved there from elsewhere in the Khmer kingdom. It may have functioned both as a religious icon and as a memorial dedicated by a king. The personalized facial features reinforce the idea that this is a portrait as well as an image of a deity, possibly a deified royal guru figure who identified himself with Shiva.

MILAREPA ON MOUNT KAILASH

Tibet, c. 1500

Pigment on cloth; 45.5 × 30 cm (17 $^7/_8$ × 11 $^{13}/_{16}$ in.)

Asian Purchase Campaign Endowment and Robert Ross Fund, 1995.277

Milarepa (1040–1123) was a beloved Tibetan singer-poet, mystic, teacher, and saint whose name means "cotton-clad," is usually shown clothed in thin white cotton and cupping a hand to his ear—a gesture typical of singers in India and the Himalayas—to enhance his hearing while blocking out extraneous noise. In this *thangka*, a painted cloth that can be rolled up for portability, Milarepa sits in a cave on Mount Kailash, which is sacred to both Buddhists and Hindus. In front of him, Lake Manasarovar (Marpam) flows by in wavy blue and green bands. Milarepa is flanked by his disciples, and his teacher, Marpa, appears in a medallion above him. The dazzling snow-covered peaks frame each of the central figures, and below them multicolored foothills appear as prismatic spikes refracting the sun's rays like jewels. Along the perimeter of the *thangka*, the five sisters of long life ride their mounts, accompanying Milarepa wherever he preaches his doctrine. The sacred peaks and lakes of the Himalayas have inspired numerous works of art—Milarepa, for example, wrote one hundred thousand songs about them. The other side of this textile contains a long inscription in Tibetan, demonstrating that this is one of the earliest representations of Milarepa.

NECKLACE INSCRIBED WITH THE NAME OF KING PRATAPAMALLADEVA
Kathmandu Valley, Nepal, c. 1650

Gilt copper with semiprecious stones; 36.2 × 35.6 × 8.9 cm (14 ¼ × 14 × 3 ½ in.)

Gift of the Alsdorf Foundation, 2010.575

This ornament may have been given by King Pratapamalla (r. 1641–74), ruler of the Malla dynasty of Nepal, to Taleju Bhavani, the revered patron goddess of the old palace in Kathmandu and the chief protective deity of Nepal and its royal family. King Pratapamalla may also have worn this collar when he participated in rituals. This complex piece is composed of five principal strands and bears the inscription: "Victory to the Mother-Goddess [*Bhagavati devi Janani*]. Hail! [This] is the necklace of the king of kings, lord of kings, lord of the poets, the victorious Pratapamalladeva (may it be) auspicious!"

The two innermost strands resemble rudraksha beads, made from the seeds of a large evergreen tree whose berries are commonly made into rosaries of 108 beads. Such prayer beads are most often worn by Shaivite ascetics, either around the neck or woven into their topknots. The third and fourth strands consist of tubular forms in a crescent shape known as *hansuli*. Each terminates in elaborate clasps, with the inner strand attached to a central amulet case. The outermost ring contains thirteen images of deities, including roundels of the eight mothers (*ashtamatrikas*), each depicted as the goddess Durga slaying the buffalo demon (Mahishasura). As this necklace was a royal commission, the finest Newari artists would have crafted it.

TWO TILES WITH CONTINUOUS FLORAL PATTERN
İznik, Turkey, Ottoman dynasty (1299–1923), c. 1560

Fritware painted in blue, turquoise, red, green, and black under a transparent glaze;
left: 27.9 × 22.2 × 2 cm (11 × 8 ³/₄ × ⁷/₈ in.); right: 27.9 × 22.4 × 2.1 cm (11 × 8 ¹³/₁₆ × ⁷/₈ in.)
Mary Jane Gunsaulus Collection, 1917.219a–b

During the sixteenth and seventeenth centuries, at the height of the Ottoman Empire, ceramic vessels and tiles of remarkable artistic and technical quality were produced at İznik, a city in northwestern Anatolia. The middle of the sixteenth century was an important moment in the evolution of İznik wares. To the existing blue-and-white palette was added color: first turquoise, green, and purple, then a red slip. The earlier focus on tableware was supplemented by a new demand for architectural tilework. Also at this time a new style emerged that emphasized floral motifs, such as familiar flowers (roses, carnations, tulips, etc.), as well as compositions of leaves and palmettes. The enduring quality of İznik at its best and most representative is the effect of bold patterning in brilliant polychrome set against a pure white ground.

The design here consists of elaborate palmettes and sinuously writhing leaves with serrated edges. Rosettes are half-covered by leaves, which, in turn, are pierced by stems. This pattern is typical of the so-called *saz* style, a term that derives from the words *saz kalem*, or "reed pen." The style developed in album drawings in black ink executed during the second half of the sixteenth century and became widely popular in various media. The two works in the Art Institute's collection can be dated to about 1560, the apogee of İznik tile production. They were meant to be contiguous since the pattern continues effortlessly from one to the other.

WINE CISTERN 1553
Francesco Durantino (Italian, active 1543–53)

Tin-glazed earthenware (maiolica); 53.3 × 26.7 cm (21 × 10 ½ in.)

Mary Waller Langhorne Endowment, 1966.395

Elaborately fashioned platters, vessels, and containers, often with decorative embellishments that indicated their specialized function or their owner's social status, were displayed on the banquet tables of Renaissance Italy. Cisterns such as this were filled with cold water and used to cool wine bottles at feasts. Skillfully decorated by the Italian ceramic painter Francesco Durantino, this work typifies the Renaissance interest in both Christian imagery and scenes from pagan antiquity. It is covered with depictions of two famous battle scenes, one on land and one at sea. Although the exterior, adapted from frescoes by Raphael's followers, represents a land battle culminating in the conversion of the Roman emperor Constantine I to Christianity, the cistern's interior depicts a legendary naval disaster: the sinking of the Trojan hero Aeneas's ships by the jealous goddess Hera. At the cistern's center, the ships disappear beneath the waves, a playful conceit that was no doubt even more effective when the cistern was filled with water. The generously sized vessel displays all the characteristics that made maiolica, a tin-glazed earthenware, popular: brilliant colors, lively painting, and riveting narratives mixed with fanciful design. The term *maiolica* probably comes from Majorca, the port through which pottery from Moorish Spain was first exported to Italy.

PORTIONS OF A FIELD ARMOR 1588/90
Jacob Halder (German, active in England, 1558–1608)
Royal Workshops of Greenwich (English, 1511–1649)
Steel, brass, gilding, leather, and silk velvet textile; h. (mounted with arm defenses): 61 cm (30 in.)
George F. Harding Collection, 1982.2241a–f

During the late Middle Ages and Renaissance, some of the finest armorers worked exclusively for royal patrons in the workshops set up to meet their needs. In 1511 King Henry VIII of England established such a workshop at Greenwich Palace outside London, which produced outstanding armor for the English court for over a century. It was staffed largely by German craftsmen, among them Jacob Halder, who was master workman at Greenwich when this half-armor was produced around 1588–90. Made for a high-ranking nobleman, it features crisply decorated bands of etching and gilding and a silhouette mimicking fashionable dress. The shape of the breast-plate, broad at the shoulders, narrow at the waist, and dipped at the belly, imitates the peasecod (peapod-shaped) cut of a gentleman's doublet of the same period. Despite the lavish decoration and exaggerated shape, this armor, intended for the field of battle, was capable of withstanding musket fire. Indeed, it was commissioned in 1588, at the very moment England was preparing for invasion by the Spanish Armada. But to the fashionable noble who commissioned this harness, demonstrating wealth and status was as important as protecting life and limb.

HORSE AND RIDER

1630

Hans Ludwig Kienle (German, 1591–1653)

Ulm, Germany

Silver and silver gilt; h. 31.5 cm (12 3/8 in.)

Eloise W. Martin fund; through prior acquisition of the George F. Harding Collection; Henry Horner Strauss, Pauline S. Armstrong, Harry and Maribel G. Blum, Tillie C. Cohn, Richard T. Crane, Jr., Memorial, Stanford Marks, Michael A. Bradshaw and Kenneth S. Harris, Mrs. Edgar J. Uihlein Art Purchase, European Decorative Arts Capital Campaign funds; through prior acquisition from Albert D. Lasker; European Decorative Arts General, Mr. and Mrs. Joseph Varley funds; through prior acquisition of the Kate S. Buckingham Gothic fund; Mary Swissler Oldberg fund; through prior acquisitions of the Howard V. Shaw Memorial and Kate S. Buckingham funds, 2003.114

This extraordinary sculptural group, which consists of a male nude astride a rearing horse, is a rare example of the work of Hans Ludwig Kienle, a German silversmith who specialized in depicting animals. Conceived as a drinking cup, this work was destined for display on a buffet or sideboard. Kienle's work belongs to a larger body of German Renaissance and Baroque sideboard silver that includes cups in the form of three-dimensional horses, lions, stags, and other animals. Horse-and-rider figural groups have their roots in earlier Greek and Roman sculpture. Renaissance princes often had themselves depicted in monumental form, wearing Classical dress or contemporary armor and sitting atop prancing or rearing steeds. That Kienle based this silver cup on an earlier sculptural model is suggested by the existence of a bronze group of virtually identical subject, composition, and scale, made in northern Italy during the second half of the sixteenth century. Kienle masterfully rendered the differentiation of human and equine musculature through the contrast of silver and silver-gilt surfaces, thus animating the already dynamic subject.

CABINET

c. 1660

Augsburg, Germany

Ebony, ivory, various woods, bronze, and iron; 160 × 110.5 × 64.8 cm (63 × 43 ½ × 25 ½ in.)

Anonymous Purchase Fund, 1970.404

Cabinets made in the southern German town of Augsburg during the sixteenth and seventeenth centuries are famous for their ornate decoration, which was typically executed in ebony veneer and ivory inlay. This exceptional example also includes delicately carved figures, bronze mounts, and narrative panels made from ivory and stained wood relief. The exquisite craftsmanship of this decoration is matched in inventiveness by the cabinet's interior structure, which is part display case, part tool chest, and part safe-deposit box. Hidden compartments to the right of a built-in clock (a 1715 replacement of an earlier timepiece) contain a set of five medicine canisters and at least twenty-two other utensils, including hammers, scissors, and a mortar and pestle. These and the other compartments in the cabinet would often have housed jewelry, gems, and important papers, among other precious items. Thematically, the cabinet's decoration ranges from pure ornament to hunting themes (especially related to the sport of falconry, which may have been a favorite pastime of the cabinet's owner) and from mythological tales to the allegorical figure of the Christian virtue Charity, who crowns the object.

COFFER

1700/1720

Attributed to André-Charles Boulle (French, 1642–1732)

Paris, France

Oak, tortoiseshell, brass, gilt copper, pewter, ebony, and gilt bronze mounts; 44.5 × 73 × 48.3 cm
(17 ½ × 28 ¾ × 19 in.)

Michael A. Bradshaw and Kenneth S. Harris, Eloise W. Martin, Richard T. Crane, Jr., Memorial,
and European Decorative Arts Purchase funds; through prior acquisitions of Mrs. C. H. Boissevain
in memory of Henry C. Dangler, Kate S. Buckingham Endowment, David Dangler, Harold T. Martin,
and Katherine Field-Rodman, 2001.54

The cabinetmaker André-Charles Boulle was responsible for some of the finest examples of French furniture made during the reign of Louis XIV (1643–1715). Boulle perfected the technique of veneering furniture with a rich marquetry of tortoiseshell, pewter, and gilt copper, and he further enriched his surfaces with sculptural gilt bronze mounts. Acclaimed for his brilliant designs and superb execution, Boulle was commissioned by the most discerning and demanding patrons in France, among them members of the royal family, aristocrats, ministers, and financiers.

This rectangular coffer is a visually powerful example of Boulle's work from the early eighteenth century. Such objects served as containers for medals or jewels. This example is richly veneered with marquetry panels of scrolls, strapwork, and vines executed in engraved gilt copper on a ground of tortoiseshell. Framing the panels are strips of ebony and pewter. The coffer also features gilt bronze mounts in the form of male, female, and animal heads. The escutcheon in the center of the front panel may depict the head of Apollo, his long hair braided on either side of his face and gathered in a knot below his chin. The lid contains a grinning, bearded male face, perhaps that of a satyr, crowned with a radiating headdress, the whole of which supports a handle.

KING VULTURE

1734
Meissen Porcelain Manufactory
(German, founded 1710)
Modeled by Johann Joachim Kändler
(German, 1706–1775)

Hard-paste porcelain, polychrome enamels; 58 × 43 cm (22 ⁷/₈ × 16 ⁷/₈ in.)

Harry and Maribel G. Blum Endowment Fund, restricted gift of the Antiquarian Society, Kate S. Buckingham Fund, Charles H. and Mary F. Worcester Collection Fund, Auction Sales Proceeds Fund, Centennial Major Acquisitions Income Fund, Robert Allerton Trust, the Mary and Leigh Block Endowment Fund, Ada Turnbull Hertle Fund, restricted gift of Harry A. Root, Wirt D. Walker Trust, Gladys N. Anderson Fund, Pauline Seipp Armstrong Fund, Edward E. Ayer Fund in memory of Charles L. Hutchinson, European Decorative Arts Krehbiel Fund, restricted gift of Mr. and Mrs. Stanford Marks, Helen A. Regenstein Endowment, Samuel A. Marx Purchase Fund for Major Acquisitions, Laura T. Magnuson Acquisition Fund, Marian and Samuel Klasstorner Fund, Maurice D. Galleher Endowment, Robert Allerton Purchase Fund, Bessie Bennett Fund, European Decorative Arts General fund, Edward Johnson Fund, Elizabeth R. Vaughn Fund, Annette Mathby Chapin Fund, Wentworth Greene Field Memorial Fund, Director's Fund, restricted gift of the Edward Byron Smith, Jr. Family Foundation, Samuel P. Avery Fund, Hugh Leander and Mary Trumbull Adams Memorial Endowment, restricted gift of the G-Bar Charitable Foundation, Betty Bell Spooner Fund, restricted gift of Elizabeth Souder Louis, Irving and June Seaman Endowment Fund, Charles U. Harris Endowed Acquisition Fund, S. DeWitt Clough Fund, restricted gift of the Woman's Board of the Alliance Française of Chicago, Grant J. Pick Purchase Fund, restricted gift of Ghenete Zelleke, 2007.105

As elector of Saxony and king of Poland, Augustus II (r. 1694/97–1733) presided over the ambitious transformation of his capital, Dresden, through advances in architecture, the arts, science, and technology. Produced beginning in 1710 through royal sponsorship and funding, Meissen porcelain was an exclusive luxury good of its time. Around 1728 Augustus conceived of replicating the animal kingdom in porcelain for display in a Baroque palace that he was transforming into a showcase for his collections of Asian and Meissen ceramics. This porcelain zoo was intended for the long gallery on the main floor of the palace. By 1733, the year the king died, more than thirty different models of birds and almost forty animals had been made, many by the sculptor Johann Joachim Kändler, who worked at Meissen from 1731 to 1775. Kändler drew this vulture from life, which allowed him to animate his work with the creature's quintessential spirit. Such porcelain animals remain the most vivid expression of Augustus's wish, as elector and king, to possess and rule over the natural world.

WALL CLOCK

1735/40
Case attributed to Jean-Pierre Latz
(French, c. 1691–1754)
Clockwork made by Francis Bayley
(Belgian, active 18th century)
Paris, France

Oak, tortoiseshell, kingwood, brass, gilt bronze,
and glass; 147.3 × 64.8 × 53.3 cm (58 × 25 ½ ×
21 in.)

Ada Turnbull Hertle Fund, 1975.172

An exuberant and lavish example of
the French Rococo style, this sculptural
wall clock epitomizes the extravagant
era of Louis XV (r. 1715–74). Festooned
with ormolu (gilt bronze) swirls and
floral swags, the clock required the
collaboration of numerous specialized
artisans. Its case, candelabra, and wall
bracket were created by the eminent
Jean-Pierre Latz, who was appointed
ébéniste (furniture maker) to the king in
1741. The clock's eight-day movement
was manufactured in the Flemish city
of Ghent by Francis Bayley, possibly a
member of the large London dynasty
of clockmakers of that name. Opulent
clocks such as this did more than tell
time; they delighted the ear with music
(six melody titles are engraved in the
dial's arch) and dazzled the eye with
dramatic scenes. Here the Greek god
Apollo is poised at the top of the clock
case to slay the serpent Python. The
space between the clock and the wall
bracket was cleverly used to suggest the
beast's home, the cave of Mount Parnas-
sus in Greece. In the triangular base are
the faces of Zeus, symbolizing time, and
Hera, presiding over marriage and child-
birth. They are surmounted by two small
coats of arms belonging to the Flemish
bride and groom whose union the clock
was probably created to celebrate.

GAMING SET

1735/40
Du Paquier Porcelain Manufactory (Austrian, 1718–44)
Vienna, Austria

Hard-paste porcelain, polychrome enamels, gilt mounts, diamonds, and gilding; overall: 16.8 × 14.8 cm
(6 5/8 × 5 13/16 in.); each gaming piece: 3.8 × 2.5 cm (1/2 × 1 in.)

Eloise W. Martin fund; Richard T. Crane and Mrs. J. Ward Thorne endowments; through prior gift
of the Antiquarian Society, 1993.349

Additional gaming pieces: Gift of the Antiquarian Society, 1995.95.1–4

This richly decorated gaming box ranks among the most exceptional works of art
produced by the Du Paquier Porcelain Manufactory during its short twenty-five-year
existence. Mounted with gold plaques and painted with colored enamels and gilding,
the box opens to reveal four small, similarly decorated porcelain containers. These
smaller boxes are mounted with gold and set with diamonds; each, when opened,
reveals two types of porcelain gambling chips. The boxes were painted according to
a complex, tightly organized decorative scheme. The lid of the large box depicts three
trompe l'oeil playing cards that appear to have been carelessly thrown down. Each of
the corners of the box and lid is painted with a network of violet and gold ornaments
characteristic of the factory's mature, late-Baroque style. With its liberal use of gold
and diamonds, this work was certainly among the most extravagant objects crafted at
the Du Paquier manufactory. The box may have been presented as a diplomatic gift,
perhaps from the Austrian Habsburgs to their Russian Romanov counterparts.

CENTERPIECE AND STAND WITH A PAIR OF COVERED SUGAR CASTERS AND AN OIL OR VINEGAR CRUET

c. 1737
Meissen Porcelain Manufactory (German, founded 1710)
Modeled by Johann Joachim Kändler (German, 1706–1775)
Meissen, Germany

Hard-paste porcelain, polychrome enamels, gilding, and gilt bronze mounts; bowl: 28 × 44.4 × 25.4 cm
(11 × 17 ½ × 10 in.); stand: 15.2 × 66 × 50.8 cm (6 × 26 × 20 in.)

Centerpiece and stand: Atlan Ceramic Club, Buckingham Lustre and Decorative Arts Purchase funds,
1958.405a–f

Sugar casters: Louise D. Smith, Edward Byron Smith Charitable, Robert Allerton, Mrs. Edward I.
Rothschild, and R. T. Crane, Jr., funds, 1984.1228a–b

Cruet: Gift of Mr. and Mrs. Samuel Grober in honor of Ian Wardropper and Ghenete Zelleke through
the Antiquarian Society, 1998.504a–b

Typifying the splendor of the Saxon court at Dresden during the eighteenth century, this porcelain centerpiece would have been part of an elaborate dinner service that graced ceremonial court banquet tables. Remarkable for its large size and luxurious decoration, the service was designed for Count Heinrich von Brühl, who was both administrator of the Royal Saxon Porcelain Manufactory at Meissen and prime minister to Augustus III (r. 1733–63), elector of Saxony and king of Poland. The centerpiece consists of a large, flat plateau made in sections fitted together to support a tall, four-legged, open basket decorated with fanciful roosters and Chinese figures. At either end of the plateau are sugar casters in the form of Chinese figures embracing under a canopy. Established in 1710, the Meissen factory dominated porcelain production in Europe until the mid-eighteenth century and continues to operate to this day.

EWER AND BASIN

c. 1745

Capodimonte Porcelain Factory (Italian, founded 1743)

Modeled by Giuseppe Gricci (Italian, c. 1700–1770)

Capodimonte, Italy

Soft-paste porcelain, polychrome enamels, and gilding; basin: 16.5 × 38.7 × 34.3 cm (6 $\frac{1}{2}$ × 15 $\frac{1}{4}$ × 13 $\frac{1}{2}$ in.); ewer: h. 30.5 cm (12 in.)

Gift of Mr. and Mrs. Robert Norman Chatain in memory of Professor Alfred Chatain, 1957.490a–b

Made during the first years of the royal porcelain factory in Capodimonte, this rare set is one of the great masterpieces of European porcelain. With its malleability and whiteness, porcelain was especially suited to the Rococo emphasis on asymmetry, natural motifs, and a palette that was lucid and light. These soft-paste porcelain surfaces, probably designed by Capodimonte's master modeler, Giuseppe Gricci, conjure up the textures and luminescence of sea-washed shells and natural mother-of-pearl. The allusion to the marine world—so appropriate to these water-bearing vessels—is furthered by the use of shell-like forms for both the shape and decoration of the ewer and basin. The surfaces of the vessels are also encrusted with marine elements, and a trompe l'oeil coral branch cleverly serves as the ewer's handle. Swirling lines and irregular surfaces contribute to the ewer's sense of lightness and complete the allusion to the sea.

FALL-FRONT DESK

c. 1810

Vienna, Austria

Various woods and gilt bronze mounts; 141 × 91.4 × 39.4 cm (55 ½ × 36 × 15 in.)

Gift of the Centennial Fund; Mrs. Burton W. Hales, Mrs. William O. Hunt, Jessie Spaulding Landon, Mrs. Harold T. Martin, Adelaide Ryerson, Mrs. E. Hall Taylor, Mrs. Chester D. Tripp, and Mrs. Philip K. Wrigley funds, 1976.39

The inventive lyre shape of this secretary, surmounted by three stepped drawers and supported by griffins, identifies it as an elaborate, complex case form made in Vienna during the Napoleonic era. The upper half of the front falls forward to serve as a writing surface revealing interior compartments, drawers, and shelves. The secretary shares characteristics with the Empire style developed in France, a bolder and more severe expression of the Neoclassical interest in ancient Greek and Roman art. Though craftsmen throughout Europe studied French handbooks detailing new designs, models were not merely imitated; this example was made with materials and techniques typical of Viennese workshops. Its form has no direct source in antiquity, although the lyre shape and abundant decorative details—griffins, cornucopias, paw feet, and interior caryatid figures—are familiar classical motifs. The variety of woods, selected to create contrast between light areas and dark borders, matches the pastiche of decorative forms. Vienna was a major European design center in the early nineteenth century, and this desk type enjoyed wide popularity. Production continued throughout the ensuing Biedermeier era, into the 1840s.

LONDONDERRY VASE

1813

Sèvres Porcelain Manufactory (French, founded 1740)

Designed by Charles Percier (French, 1764–1838); decoration designed by Alexandre-Théodore Brongniart (French, 1739–1813); painted by Gilbert Drouet (French, 1785–1825) and Christophe-Ferdinand Caron (French, active 1792–1815)

Sèvres, France

Hard-paste porcelain, polychrome enamels, gilding, and gilt bronze mounts; h. 137.2 cm (54 in.)

Gift of the Harry and Maribel G. Blum Fund and the Harold L. Stuart Endowment, 1987.1

This vase epitomizes the great achievements of the royal porcelain factory at Sèvres during the Napoleonic period. Sèvres was a chief beneficiary of Napoleon's policy of resuscitating factories after the trauma of the French Revolution; demonstrating the supremacy of French craftsmanship, the emperor used sumptuous porcelain in his palaces as well as for state gifts. With its monumental size, rigorous symmetry, and unabashed splendor, this vase is a superb example of the Empire style inspired by Greco-Roman art. It is a triumph of the collaborative practice of the Sèvres factory; documents reveal the precise roles played by each artist in its creation. Napoleon's chief architect, Charles Percier, created the Etruscan scroll-handled design. The vase was commissioned by Napoleon in 1805 but was produced only in 1813 and was still at the factory when he was exiled the following year. It was used as a diplomatic gift from his successor, King Louis XVIII, to Viscount Castlereagh, the British foreign secretary and, from 1821, the 2nd Marquess of Londonderry.

SIDEBOARD

c. 1876
Designed by Edward William Godwin (English, 1833–1886)
Made by William Watt (English, 1834–1885)
London, England

Ebonized mahogany, glass, and silvered brass; 181.6 × 255.3 × 50.2 cm (71 $\frac{1}{2}$ × 100 $\frac{1}{2}$ × 19 $\frac{3}{4}$ in.) (with leaves extended)

Restricted gift of Robert Allerton, Harry and Maribel G. Blum, Mary and Leigh Block, Mary Waller Langhorne, Mrs. Siegfried G. Schmidt, Tillie C. Cohn, Richard T. Crane, Jr., Memorial, Eugene A. Davidson, Harriott A. Fox, Florence L. Notter, Kay and Frederick Krehbiel, European Decorative Arts Purchase, and Irving and June Seaman endowments; through prior acquisition of the Reid Martin Estate, 2005.529

Celebrated as the "poet of architects and architect of all the arts," Edward William Godwin was a man of many accomplishments. In a career that spanned more than thirty-five years, he was an architect of civic, domestic, and ecclesiastical buildings; an innovative interior decorator and designer of furniture, textiles, and theater sets; and an articulate critic of art and architecture. Godwin first designed his ebonized sideboard, of which this is a variant model, for his own dining room in 1867, and he subsequently reconsidered the form over the next two decades. In its appearance, the sideboard represents a turning away from the weight of contemporary Gothic Revival aesthetics and a move toward a reductionist sensibility expressed through the balance of solids and voids. This spare style gained Godwin some notable contemporary clients, among them James McNeill Whistler and Oscar Wilde. In his 1904 study *The English House*, the influential German critic Hermann Muthesius wrote that Godwin's furniture, including this sideboard, foreshadowed the more modern look that emerged at the turn of the twentieth century. While calling Godwin's creations "wildly picturesque," Muthesius concluded that the overall effect was "one of elegance."

MANXMAN PIANOFORTE

1897

Designed by Mackay Hugh Baillie Scott (English, 1865–1945)

Made by John Broadwood and Sons (English, founded 1728)

London, England

Oak and ebony with marquetry decoration, ivory, mother-of-pearl, and copper; 128.9 × 143.2 cm

(50 ³/₄ × 56 ¹/₂ × 27 ¹/₂ in.)

Restricted gifts of Robert Allerton, Mrs. Joseph Regenstein, Sr., Walter S. Brewster, Mrs. Emily

Crane Chadbourne, Richard T. Crane, Jr., Mr. and Mrs. Leopold Blumka, Henry Manaster, Jack Linsky,

Mrs. Margaret Day Blake, Mr. and Mrs. John Wilson, Mrs. Henry C. Wood, by exchange; Florene May

Schoenborn and Samuel A. Marx Fund; European Decorative Arts Purchase Fund, 1985.99

A product of the Arts and Crafts movement in England, the Manxman Pianoforte represents an innovative solution to the somewhat awkward form of the upright piano. Motivated by the shoddy results of industrial mass production, the movement advocated the recognition of furniture and decorative arts as works of art. Here the celebrated English architect and designer Mackay Hugh Baillie Scott created an object that is both cleverly functional and aesthetically pleasing. When opened, the lid and doors of the strikingly decorated cabinet act as acoustical sounding boards. Revealed inside is the musical instrument itself, along with a profusion of exquisite handcrafted metalwork, including candleholders fixed to the sides of the case. The overall design, like the keyboard, is a study in contrasts of light and dark; the lower section's alternating pattern echoes the piano's keys. A Manxman is an inhabitant of the Isle of Man, and the term derives from Scott's early residence there. This piano is one of a number executed around 1900 with John Broadwood and Sons of London, who made the musical movements.

SAMOVAR

1897/1907

Designed by Henry van de Velde
(Belgian, 1863–1957); made by the
workshop of Theodor Müller (German,
active late 18th/early 19th century)
Weimar, Germany

Silvered brass and teak; h. 37.9 cm (14 7/8 in.)
Gift of the Historical Design Collection; Mr. and
Mrs. F. Lee Wendell and European Decorative
Arts Purchase funds; Edward E. Ayer Endow-
ment in memory of Charles L. Hutchinson;
Bessie Bennett Endowment; Edward Chase
Garvey Memorial; Walter C. Clark, Mrs. Oscar
Klein, Mrs. R. W. Morris, and Mrs. I. Newton
Perry, 1989.154a–e

The Belgian architect and designer Henry
van de Velde was one of the primary
exponents of Art Nouveau, an international design style informed by the
English Arts and Crafts Movement (see
p. 139) that was born in the 1880s and
flourished at the turn of the twentieth
century. This samovar, or Russian tea-
kettle, beautifully illustrates the adroit
mixture of taut lines and curvilinear
motifs that characterizes Van de Velde's
mature Art Nouveau style. The sinuous
organic lines of its base twist and snake
around upright brackets and pick up
again in the braided band motif of the
teak handle. The kettle itself is simple in
form, unornamented, and, with a prominent hinge on the spout cover, appears
to be more engineered than crafted. This
example was made from silvered brass
and teak in accord with Van de Velde's
philosophy that art should be accessible
and affordable to a broad public (though
other examples were made of more
costly silver). The kettle was designed
at the Weimar School of Applied Arts,
where Van de Velde became director in
1904. That school later became the Bauhaus, the bastion of modern design.

TALL-CASE CLOCK

c. 1906
Case designed by Josef Hoffmann (Austrian, 1870–1956); metalwork designed by Carl Otto Czeschka (Austrian, 1878–1960); made by Wiener Werkstätte (Austrian, 1903–32)
Vienna, Austria

Painted maple, ebony, mahogany, gilt brass, glass, silver-plated copper, patinated bronze-bands, and clockworks; 179.5 × 46.5 × 30.5 cm (70 5/8 × 18 1/4 × 12 in.)
Laura Matthews and Mary Waller Langhorne endowments, 1983.37

This tall-case clock represents a masterful collaboration between two major figures in the Vienna Secession movement: the architect Josef Hoffmann and the designer Carl Otto Czeschka. Like their English counterparts in the Arts and Crafts movement, the Secessionists initially supported the credo that art is for everyone and worked to create beautiful, simple objects for everyday use. A manifestation of this philosophy was the Wiener Werkstätte, or Vienna Workshop, of which Hoffmann was a founder and Czeschka a member. Produced by the Werkstätte's specialist craftsmen, this clock embodies the unexpected dichotomy that arose within the workshop: its early reformist ideals resulted in progressive, even avant-garde, products that appealed primarily to a privileged, sophisticated clientele. Hoffmann's design consists of simple, architectonic forms emphasized through the bold use of stark white-painted maple and an inlaid checkered pattern. In contrast to the case's austere rectilinearity, Czeschka designed a luxurious, hand-wrought scheme for its dial and door. The door is fashioned from hand-embossed gilt brass inset with cut-glass prisms. Its richly patterned surface decoration depicts a stylized tree of life motif.

CORNER CABINET

c. 1916
Designed by Émile-Jacques Ruhlmann (French, 1879–1933)
Paris, France

Oak, mahogany, amboyna, ebony, and ivory veneer; 127.3 × 82.9 × 52.1 cm (50 1/8 × 32 5/8 × 20 1/2 in.)
Restricted gift of Mrs. James W. Alsdorf, Mrs. T. Stanton Armour, Mrs. DeWitt W. Buchanan, Jr., Mrs. Henry M. Buchbinder, Quinn E. Delaney, Mrs. Harold T. Martin, Manfred Steinfeld, Mrs. Edgar J. Uihlein; Mrs. T. Stanton Armour, Mr. and Mrs. Robert O. Delaney, Mr. and Mrs. Fred Krehbiel, and Mrs. Eric Oldberg funds; Mrs. Pauline S. Armstrong, Harry and Maribel G. Blum, Richard T. Crane, Jr., Memorial, Mr. and Mrs. Fred Krehbiel, Mary Waller Langhorne, and European Decorative Arts endowments; through prior acquisitions of the Antiquarian Society, European Decorative Arts Purchase Fund, Howard Van Doren Shaw, and Mr. and Mrs. Martin A. Ryerson, 1997.694

This sumptuously veneered corner cabinet is arguably a signature piece of the Art Deco era. The term *Art Deco*, used since the 1960s to refer to the high-style interiors of the years between the two world wars, is derived from the title of the 1925 Paris Exposition Internationale des Arts Décoratifs et Industriels Modernes. This cabinet's triangular form, with its serpentine door, is supported on short, fluted legs that are shod with ivory on the two front feet and terminate at the knees with a scroll flourish. Émile-Jacques Ruhlmann employed ebony and ivory to depict the large urn from which an abundance of stylized flowers and leaves cascades, overflowing the limits of the container to form a black-and-white oval that contrasts with the warm tone of the amboyna wood.

ENGLISH DINING ROOM OF THE GEORGIAN PERIOD, 1770–90
c. 1937

Miniature room, mixed media; interior: 50.8 × 89.5 × 65.1 cm (20 × 35 1/4 × 25 5/8 in.)

Gift of Mrs. James Ward Thorne, 1941.1195

The sixty-eight fascinating Thorne Miniature Rooms feature highlights from the history of interior design and decorative arts from the thirteenth century to 1940. These enchanting miniature stage sets were conceived by Mrs. James Ward Thorne of Chicago and constructed between 1934 and 1940 by master craftsmen according to her exacting specifications, on a scale of one inch to one foot. The harmonious elegance seen here is based on two dining rooms designed by Robert Adam, the successful eighteenth-century London architect whose precise and delicate interpretation of the antique (stimulated by then-recent excavations at Herculaneum and Pompeii) dictated English taste for a quarter of a century. To insure perfect conformity, Adam undertook the entire design of a house and every detail of its interior, hiring cabinetmakers to execute furniture that blended Neoclassical elements with current English forms. Instead of using wood and wallpaper, Adam carved low-relief ornament in plaster against painted panels in the style of Roman stuccos, as seen in this dining room. His furniture was often gilded in the Continental fashion, as is the side table in this room. The landscape over the table, painted by one of the many artists that Mrs. Thorne commissioned for the project, is in the style of Claude Lorrain (see p. 307).

EUROPEAN PAINTING AND SCULPTURE

RELIQUARY CASKET OF SAINTS ADRIAN AND NATALIA
1100/1150
Spanish; Léon
Silver and oak core; 15.9 × 25.4 × 14.5 cm (6 ¼ × 10 × 5 ¾ in.)
Kate S. Buckingham Endowment, 1943.65

This rare casket was made to contain the sacred relics of Saint Adrian. It was fashioned like a miniature tomb, complete with a tiled roof and Romanesque columns.
Adrian was revered as the patron saint of soldiers and a protector against the plague.
A Roman officer in charge of the persecution of Christians, Adrian so admired the
virtues of those whom he oppressed that he converted to their faith. After declaring
himself a Christian, Adrian was arrested and brutally martyred in the early fourth
century. Unflinchingly illustrated on the sides of this reliquary (and reinforced by the
inscription) is the story of Adrian's trial, his dismemberment, and the transport of
his remains to a city near Constantinople by his devoted wife, Saint Natalia.

The casket's design was hammered out from the reverse on thin sheets of silver,
a technique called repoussé. The figures were reduced to simple, monumental forms
composed of convex bulges, reflecting the style of Romanesque relief sculpture and
manuscript illumination in northern Spain.

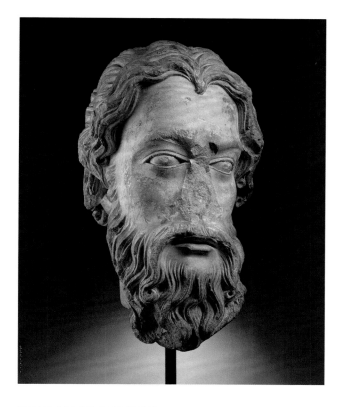

HEAD OF AN APOSTLE

c. 1210

French; Paris

Limestone; h. 43 cm (17 in.)

Kate S. Buckingham Endowment, 1944.413

This imposing head probably comes from a full-length sculpture of an apostle that was one of the column or jamb figures flanking the portals of the west facade of Notre-Dame Cathedral in Paris. Showing the heritage of ancient and Byzantine models, it bears all the stylistic hallmarks of the beginning of the Gothic style in the region around the year 1200. The object's origin was the subject of heated scholarly debate for several decades. Neutron activation analysis has shown that the limestone came from a quarry that also supplied stone for other carvings on Notre-Dame. The discovery of sculptural fragments from the cathedral's Gallery of Kings above the west portals, dated to between 1220 and 1235 (and now in the Musée National du Moyen Âge, Paris), provided an important point of comparison. The Art Institute's head is said to have been found during excavations for the modernization of Paris in the mid-nineteenth century. Medieval sculpture from Notre-Dame was purposefully damaged in the 1790s during the French Revolution because of its presumed royal associations. Fragments of some of the sculpture removed at the order of the revolutionary tribunal were buried out of a lingering respect for its tradition and quality, to be rediscovered in later years.

TRIPTYCH WITH SCENES FROM THE LIFE OF CHRIST
1350/75
German; Cologne
Ivory with traces of gold; 25.7 × 17.5 cm (10 1/8 × 6 15/16 in.)
Mr. and Mrs. Martin A. Ryerson Collection, 1937.827

Ivory was used to make highly prized devotional objects in the Gothic era. This trip-tych features scenes from the infancy and Passion of Christ, arranged in a chrono-logical sequence from left to right, starting at the bottom with the Annunciation, the Adoration of the Magi, and the Presentation in the Temple. The narrative continues in the top register with the Road to Calvary, Christ on the Cross, and the encounter of Christ and Mary Madgalen after the Resurrection. Such small devotional objects might be kept on a stand or cabinet in a bedroom, ready to be used as a focus for prayer by the layperson who owned them, along with an illuminated Psalter or Book of Hours. The intimate scale and movable wings of the triptych made it easy to store in a chest or to carry from one residence to another as needed. Although Paris has long been recognized as a great center for ivory carving in the Gothic era, recent scholarship has also emphasized the importance of workshops in England, Germany, and Italy—affirming the popularity of the medium throughout medieval Europe. This triptych was most likely made by a master artist and his atelier working in Germany, probably in Cologne.

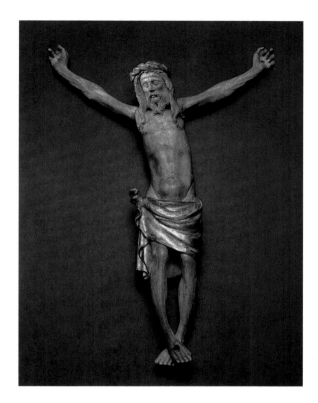

JACQUES DE BAERZE Netherlandish, active before 1384–after 1399
MELCHIOR BROEDERLAM Netherlandish, c. 1355–c. 1411
Corpus of Christ, from *Altarpiece of the Crucifixion*, 1391/99
Walnut with traces of polychromy and gilding; h. 27.7 cm (11 in.)
Gift of Honoré Palmer, 1944.1370

Corpus of Christ was originally the focal point of a large triptych combining painting
and sculpture that was commissioned in 1390 by Philip the Bold, Duke of Burgundy,
for the newly founded Charterhouse of Champol outside Dijon. Philip intended this
monastery as a dynastic burial place, and he and his successors endowed it with artistic
treasures. The triptych was a collaboration between two important artists from the
Flemish territories controlled by Philip the Bold: the sculptor Jacques de Baerze and
the painter Melchior Broederlam. When open, the altarpiece showed carved reliefs of
the Crucifixion, the Adoration of the Magi, and the Entombment together with standing figures of saints. The gilded center could be covered by movable wings whose backs,
painted with scenes from the Infancy of Christ by Broederlam, were visible when the
altarpiece was closed. The triptych still survives in Dijon (Musée des Beaux-Arts), but
the central figure of the crucified Christ was removed during the French Revolution.
Even separated from its context within the altarpiece, however, the crucified Christ
remains a powerfully expressive work. Christ's tensed hands and feet and earthy features are realistically observed, while the curving contour of his torso and the folds
of his loincloth reflect a more courtly ideal.

LORENZO MONACO
Italian, c. 1370–c. 1422/23
Processional Cross, 1392/95
Tempera on panel; panel (including frame):
57.3 × 28 cm (22 ½ × 11 ¹/₁₆ in.); painted surface:
51 × 23.3 cm (20 ⅛ × 9 ³/₁₆ in.)
Mr. and Mrs. Martin A. Ryerson Collection,
1933.1032

Representative of the early work of
Lorenzo Monaco, a Camaldolese monk
and leading Florentine painter of the
end of the fourteenth century and the
beginning of the fifteenth century, the
delicate colors and simplified forms of
this Crucifixion are exceptionally well
preserved. The medallion above the
crucified Christ contains an image of
Christ in Glory, holding a palm in each
hand to symbolize his victory over death.
Below, the crowned figure of King David
holds an inscribed scroll. More often
in Crucifixion scenes of this period, a
pelican appears at the top of the cross
and the skull of Adam lies at the foot.
A penitential theme is suggested by
the figures kneeling under the Cross:
on the right is a haloed Magdalen in
a red robe; on the left, a man with the
incised rays of a *beatus,* or blessed one,
emanating from his head wears the
torn brown cloak of a hermit. He was
probably meant to represent a specific
hermit within the Camaldolese order.
The panel has a hole drilled at the base,
allowing it to be mounted on a pole and
used as a processional cross, likely in the
monastic Camaldolese community of
Santa Maria degli Angeli, where Lorenzo
lived and worked.

BERNAT MARTORELL Spanish, c. 1400–1452
Saint George and the Dragon, 1434/35
Tempera on panel; 155.6 × 98.1 cm (61 ¼ × 38 ⅝ in.)
Gift of Mrs. Richard E. Danielson and Mrs. Chauncey B. McCormick, 1933.786

Bernat Martorell was the greatest painter of the first half of the fifteenth century in Catalonia in northeastern Spain. Depicted here is the most frequently represented episode from the popular legend of Saint George, in which the model Christian knight saves a town and rescues a beautiful princess. Conceived in the elegant, decorative International Gothic style, the painting was originally the center of an altarpiece dedicated to Saint George that was apparently made for the chapel of the palace of the Catalan government in Barcelona. This central scene was surrounded by four smaller narrative panels, now in the Musée du Louvre, Paris, and was probably sur-mounted by a lost image of Christ on the Cross. Here Saint George, on his white steed, triumphs over the evil dragon. A wealth of precisely observed details intensifies the drama. Dressed in an ermine-lined robe, the princess wears a sumptuous gilt crown atop her wavy red-gold hair. Her parents and their subjects watch the spectacle from the distant town walls. George's halo and armor and the scaly body of the dragon are richly modeled with raised stucco decoration. Martorell also treated the ground, littered with bones and crawling with lizards, in a lively manner, giving it a gritty texture.

GIOVANNI DI PAOLO Italian, 1398–1482
The Beheading of Saint John the Baptist, 1455/60
Tempera on panel; 68.6 × 39.1 cm (27 × 15 ³/₈ in.)
Mr. and Mrs. Martin A. Ryerson Collection, 1933.1014

Among the most impressive achievements of the Sienese master Giovanni di Paolo
is his narrative series of twelve panels illustrating the life of Saint John the Baptist—from his birth, prophecy, and the baptism of Christ through his beheading at
the request of Salome. These scenes are enacted in complex settings that exploit the
tall, slender proportions of the panels and set off the expressive poses of the figures.
The Beheading of Saint John the Baptist depicts the henchmen of Queen Herodias
placing his head on a golden platter. The execution has just occurred; blood spews
profusely from the elongated neck of the saint. The rich patterning of the architecture, painted in a light, delicate palette, contrasts with the gruesome trails of blood
falling to the ground and collecting beneath the decapitated corpse. The distant landscape was inspired by the hills around Siena. Throughout the series, Giovanni skillfully repeated colors, settings, and patterns to create a unified narrative. Eleven of the
original twelve panels survive, six of which are in the Art Institute. The panels were
arranged in three rows to form two large, movable doors, possibly once enclosing a
sculpture or relic.

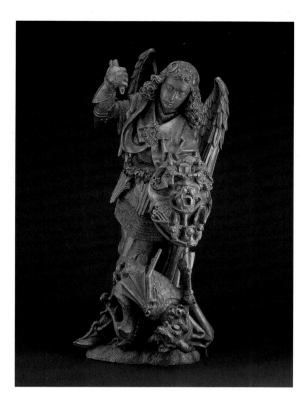

SAINT MICHAEL AND THE DEVIL
1475/1500
Spanish

Poplar, formerly polychromed and gilded; 52.4 × 22.9 × 21.3 cm (20 5/8 × 9 × 8 3/8 in.)

Chester D. Tripp Endowment, 2004.721

Saint Michael was one of the seven archangels of God in the Old Testament, and he led the heavenly host against God's enemies in the book of Revelation. This sculpture represents Michael's battle against Satan, who lies at his feet, pierced by the saint's lance. This subject would inevitably have been associated with the hope of salvation, since Saint Michael was often depicted weighing the souls of the blessed and the damned in images of the Last Judgment. This wood sculpture is a powerful example of the influence of trends from northern Europe on the art of Spain in the second half of the fifteenth century through the importation of works of art and craftsmen. The angular, dancing rhythm of the saint's pose and the tight, graphic quality of the details of his shield, hair, and wings may reflect sources in northern European prints, such as the engravings of Master E. S. These elements would originally have been enhanced by a painted and gilded surface, which at some point was stripped away.

JEAN HEY (MASTER OF MOULINS) French, active c. 1475–c. 1505
The Annunciation, 1490/95
Oil on panel; 72.5 × 50.1 cm (28 ½ × 19 ¹¹/₁₆ in.)
Mr. and Mrs. Martin A. Ryerson Collection, 1933.1062

The archangel Gabriel's announcement to Mary that she will give birth to a son, and her immediate acceptance of this news, represent the moment of Christ's Incarnation. Although *The Annunciation* appears to be an independent painting, it is actually a fragment that once formed the right side of an altarpiece; the left side, now in the National Gallery, London, depicts the moment of Mary's own Immaculate Conception, believed to have occurred when her parents, Joachim and Anne, greeted each other at the Golden Gate. A central section, now lost, probably featured the enthroned Virgin and Child, perhaps with Saint Anne. Jean Hey, known as the Master of Moulins,was the leading painter working in France in the last decades of the fifteenth century. He worked in Moulins in central France for Duke Pierre II of Bourbon and his wife, Anne of France, who played a large role in the government of of the kingdom during the minority of Anne's brother Charles VIII. As their court painter, Hey, who was probably of Netherlandish origin, fused the intense naturalism and preciousness of Flemish and French painting and manuscript illumination with the emerging Renaissance interest in antiquity, as is evident in this painting's Italianate architecture.

FRA BARTOLOMMEO (BACCIO DELLA PORTA) Italian, 1472–1517
The Nativity, 1504/7

Oil on panel; 34 × 24.5 cm (13 ³/₈ × 9 ⁵/₈ in.)

Ethel T. Scarborough Fund; John G. Searle Family Trust, L. L. and A. S. Coburn, Mr. and Mrs. Lester King, John and Josephine Louis, Samuel A. Marx, Alexander McKay, Chester D. Tripp, and Murray Vale endowment funds; restricted gift of Marilynn Alsdorf, Anne Searle Bent, David and Celia Hilliard, Alexandra and John Nichols, Mrs. Harold T. Martin, Mrs. George B. Young in memory of her husband, and the Rhoades Foundation; gift of John Bross and members of the Old Masters Society in memory of Louise Smith Bross; through prior gift of the George F. Harding, Mr. and Mrs. W. W. Kimball, Mr. and Mrs. Martin A. Ryerson, and Charles H. and Mary F. S. Worcester collections, 2005.49

The young Baccio della Porta came under the spell of the charismatic Dominican friar Girolamo Savonarola, joining his monastic order as Fra (Friar) Bartolommeo in 1500 and forsaking his painting career for several years. Returning to painting in 1504, he looked to the most lyrical and harmonious recent works of Leonardo da Vinci, Raphael, and Michelangelo to form his own style, which was characterized by a new, quiet spirituality. The palette of saturated blue, red, and green announces the Holy Family, while the muted tones of the angels' garments establish an otherworldly presence. Here he treated the Nativity in a traditional, though especially intimate, manner. The Virgin kneels humbly as she gazes at the Christ Child, while Joseph assumes a pose of restrained wonderment, as if suddenly aware of the infant's divine nature. The family shelters in a rustic stall erected within the ruins of an edifice understood to be the palace of David at Bethlehem. This juxtaposition of architecture symbolizes Christ's establishment of his new church on the Old Testament order of the Jews. Reinforcing this device is a young tree springing from a remnant of ancient stones directly above the infant.

CORREGGIO (ANTONIO ALLEGRI) Italian, 1489–1534
Virgin and Child with the Young Saint John the Baptist, c. 1515
Oil on panel; 64.2 × 50.2 cm (25 ¼ × 19 ¾ in.)
Clyde M. Carr Fund, 1965.688

Correggio spent most of his brief career in the northern Italian city of Parma. Removed from the great centers of Renaissance art, he was able to create a remarkably innovative body of work. This intimate devotional panel is a product of the artist's youth. Here Correggio revealed his own evolving style while assimilating lessons from other masters. The panel's pyramidal grouping of figures reflects the High Renaissance manner of Raphael, while their soft outlines and the Virgin's enigmatic smile recall Leonardo da Vinci. The evocative use of the distant landscape demonstrates the young artist's awareness of Northern European precedents. The gentle sensuousness of the figures and the tenderness they show one another through glance are unique to Correggio. The artist used light, shadow, and color to bathe the panel in a gentle glow; skin and fabrics appear to take on a velvety texture. The expressive, idyllic quality of this painting presages the radiant ceiling frescoes of Correggio's maturity, especially those in Parma's Cathedral.

ALESSANDRO VITTORIA Italian, 1525–1608
The Annunciation, c. 1583
Bronze; 97.8 × 61.6 cm (38 ½ × 24 ¼ in.)
Edward E. Ayer Endowment in memory of Charles L. Hutchinson, 1942.249

This masterpiece of Renaissance relief sculpture by the Venetian artist Alessandro
Vittoria was commissioned in 1580 by Hans Fugger, a member of a noted Augsburg
banking family, to decorate an altarpiece for the chapel of his family's castle in
Kirchheim, Swabia. Here Vittoria translated into bronze the flickering light and colorful palette of the great Venetian painters of the period; his composition is specifically
adapted from altarpieces by Titian. Working in wax (from which the finished relief
was then cast in bronze), Vittoria manipulated the relief's form and edges to catch the
light. The result is a highly animated surface in which everything—figures, drapery,
clouds, and sky—seems to move with excitement, heightening the drama between
the sharply turned, startled Virgin and the powerful figure of Gabriel, who has suddenly descended from heaven to announce that she will be the mother of Christ. Fully
sculpted in the round, the archangel's arm points to the smallest feature in the scene:
the dove, representing the Holy Ghost of the Christian Trinity. The plasticity and depth
of the relief, the dramatic movement, and the handling of detail make this one of the
artist's finest creations.

EL GRECO
(DOMENIKOS THEOTOKOPOULOS)
Greek, active in Spain, 1541–1614
The Assumption of the Virgin, 1577–79
Oil on canvas; 403.2 × 211.8 cm (158 ³/₄ × 83 ³/₄ in.)
Gift of Nancy Atwood Sprague in memory of Albert Arnold Sprague, 1906.99

This painting was the central element of the altarpiece that was El Greco's first major Spanish commission and first large public work. After living in Venice and Rome, where he absorbed the late Mannerist style, the Greek-born artist settled in the Spanish city of Toledo in 1577 to work on the high altar of the convent church of Santo Domingo el Antiguo. The church of this ancient Cistercian convent was being rebuilt as the funerary chapel of a pious widow, Doña Maria de Silva. In El Greco's grand design, the Assumption was surmounted by a representation of the Trinity and was flanked by two side altars decorated with paintings of the Adoration of the Shepherds and the Resurrection. The visionary imagery of the Assumption and the Trinity aptly expressed the patron's hope of salvation. Here the Virgin floats upward, supported on the crescent moon that is symbolic of her purity, while the boldly modeled heads of the crowd of apostles gathered around her empty tomb express amazement and concern. The vigor of El Greco's broad brushstrokes proclaims the confident achievement of this early work, as does this artist's large signature in Greek, painted as though affixed to the surface of the picture at the lower right.

JUAN SÁNCHEZ COTÁN Spanish, 1560–1627
Still Life with Game Fowl, 1600/1603
Oil on canvas; 67.8 × 88.7 cm (26 ¹¹/₁₆ × 34 ¹⁵/₁₆ in.)
Gift of Mr. and Mrs. Leigh B. Block, 1955.1203

This work, the earliest European still life in the Art Institute's collection, was painted by a leading Spanish practitioner of this new genre. It employs Juan Sánchez Cotán's signature format: commonplace edibles placed in a shallow, niche-like embrasure with an impenetrable, dark background evoking the larders in Spanish homes used to keep food fresh. Some of the artist's still lifes contain few objects, while in others, such as this one, the recess is filled. The objects are painstakingly rendered, and their place-ment seems mathematically exact. The hanging quince and game birds are arranged not perpendicular to the bottom edge of the painting, but on a barely perceptible diagonal. Further enlivening the composition is the strong light that sweeps over the still life and creates a dramatic contrast of light and shade, of precise realism and abstract form. After 1603 the artist stopped creating these austere and powerful images. Sánchez Cotán left his successful artistic career in Toledo to join the Carthusian order as a lay brother at the Charterhouse of Granada. Thereafter, his work consisted solely of idealized religious images.

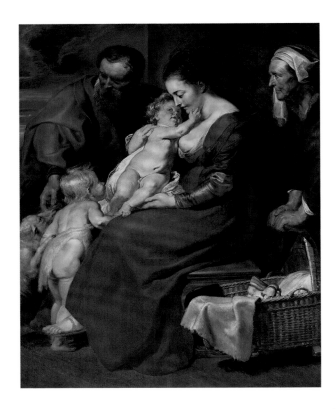

PETER PAUL RUBENS Flemish, 1577–1640

The Holy Family with Saints Elizabeth and John the Baptist, c. 1615

Oil on panel; 114.5 × 91.5 cm (45 ⅛ × 36 in.)

Major Acquisitions Fund, 1967.229

This painting of the Holy Family is one of several completed in the decade after Peter Paul Rubens returned to his native Antwerp, following an eight-year stay in Italy. Fully immersed in Italian art, the prodigiously productive artist had acquired such facility in handling brush, color, figures, and drapery and in arranging large-scale compositions that he was unrivaled north of the Alps. Here he displayed these skills not only by bringing a sacred subject to life but also by bringing it down to earth. Vital and believable Flemish figures fill the composition, which is dominated by the Virgin clad in a brilliant red dress. The bold, diagonal movement of the playful infants is an effective counterbalance to the full, rounded figure of Mary. Joseph (Mary's husband) and Elizabeth (her cousin, and the mother of John the Baptist) frame the pyramidal group as aged and more passive protectors. The atmosphere of joyful solemnity—of light, color, and life—is typical of Rubens and made him the quintessential Baroque artist, in demand as the designer of grand decorative schemes for churches and palaces across Europe.

FRANCESCO MOCHI Italian, 1580–1654

Bust of a Youth (Saint John the Baptist?), 1630/40

Marble, on variegated black marble socle; 40.5 × 33 × 29 cm (15 7/8 × 13 × 11 3/8 in.)

From the collection of the estate of Federico Gentili di Giuseppe; restricted gift of Mrs. Harold T. Martin through the Antiquarian Society; Major Acquisitions Centennial Endowment; through prior gift of Arthur Rubloff; European Decorative Arts Purchase Fund, 1989.1

One of the most individual sculptors of his age, Francesco Mochi possessed an astounding technical prowess. Although his output was relatively small, Mochi was one of the most original artists to emerge in seventeenth-century Italy. His art is distinguished by energetic lines, dramatic movement, and subtle psychology. Here a taut precision characterizes the youth's garment, and a carefully composed rhythm governs Mochi's virtuoso treatment of the corkscrew curls. In contrast to the greater precision of the hair and drapery, the wistful expression of the youth, with his slightly parted lips, endows the sculpture with life. This work may have been conceived as a portrait, but it is more likely a biblical or mythological subject. The almost transcendent expression suggests that the sculpture may represent a religious figure, such as the youthful Saint John the Baptist. Its small scale suggests that the work was intended as an object for private contemplation.

REMBRANDT HARMENSZ. VAN RIJN Dutch, 1606–1669

Old Man with a Gold Chain, 1631

Oil on panel; 83.1 × 75.7 cm (32 ³/₄ × 29 ³/₄ in.)

Mr. and Mrs. W. W. Kimball Collection, 1922.4467

This evocative character study is an early example of a type of subject that preoccupied the great Dutch master Rembrandt van Rijn throughout his long career. Although his large output included landscapes, genre paintings, and the occasional still life, he focused on biblical and historical paintings and on portraits. As an extension of these interests, the artist studied the effect of a single figure, made dramatic through the use of costume and rich, subtle lighting. Rembrandt collected costumes to transform his models into characters. Here, the gold chain and steel gorget suggest an honored military career, while the plumed beret evokes an earlier time. The broad black mass of the old man's torso against a neutral background is a powerful foil for these trappings. The face is that of a real person, weathered and watchful, glowing with pride and humanity. The unidentified sitter, once thought to be the artist's father, was a favorite model, appearing in many of the artist's early works. The confident execution suggests that the young Rembrandt completed this picture about 1631, when he had left his native Leiden to pursue a career in the metropolis of Amsterdam; perhaps he wished to use this work to demonstrate his skill in a genre that combined history painting and portraiture.

GUIDO RENI Italian, 1575–1642
Salome with the Head of Saint John the Baptist, 1639/42
Oil on canvas; 248.5 × 174 cm (97 ³/₄ × 68 ¹/₂ in.)
Louise B. and Frank H. Woods Purchase Fund, 1960.3

In this large canvas, Guido Reni, a leading seventeenth-century Bolognese painter, depicted one of the New Testament's more macabre stories. Salome, the daughter of Queen Herodias, so pleased her stepfather, Herod Antipas, by dancing at his birth-day feast that he promised to grant her any wish. Prompted by her vengeful mother, Salome asked for the head of the prophet John the Baptist, whom Herod had imprisoned for denouncing his marriage. The painting illustrates the moment when the head of the saint is presented to the beautiful young woman. Highly selective in his palette, Reni depicted this gory event with rhythmic grace, soft modeling, and elegant remove. No blood drips from John's head, and the color and illumination are cool; indeed, there is no specific setting, nor are any strong emotions depicted. In this late work, the handling of the figures is broad, especially in the legs of the young page and the feet of Salome, which are only summarily brushed in. This raises the central, unresolved question of much of Reni's late work: whether or not this picture should be considered finished.

NICOLAS POUSSIN French, 1594–1665
Landscape with Saint John on Patmos, 1640
Oil on canvas; 100.3 × 136.4 cm (39 ½ × 53 ⅝ in.)
A. A. Munger Collection, 1930.500

Although French by birth and training, Nicolas Poussin spent most of his career in Rome, immersed in the study of ancient art, where he painted classically inspired works for an educated elite. His art has long been considered the embodiment of the ideals of seventeenth-century classicism. In this painting, Saint John, one of the four Evangelists who wrote the Gospels of the New Testament, reclines beside his attribute, the eagle. He is here depicted as a powerful old man, presumably after retiring to the Greek island of Patmos to write his gospel and the book of Revelation at the end of his life. To suggest the vanished glory of the ancient world, Poussin carefully constructed an idealized setting for the saint, complete with an obelisk, a temple, and column fragments. Man-made and natural forms were adjusted according to principles of geometry and logic to convey the measured order of the scene. Even the profile view of Saint John is in harmony with the classical landscape. This painting may have been part of a projected series on the four Evangelists—in addition to this work, Poussin completed a companion, *Landscape with Saint Matthew* (1640; Gemäldegalerie, Berlin).

JACOB VAN RUISDAEL Dutch, c. 1628–1682
Landscape with the Ruins of the Castle of Egmond, 1650/55
Oil on canvas; 98 × 130 cm (38 ⁷/₈ × 51 ³/₈ in.)
Potter Palmer Collection, 1947.475

The heroic but ephemeral edifices of humankind and the enduring power and
grandeur of nature are evocatively expressed in this work by the landscape painter
Jacob van Ruisdael. A shepherd and his flock are dwarfed by the ruins of a castle, a
massive hill in the background, and dark, swollen clouds gathering overhead. Ruisdael's skillful use of color also enhances the painting's poetic effect. Other than the
glowing terra-cotta of the ruins and the restrained use of creamy whites, his palette
consists mostly of the greens and browns of nature. There is only one small point
of bright color in the entire painting: the shepherd's red jacket. Although the artist's
choice of ruins as his subject followed an established pictorial tradition in the Netherlands, he was not concerned with topographical accuracy; indeed, the prominent hill
behind the structure was a product of his imagination. The castle, once the seat of the
Counts of Egmond, had powerful associations. It was destroyed at the command of
the Prince of Orange to prevent the Spanish Army from occupying it during the Dutch
struggle for independence from Spanish rule in the late sixteenth century.

GIOVANNI BATTISTA TIEPOLO Italian, 1696–1770
Armida Encounters the Sleeping Rinaldo, 1742/45
Oil on canvas; 187.5 × 216.8 cm (73 ¹³/₁₆ × 85 ³/₈ in.)
Bequest of James Deering, 1925.700

Giovanni Battista Tiepolo's monumental ceiling and wall decorations epitomize the brilliant exuberance of the late Baroque style. Tiepolo enjoyed an international career and was called upon to use his mastery of light, color, and illusion to transform palaces and monasteries in his native Venice and elsewhere in Italy, as well as in Germany and Spain. This painting and three others at the Art Institute, together with smaller decorative panels and a ceiling painting, once graced the cabinet of mirrors, a richly decorated room in the Venetian palace of the powerful Cornaro family. The suite illustrates Torquato Tasso's popular sixteenth-century epic romance *Jerusalem Delivered,* which is set in the eleventh century, during the First Crusade, when Western knights sought to take Jerusalem from the Muslims. The canvas captures the moment of Rinaldo's seduction: the beautiful sorceress Armida has just arrived to divert the sleeping hero from his crusade. Accompanied by her attendant nymph and a cupid figure, she appears like a beautiful mirage, enthroned on a billowing cloud, her drapery and shawl wafting gently behind her. Altough Tasso's story symbolizes the conflict between love and duty, Tiepolo's depiction of a magical, bucolic world—enhanced by effervescent colors, luminous atmosphere, and dense, creamy paint—seems to evoke only love's enchantment.

SIR JOSHUA REYNOLDS English, 1723–1792
Lady Sarah Bunbury Sacrificing to the Graces, 1763–65
Oil on canvas; 242.6 × 151.5 cm (95 ¹/₂ × 59 ³/₄ in.)
Mr. and Mrs. W. W. Kimball Collection, 1922.4468

Lady Sarah Bunbury was famous as the society beauty who attracted the attention of
the future King George III when she was only fifteen. George was persuaded to marry
a German princess instead of her, and a year after the royal marriage, Lady Sarah
wed Sir Charles Bunbury in a match that lasted only a short while. In this portrait,
Sir Joshua Reynolds—the first president of the Royal Academy and a champion of
the importance of classical artistic models—conferred upon her a flattering honorary
citizenship in the ancient world. Dressed in a loose, vaguely Roman costume and
surrounded by the art and artifacts of antiquity, Lady Sarah is cast as a devotee of the
Three Graces, symbols of generosity and the mythical companions of Venus, the
Roman goddess of love and beauty. Lady Sarah pours a libation into a smoking tripod,
and one of the Graces seems to offer her a wreath, as if inviting the aristocratic
beauty to join their number. As an academician, Reynolds valued historical subjects,
but as a practicing painter, he made his living largely through portraiture. In this and
other grand portraits, he found a way of combining the requirements of his patrons
with the prestige of the classical tradition.

JEAN-HONORÉ FRAGONARD French, 1732–1806
Portrait of a Man in Spanish Costume, 1768/70
Oil on canvas; 80.3 × 64.7 cm (31 ⅝ × 25 ½ in.)
Gift of Mary and Leigh Block in honor of John Maxon, 1977.123

One of the most brilliant eighteenth-century French artists, Jean-Honoré Fragonard excelled at painting light-hearted, amorous subjects, landscapes, and scenes of everyday life but only rarely turned his hand to those subjects drawn from antiquity that were most esteemed by the Royal Academy of Painting and Sculpture. His paintings avoided the high finish then deemed appropriate for a carefully prepared and executed work. Instead, he applied paint directly and impetuously, so that his compositions often have the character of quick sketches.

Portrait of a Man in Spanish Costume is closely related to a series of fantasy portraits that, in many ways, summarizes Fragonard's highly personal art. Loosely based on the artist's circle of patrons and friends, these half-length figures endow their sitters with extraordinary vitality while playfully dressing them up in the trappings of the past through pose and costume. Details of dress—ruffs, padded shoulders, jaunty hats—evoke historical costume and reflect Fragonard's fascination with earlier painting and his appropriation of the styles and subjects of his great predecessors, notably Peter Paul Rubens (see p. 158). In the case of *Portrait of a Man*, the identity of the sitter is unknown, and he have been intended as an imaginative type. Because of his air of world-weary gallantry, this figure has sometimes been associated with Don Quixote, the hero of Miguel de Cervantes's great early seventeenth-century novel, though there is nothing to support this identification in the painting's history. In any case, his beard and mustache and the striped garment with extended shoulders relate to the fashions of the early Baroque period. The restricted color range gives added force to the man's head, silhouetted against a luminous background. His large eyes dominate the image and, in their stillness, contrast poignantly with the active, undulating contours of his costume.

HUBERT ROBERT French, 1733–1808
The Fountains, 1787/88
Oil on canvas; 255.3 × 221.2 cm (100 ½ × 88 ⅛ in.)
Gift of William G. Hibbard, 1900.385

The painting of Classical ruins had reached the zenith of its popularity when Hubert
Robert, the leading French practitioner of this specialty, was commissioned in 1787
to paint a suite of four canvases for a wealthy financier's château at Méréville, near
Paris. *The Fountains* and its companion pieces were set into the paneled walls of a salon
in the château, creating an alternate space that played off of the elegant, Neoclassical
decor of the room. Robert has studied in Rome from 1754 to 1765 and there had
gleaned his artistic vocabulary. Like the other three large paintings from the group
painted for Méréville, all in the Art Institute, *The Fountains* exploits Robert's typical
vocabulary of fictive niches, arches, coffered vaults, colonnades, majestic stairwells, and
Roman statuary to create a fantasy of expansive space. The four paintings are inhab-
ited by tiny figures in the foreground; these serve only to set the scale and animate the
scene, for the ruins themselves are the true subject of the pictures. In his use of ruins,
Robert embodied the notion of the relationship of mankind and the built environment
to nature that was expressed by the French philosopher and encyclopedist Denis Diderot:
"Everything vanishes, everything dies, only time endures."

JACQUES-LOUIS DAVID French, 1748–1825
Madame de Pastoret and Her Son, 1791/92
Oil on canvas; 129.8 × 96.6 cm (51 ⅛ × 38 in.)
Clyde M. Carr Fund and Major Acquisitions Endowment, 1967.228

The volatile events of the early years of the French Revolution make it impossible to determine with certainty the date of Jacques-Louis David's warm, fresh portrait of Adélaïde de Pastoret. They also probably account for the portrait's unfinished state. David, a renowned Neoclassical painter, was at the time an ardent revolutionary; Madame de Pastoret was the wife of a staunch royalist. The sittings must have occurred after the birth, early in 1791, of her son, who is portrayed asleep by her side, and before her brief imprisonment during the Reign of Terror in 1792. Here David completed the stippled, almost monochromatic underpainting but did not create the stark, enamel-smooth surface that is characteristic of his finished paintings. He did not even get far enough to place a needle and thread in Madame de Pastoret's hand. Nevertheless, this large portrait of unaffected domesticity captures the youthful mother with charm as well as dignity and displays David's skill as a portraitist. Objecting to David's revolutionary ideals, Madame de Pastoret (who became the Marquise de Pastoret in 1817) refused the painting during the artist's lifetime. After David's death, she had her son, by then an adult (see p. 171), purchase the portrait from the artist's estate.

FRANCISCO JOSÉ DE GOYA Y LUCIENTES Spanish, 1746–1828

Friar Pedro Shoots El Maragato As His Horse Runs Off, c. 1806

Oil on panel; 29.2 × 38.5 cm (11 ½ × 15 ⅝ in.)

Mr. and Mrs. Martin A. Ryerson Collection, 1933.1075

When the dreaded bandit El Maragato was seized in 1806 by the humble monk
Pedro de Zaldivia, a lay brother of a Franciscan barefoot order, the story swept
through Spain. Not only did daily newspapers and pamphlets publicize it, but songs,
ballads, and popular prints also praised the heroic deed. Although Francisco de Goya
was chief painter to the Spanish king at the time, he was interested in the whole range
of human experience, including contemporary Spanish events. The tale of Zaldivia
and Maragato evidently captured his imagination. This small, lively painting belongs
to a series of six in the Art Institute, which, like a modern-day comic strip, dramatically illustrates the event. This is the climactic scene, presenting the bandit's humiliat-
ing and somewhat comical downfall at the hands of the brave monk. Here, as in all
the panels, the artist's broad, quick brushwork dispenses with unnecessary detail to
pinpoint the essential drama of the event. Goya may have made these paintings for
himself rather than for a commission, since they were still listed among his posses-
sions in an 1812 inventory.

ANTONIO CANOVA Italian, 1757–1822
Bust of Paris, 1809
Marble; h. 66 cm (26 in.)
Harold Stuart Endowment; restricted gift of Mrs. Harold T. Martin, 1984.530

The enormously popular Neoclassical sculptor Antonio Canova frequently made replicas or variants of his major works to satisfy the demand for his art. While executing a commission from Empress Josephine of France for a full-length statue of Paris (State Hermitage Museum, Saint Petersburg), Canova carved this bust for his friend Antoine Quatremère de Quincy, a French Neoclassical theorist and critic who greatly influenced the sculptor's artistic ideals. It depicts the moment in Greek mythology when the shepherd Paris, called upon by Zeus to judge who was the most beautiful among Hera, Athena, and Aphrodite, turns to gaze at the three goddesses. Canova exploited the subject to create an ideal head, balancing the geometry of pure forms with the sensuousness of Paris's expression. Upon receipt of the gift, Quatremère stated: "There is in [the bust] a mixture of the heroic and the voluptuous, the noble and the amorous. I do not believe that in any other work you have ever combined such life, softness, and chaste purity." Documents indicate that Canova made four full-length marble statues and at least seven busts of Paris, a clear indication of the sculpture's popularity.

JEAN-AUGUSTE-DOMINIQUE INGRES French, 1780–1867

Amédée-David, the Comte de Pastoret, 1823–26

Oil on canvas; 103 × 83.5 cm (40 ½ × 32 ¾ in.)

Estate of Dorothy Eckhart Williams; Robert Allerton, Bertha E. Brown, and Major Acquisitions funds, 1971.452

Jean-Auguste-Dominique Ingres, who championed Classical ideals throughout his long and productive career, began this portrait in 1823, the same year that the thirty-two-year-old count helped him become a full member of the Académie des Beaux-Arts. Ingres astutely captured the character of the suave young nobleman, from the refined line of his silhouette to his elegant costume, long fingers, and slightly swaggering pose. The artist's fastidious, impeccable technique is particularly evident in the precisely rendered details of the sword hilt and the medal of the Order of the Legion of Honor, which the count received in 1824. Ingres studied in the prestigious atelier of Jacques-Louis David; although he considered himself a history painter, portraits such as this paid his bills for many years and earned him considerable praise. This work was in progress at about the same time that the count acquired a painting of his mother by David at the artist's posthumous sale (see p. 168). In 1897 *Amédée-David, the Comte de Pastoret* was purchased by the painter Edgar Degas, an avid art collector and admirer of Ingres, who, like the older artist, became the greatest French portrait painter of his generation.

EUGÈNE DELACROIX French, 1798–1863
The Combat of the Giaour and Hassan, 1826
Oil on canvas; 59.6 × 73.4 cm (23 ¹/₂ × 28 ⁷/₈ in.)
Gift of Bertha Palmer Thorne, Rose Movius Palmer, Mr. and Mrs. Arthur M. Wood, and Mr. and Mrs. Gordon Palmer, 1962.966

The Combat of the Giaour and Hassan is among Eugène Delacroix's finest early representations of battle. The painting was inspired by *The Giaour*, a lengthy poem by England's famous Romantic poet, Lord Byron. Written in 1813 and translated into French in 1824, the poem presents a subject and setting—passion avenged on a Greek battlefield—that perfectly suited the artist's Romantic imagination. The painting depicts the poem's dramatic climax, when the Venetian giaour (a Turkish word for a non-Muslim) avenges his lover's death at the hands of the Turk Hassan. Weapons poised, the two enemies face off in mirroring poses: the giaour in swirling white, and Hassan with his face hidden. With its exotic costumes, intense drama, and forceful colors and forms, this painting is the most revered of the six known versions Delacroix made based on Byron's poem. Begun in 1824, the year Byron died in the struggle for Greek independence from the Turks, Delacroix finished the painting two years later, just in time for it to be included in a Parisian exhibition benefiting the popular Greek cause.

CARL BLECHEN German, 1798–1840

The Interior of the Palm House on the Pfaueninsel near Potsdam, 1834

Oil on canvas; 135 × 126 cm (52 ¹/₂ × 50 in.)

Through prior acquisitions of the George F. Harding Collection; L. L. and A. S. Coburn and Alexander A. McKay endowments; through prior gift of William Wood Prince; through prior acquisitions of the Charles H. and Mary F. S. Worcester Collection, 1996.388

Carl Blechen is regarded as a pivotal figure in nineteenth-century German painting; his short career marks the transition from Romanticism to a more realistic view of nature. Although he is best known for scenes in which a carefully observed Italian landscape served as the backdrop for mysterious or nostalgic figures, *The Palm House* represents an important detour in his work. In 1832 Blechen was commissioned by Friedrich Wilhelm III of Prussia (r. 1797–1840) to paint two views of an exotic pleasure building recently constructed near Potsdam. The architect Karl Friedrich Schinkel designed the Palm House for the king's collection of palms. It was situated on the Pfaueninsel, or Peacock Island, a favorite royal retreat dotted with whimsical buildings such as a tiny castle and a Gothic dairy. Blechen's painting is both a record of the building, with its lush palms and fragments of an Indian temple, and an evocation of a fantasy world peopled by beautiful women purposefully playing to the viewer's imagination. After completing two exquisite, small paintings for the king, Blechen made this grand version for public viewing. *The Palm House* was one of the artist's most ambitious statements, for he soon succumbed to melancholy and madness.

JOHN CONSTABLE English, 1776–1837
Stoke-by-Nayland, 1836
Oil on canvas; 126 × 169 cm (49 ⅝ × 66 ½ in.)
Mr. and Mrs. W. W. Kimball Collection, 1922.4453

Stoke-by-Nayland depicts the subject matter that the landscape painter John Constable explored throughout his life: the Suffolk countryside of his youth. Constable based his landscapes on countless studies and sketches that he often took back to his London studio to expand and then finish. Of *Stoke-by-Nayland*, he wrote to a friend: "What say you to a summer morning? July or August, at eight or nine o'clock, after a slight shower during the night." To achieve the effect of sparkling wetness and a freshness of earth and air, Constable painted as much with a palette knife as with a brush, flecking the surface with white highlights and sketching and scraping the picture into existence. The deliberate ruggedness of his style echoes nature's rough spontaneity. The unpolished execution is reminiscent of the full-scale sketches in oil that Constable made for earlier exhibition paintings; however, no more fully treated version is known, and the rich color suggests that this is a finished work, done in the artist's late style. Constable's emphasis on surface brushwork and texture in his effort to record the constantly shifting effects of natural light on land and sky exerted enormous influence on French artists like Eugène Delacroix and a younger generation of French painters, the Impressionists.

JOSEPH MALLORD WILLIAM TURNER English, 1775–1851
Fishing Boats with Hucksters Bargaining for Fish, 1837/38
Oil on canvas; 174.5 × 224.9 cm (68 ³/₄ × 88 ¹/₂ in.)
Mr. and Mrs. W. W. Kimball Collection, 1922.4472

In *Fishing Boats with Hucksters Bargaining for Fish*, Joseph Mallord William Turner translated his enduring preoccupation with the sea into a dramatic vision. The subject itself and the painting's low horizon line derive directly from seventeenth-century Dutch sea painting. But where the boats in the seascapes of the period are almost reconstructible in their exactness, Turner's minimal and more impressionistic depiction of vessels is secondary to the drama of roiling seas, billowing sails, and a threatening sky. With just a few figurative details, Turner roughly sketched in the standing, gesturing figure on the right, who is negotiating to buy fish from the larger, crowded fishing boat on the left. Between them is a mythical golden boat that seems to spring from the artist's imagination, and on the distant horizon is the suggestion of progress, a steam-driven vessel. With his manipulation of translucent and opaque pigments to create a sense of atmosphere and light, Turner alluded to the insignificance of man in the face of nature's mysterious and sublime power.

ÉDOUARD MANET French, 1832–1883
Fish (Still Life), 1864
Oil on canvas; 73.5 × 92.4 cm (28 ¹⁵/₁₆ × 36 ³/₈ in.)
Mr. and Mrs. Lewis Larned Coburn Memorial Collection, 1942.311

Although still-life ensembles were an important element in many of the major paintings of the avant-garde artist Édouard Manet, his most sustained interest in the genre itself was from 1864 to 1865, when *Fish* was painted. Manet's focus on still lifes coincided with the gradual reacceptance of the genre during the nineteenth century, due in part to the growth of the middle class, whose tastes ran to intimate, moderately priced works. This painting, like many of Manet's still-life compositions, recalls seventeenth-century Dutch models. The directness of execution, bold brushwork, and immediacy of vision displayed in the canvas, however, suggest why the public found Manet's work so unorthodox and confrontational. While *Fish* is indeed an image of "dead nature" (*nature morte* is the French term for still life), there is nothing still about the work: the produce seems fresh and the handling of paint vigorous. Further enlivening the composition is the placement of the carp, which offsets the strong diagonal of the other elements. Manet never submitted his still lifes to the official French Salon but rather sold them through the burgeoning network of art galleries in Paris and gave them to friends.

CLAUDE MONET French, 1840–1926
The Beach at Sainte-Adresse, 1867
Oil on canvas; 75.8 × 102.5 cm (29 ¹³/₁₆ × 40 ⁵/₁₆ in.)
Mr. and Mrs. Lewis Larned Coburn Memorial Collection, 1933.439

In the summer of 1867, Claude Monet stayed with his aunt at Sainte-Adresse, an affluent suburb of the port city of Le Havre, near his father's home. The paintings he produced that summer, few of which survive, reveal the beginnings of the young artist's development of the revolutionary style that would come to be known as Impressionism. In his quest to capture the effects of shifts in weather and light, Monet painted *The Beach at Sainte-Adresse* out-of-doors on an overcast day. He devoted the majority of the composition to the sea, sky, and beach. These he depicted with broad sheets of color, animated by short brushstrokes that articulate gentle azure waves, soft white clouds, and pebbled ivory sand. While fishermen go about their chores, a tiny couple relaxes at the water's edge. Monet did not exhibit this work publicly for almost ten years after he completed it. In 1874 he banded together with a diverse group of like-minded, avant-garde artists to mount the first of what would be eight independent exhibitions. He included *Sainte-Adresse* in the second of these Impressionist shows, in 1876.

JEAN-BAPTISTE-CAMILLE COROT French, 1796–1875

Interrupted Reading, c. 1870

Oil on canvas, mounted on board; 92.5 × 65.1 cm (36 ⁵/₁₆ × 25 ⁵/₈ in.)

Potter Palmer Collection, 1922.410

Interrupted Reading is among the most compelling of Camille Corot's late figure paintings. Corot almost never exhibited these studies of the human form, preferring instead to publicize the idyllic landscapes that were his specialty. To emphasize the private nature of *Interrupted Reading*, Corot enclosed his model within the protective environment of the artist's studio. The mood of the painting is introspective and somewhat melancholic, the very essence of the Romantic sensibility. The muse-like image of a woman reading a book was a popular one in nineteenth-century art, but Corot chose to show his model pausing, looking up from this activity. Having spent a number of years in Italy and being a lover of everything Italian, the artist often furnished his models with Italianate costumes such as the one worn here. Whereas Corot's subject matter is traditional, his technique is not. With direct and bold brushwork, he explored the human form as a construction of masses that support and balance one another. This broad handling is complemented by the artist's obvious delight in detail—the ribbon in the model's hair, the delicate earrings, the deep folds in the skirt. Here he combined a profound sense of formal structure with the dreamy softness and intimacy that characterize his most famous landscapes.

BERTHE MORISOT French, 1841–1895
Woman at Her Toilette, 1875/80
Oil on canvas; 60.3 × 80.4 cm (23 ³/₄ × 31 ⁵/₈ in.)
Stickney Fund, 1924.127

Consistent with the Impressionist aesthetic that Berthe Morisot fervently espoused, *Woman at Her Toilette* attempts to capture the essence of modern life in summary, understated terms. The painting also moves discreetly into the realm of female eroticism explored by Edgar Degas, Édouard Manet, and Pierre-Auguste Renoir but seldom broached at this time by women artists. Rendered with soft, feathery brushstrokes in nuanced shades of lavender, pink, blue, white, and gray, the composition resembles a visual tone poem, orchestrated with such perfumed and rarified motifs as brushed blonde hair, satins, powder puffs, and flower petals. The artist even signed her name along the bottom of the mirror, as if to suggest that the image in her painting is as ephemeral as a silvery reflection. Morisot exhibited in seven of the eight Impressionist group shows; this painting was included in the fifth exhibition, in 1880, where her work received great acclaim. She was a particularly close friend of and frequent model for Manet, and she married his younger brother Eugène the year before she completed this painting. In addition to domestic interiors such as this one, Morisot's pictorial realm included studies of women and children, gardens, fields, and seaside vacation homes.

GUSTAVE CAILLEBOTTE French, 1848–1894
Paris Street; Rainy Day, 1877
Oil on canvas; 212.2 × 276.2 cm (83 ½ × 108 ¾ in.)
Charles H. and Mary F. S. Worcester Collection, 1964.336

This complex intersection, just minutes away from the Saint-Lazare train station, represents in microcosm the changing urban milieu of late nineteenth-century Paris. Gustave Caillebotte grew up near this district when it was a relatively unsettled hill with narrow, crooked streets. As part of a new city plan designed by Baron Georges-Eugène Haussmann, these streets were relaid and their buildings razed during the artist's lifetime. In this monumental urban view, which measures almost seven by ten feet and is considered the artist's masterpiece, Caillebotte strikingly captured a vast, stark modernity, complete with life-size figures strolling in the foreground and wearing the latest fashions. The painting's highly crafted surface, rigorous perspective, and grand scale pleased Parisian audiences accustomed to the academic aesthetic of the official Salon. On the other hand, its asymmetrical composition, unusually cropped forms, rain-washed mood, and candidly contemporary subject stimulated a more radical sensibility. For these reasons, the painting dominated the celebrated Impressionist exhibition of 1877, largely organized by the artist himself. In many ways, Caillebotte's frozen poetry of the Parisian bourgeoisie prefigures Georges Seurat's luminous *Sunday on La Grande Jatte—1884* (p. 186), painted less than a decade later.

PIERRE-AUGUSTE RENOIR French, 1841–1919

Acrobats at the Cirque Fernando (Francisca and Angelina Wartenberg), 1879

Oil on canvas; 131.2 × 99.2 cm (51 ¹/₂ × 39 ¹/₁₆ in.)

Potter Palmer Collection, 1922.440

The two little circus girls in this painting are Francisca and Angelina Wartenberg, who performed as acrobats in the famed Cirque Fernando in Paris. Although they were depicted in the center of a circus ring, the sisters actually posed in costume in Pierre-Auguste Renoir's studio, enabling him to paint them in daylight. Here he portrayed them just as they have finished their act and are taking their bows. One sister turns to the crowd, acknowledging its approval, while the other faces the viewer with an armful of oranges, a rare treat that the audience has tossed in tribute. Although *Acrobats at the Cirque Fernando* reflects the artist's enchantment with the innocence of childhood—he has enveloped the girls in a virtual halo of pinks, oranges, yellows, and whites—the partially visible, darkly clothed (mainly male) spectators allude to the less wholesome, nocturnal demimonde of the nineteenth-century circus in which these two young performers grew up. The famed Chicago collector Mrs. Potter Palmer purchased *Acrobats at the Cirque Fernando* in 1892 and was so enamored of the picture that she kept it with her at all times, even on her travels abroad.

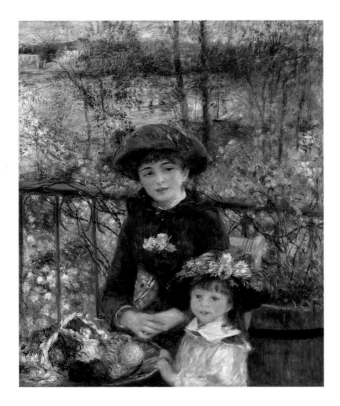

PIERRE-AUGUSTE RENOIR French, 1841–1919
Two Sisters (On the Terrace), 1881
Oil on canvas; 100.4 × 80.9 cm (39 ½ × 31 ⅞ in.)
Mr. and Mrs. Lewis Larned Coburn Memorial Collection, 1933.455

"He loves everything that is joyous, brilliant, and consoling in life," an anonymous interviewer once wrote about Pierre-Auguste Renoir. This may explain why *Two Sisters (On the Terrace)* is one of the most popular paintings in the Art Institute. Here Renoir depicted the radiance of lovely young women on a warm and beautiful day. The older girl, wearing the female boater's blue flannel, is posed in the center of the evocative landscape backdrop of Chatou, a suburban town where the artist spent much of the spring of 1881. She gazes absently beyond her younger companion, who seems, in a charming visual conceit, to have just dashed into the picture. Technically, the painting is a tour de force: Renoir juxtaposed solid, almost life-size figures against a landscape that—like a stage set—seems a realm of pure vision and fantasy. The sewing basket in the left foreground evokes a palette, holding the bright, pure pigments that the artist mixed, diluted, and altered to create the rest of the painting. Although the girls were not actually sisters, Renoir's dealer showed the work with this title, along with *Acrobats at the Cirque Fernando* (p. 181) and others, at the seventh Impressionist exhibition, in 1882.

CHARLES HENRI JOSEPH CORDIER
French, 1827–1905
Bust of Said Abdullah of the Darfour People, 1848
Bronze; with socle: h. 82.5 cm (32 ½ in.)
Bust of an African Woman, 1851
Bronze; with socle: h. 71.7 cm (31 in.)
Ada Turnbull Hertle Endowment, 1963.839–40

Charles Henri Joseph Cordier was still a student of French sculptor François Rude when his plaster-cast version of the clay portrait he had modeled of a Sudanese man was accepted to the Paris Salon. Exhibited in the same year that France extended full emancipation to all residents, including those in its African colonies and territories, Cordier's sculpture was seen as embodying the Romantic ideals of individual liberty. Its detailed realism (including the individual strands of tassels and hair) appealed to the public's growing interest in ethnographic accuracy, while its strong features and dignified expression matched the European tradition for expressing moral and physical purity. Two years later, Cordier created a female portrait that was equally acclaimed as a blend of realism (the model wears a patterned wrap, heavy earrings, and coral necklace, all associated with East Africa) and idealism (in the sitter's regal and aristocratic bearing). In 1851 casts of both sculptures were commissioned for the anthropological gallery of the National History Museum in Paris, and for the International Exhibition in London, sealing their fate as companion pendants. While Cordier came to specialize in ethnographic sculpture and made several trips to North Africa during his lifetime, it is by these two works that he is best remembered.

ARNOLD BÖCKLIN Swiss, 1827–1901

In the Sea, 1883

Oil on panel; 86.5 × 115 cm (34 ³/₈ × 45 ³/₄ in.)

Joseph Winterbotham Collection, 1990.443

Arnold Böcklin's art had little in common with Impressionism or the academic art of his time. Instead, his depictions of demigods in naturalistic settings interpret themes from Classical mythology in an idiosyncratic, often sensual manner. *In the Sea*, part of a series of paintings of mythological subjects, displays an unsettling, earthy realism. Mermaids and tritons frolic in the water with a lusty energy and abandon verging on coarseness. Occupying the center of the composition is a harp-playing triton. Three mermaids have attached themselves to his huge frame as if it were a raft; the one near his shoulder seems to thrust herself upon him. The work's sense of boisterousness is tempered by the ominously shaped reflection of the triton and mermaids in the sea and by the oddness of the large-eared heads that emerge from the water at the right. In addition to imaginative, bizarre interpretations of the Classical world, Böcklin painted mysterious landscapes punctuated by an occasional lone figure. These haunting later works made him an important contributor to the international Symbolist movement. They also appealed to some Surrealist artists, particularly Giorgio de Chirico (see p. 207), who declared, "Each of [Böcklin's] works is a shock."

EDGAR DEGAS French, 1834–1917
The Millinery Shop, 1879/86
Oil on canvas; 100 × 110.7 cm (39 3/8 × 43 9/16 in.)
Mr. and Mrs. Lewis Larned Coburn Memorial Collection, 1933.428

Of at least fifteen pastels, drawings, and paintings that Edgar Degas created on this subject during the 1880s, *The Millinery Shop* is the largest and perhaps the most ambitious. As a result of its unusual cropping and tilted perspective, it seems to capture an unedited glimpse of the interior of a small nineteenth-century millinery shop. The identity of the young woman in the painting remains unclear: she may be a shop girl or a customer. In an early version of the composition, the woman is clearly intended to be a customer; she wears a fashionable dress, though her hat—a prerequisite token of bourgeois culture—is absent. In the final painting, however, the woman appears with her mouth pursed, as if around a pin, and her hands gloved, possibly to protect the delicate fabric of the hat she holds. Degas seems to have deliberately left her role as a creator or consumer ambiguous. She is totally absorbed in her activity and, like most of the women in Degas's paintings, seems unaware of being watched. The bonnets that are displayed on the table next to her like a still life present an analogy to the artist's creative process: where they are unfinished, so too is the painting.

GEORGES SEURAT French, 1859–1891
A Sunday on La Grande Jatte—1884, 1884/86
Oil on canvas; 207.5 × 308.1 cm (81 3/4 × 121 1/4 in.)
Helen Birch Bartlett Memorial Collection, 1926.224

"Bedlam," "scandal," and "hilarity" were among the epithets used to describe what
is now considered Georges Seurat's greatest work, and one of the most remarkable
paintings of the nineteenth century, when it was first exhibited in Paris. Seurat labored
extensively over *A Sunday on La Grande Jatte—1884*, reworking the original as well
as completing numerous preliminary drawings and oil sketches (the Art Institute has
one such sketch and two drawings). With what resembles scientific precision, the
artist tackled the issues of color, light, and form. Inspired by research in optical and
color theory, he juxtaposed tiny dabs of colors that, through optical blending, form a
single and, he believed, more brilliantly luminous hue. To make the experience of the
painting even more intense, he surrounded the canvas with a frame of painted dashes
and dots, which he, in turn, enclosed with a pure white wood frame, similar to the one
with which the painting is exhibited today. The very immobility of the figures and
the shadows they cast makes them forever silent and enigmatic. Like all great masterpieces, *La Grande Jatte* continues to fascinate and elude.

PAUL CÉZANNE French, 1839–1906
The Bay of Marseilles, Seen from L'Estaque, c. 1885
Oil on canvas; 80.2 × 100.6 cm (31 ⅝ × 39 ⅝ in.)
Mr. and Mrs. Martin A. Ryerson Collection, 1933.1116

In a letter to his friend and teacher Camille Pissarro, Paul Cézanne compared the view
of the sea from L'Estaque to a playing card, with its simple shapes and colors. The
landscape's configuration and color fascinated him. This painting is one of more than
a dozen such vistas created by the artist during the 1880s. Cézanne divided the canvas
into four zones—architecture, water, mountain, and sky. Although these four elements
are seen repeatedly in Impressionist paintings, Cézanne's work is very different from
that of his fellow artists. Whereas their primary purpose was to record the transient
effects of light, Cézanne was interested in the underlying structure and composition
of the views he painted. Filling the canvas with shapes defined by strong, contrasting
colors and a complex grid of horizontal, vertical, and diagonal lines, he created a
highly compact, dynamic pattern of water, sky, land, and village that at once refers
back to traditionally structured landscape paintings and looks forward to the innovations of Cubism. Using blocklike brushstrokes to build the space, Cézanne created
a composition that seems both two- and three-dimensional. Not locked tightly in
place, his forms appear to touch and shift continually, creating a sense of volume and
space that strengthens the composition and brings it to life.

VINCENT VAN GOGH Dutch, 1853–1890
Self-Portrait, 1887
Oil on artist's board, mounted on cradled panel; 41 × 32.5 cm (16 ⅛ × 12 ¹³/₁₆ in.)
Joseph Winterbotham Collection, 1954.326

In 1886 Vincent van Gogh left his native Holland and settled in Paris, where his beloved brother Theo was a dealer in paintings. Van Gogh created at least twenty-four self-portraits during his two-year stay in the energetic French capital. This early example is modest in size and was painted on prepared artist's board rather than canvas. Its densely dabbed brushwork, which became a hallmark of Van Gogh's style, reflects the artist's response to Georges Seurat's revolutionary pointillist technique in *A Sunday on La Grande Jatte—1884* (p. 186). But what was for Seurat a method based on the cool objectivity of science became in Van Gogh's hands an intense emotional language. The surface of the painting dances with particles of color—intense greens, blues, reds, and oranges. Dominating this dazzling array of staccato dots and dashes are the artist's deep green eyes and the intensity of their gaze. "I prefer painting people's eyes to cathedrals," Van Gogh once wrote to Theo. "However solemn and imposing the latter may be—a human soul, be it that of a poor streetwalker, is more interesting to me." From Paris, Van Gogh traveled to the southern town of Arles for fifteen months (see p. 190). At the time of his death, in 1890, he had actively pursued his art for only five years.

PAUL GAUGUIN French, 1848–1903
Arlésiennes (Mistral), 1888
Oil on jute canvas; 73 × 92 cm (28 ³/₄ × 36 ³/₁₆ in.)
Mr. and Mrs. Lewis Larned Coburn Memorial Collection, 1934.391

One of seventeen canvases that Paul Gauguin completed during a brief and tumultuous visit with Vincent van Gogh in Arles (see p. 190), this powerful and enigmatic
painting depicts the public garden directly across from Van Gogh's residence, the
"Yellow House." Not only is the careful planning of the composition in marked contrast to the spontaneity seen in Van Gogh's depiction of the same scene (State Hermitage Museum, Saint Petersburg), but everything about the painting—its large, flat
areas of color; arbitrary handling of space; and enigmatic silhouettes—also exemplifies the deliberateness with which Gauguin sought pictorial harmony and symbolic
content in his work. Here four women wrapped in shawls slowly stroll through
the garden. The two closest to the viewer avert their gazes and curiously cover their
mouths. Their somber outlines echo the two orange cones, which probably represent
shrubs wrapped against the frost. The bench along the upper-left path rises steeply,
defying logical perspective. Equally puzzling is the mysterious bush on the left, in
which Gauguin consciously embedded forms that suggest eyes and a nose, creating
the impression of a strange, watchful presence. With its aura of repressed emotion
and elusive meaning, *Arlésiennes (Mistral)* explores the ambiguities, mysteries, and
emotions that Gauguin believed underlie appearances.

VINCENT VAN GOGH Dutch, 1853–1890
The Bedroom, 1889
Oil on canvas; 73.6 × 92.3 cm (29 × 36 ⅝ in.)
Helen Birch Bartlett Memorial Collection, 1926.417

Vincent van Gogh so highly esteemed his bedroom painting that he made three distinct versions: the first, now in the collection of the Van Gogh Museum, Amsterdam; the second, belonging to the Art Institute of Chicago, painted a year later on the same scale and almost identical; and a third, smaller canvas in the collection of the Musée d'Orsay, Paris, which he made as a gift for his mother and sister. Van Gogh conceived the first *Bedroom* in October 1888, a month after he moved into his "Yellow House" in Arles, France. This moment marked the first time the artist had a home of his own, and he had immediately and enthusiastically set about decorating, painting a suite of canvases to fill the walls. Completely exhausted from the effort, he spent two-and-a-half days in bed and was then inspired to create a painting of his bedroom. As he wrote to his brother Theo, "It amused me enormously doing this bare interior. With a simplicity à la Seurat. In flat tints, but coarsely brushed in full impasto, the walls pale lilac, the floor in a broken and faded red, the chairs and the bed chrome yellow, the pillows and the sheet very pale lemon green, the bedspread blood-red, the dressing-table orange, the washbasin blue, the window green. I had wished to express utter repose with all these very different tones." Although the picture symbolized relaxation and peace to the artist, to our eyes the canvas seems to teem with nervous energy, instability, and turmoil, and effect heightened by the sharply receding perspective.

CLAUDE MONET French, 1840–1926
Stacks of Wheat (End of Summer), 1890/91
Oil on canvas; 60 × 100.5 cm (23 ⅝ × 39 ⁹/₁₆ in.)
Gift of Arthur M. Wood, Sr., in memory of Pauline Palmer Wood, 1985.1103

The monumental stacks that Claude Monet depicted in his series *Stacks of Wheat*
rose fifteen to twenty feet and stood just outside the artist's farmhouse at Giverny.
Through 1890 and 1891, he worked on this series both in the field, painting simultaneously at several easels, and in the studio, refining pictorial harmonies. In May
1891, Monet hung fifteen of these canvases next to each other in one small room in
the Galerie Durand-Ruel in Paris. An unprecedented critical and financial success,
the exhibition marked a breakthrough in Monet's career, as well as in the history of
French art. In this view, and in nearly all of the autumn views in the series, the conical tops of the stacks break the horizon and push into the sky. But in most of the
winter views, which constitute the core of the series, the stacks seem wrapped by
bands of hill and field, as if bedded down for the season. For Monet, the stack was
a resonant symbol of sustenance and survival. He followed this group with further
series depicting poplars, the facade of Rouen Cathedral, and, later, his own garden
at Giverny (see p. 194). The Art Institute has the largest group of Monet's *Stacks
of Wheat* in the world.

HENRI DE TOULOUSE-LAUTREC French, 1864–1901
At the Moulin Rouge, 1892/95
Oil on canvas; 123 × 141 cm (48 ⁷⁄₁₆ × 55 ¹⁄₂ in.)
Helen Birch Bartlett Memorial Collection, 1928.610

In *At the Moulin Rouge* Henri de Toulouse-Lautrec memorialized Parisian night-life at the end of the nineteenth century. The painting is noted for its daring composition, dramatic cropping, and flat planes of strident color. A regular patron of the Moulin Rouge, one of the most famous cabarets of the Montmartre district, Toulouse-Lautrec here turned his acute powers of observation on the club's other habitués. The flaming red-orange hair of the entertainer Jane Avril is the focal point of the central seated group. Preening in the greenish mirror in the background is the dancer La Goulue. The stunted figure of the aristocratic artist appears, as it often did in life, next to his devoted, much taller cousin, Dr. Gabriel Tapié de Céleyran. But it is the frozen, acid-green face of the dancer May Milton that dominates the canvas and haunts the action. The painting comprises two joined parts: a small main canvas and an L-shaped panel to the lower and right edges. The canvas was severed after the artist's death, perhaps by his dealer (to make the composition less radical and more saleable), and restored sometime before 1914.

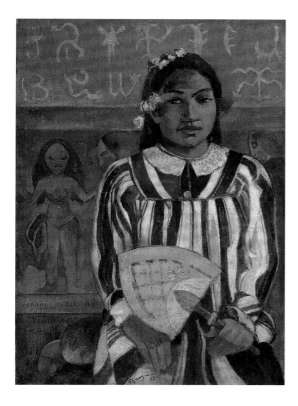

PAUL GAUGUIN French, 1848–1903

Merahi metua no Tehamana (*Tehamana Has Many Parents* or *The Ancestors of Tehamana*), 1893

Oil on jute canvas; 75 × 53 cm (29 ¹/₂ × 20 ⁷/₈ in.)

Gift of Mr. and Mrs. Charles Deering McCormick, 1980.613

Paul Gauguin traveled to rural France and then abroad in search of inspiration for his art. His quest took the former stockbroker to the French regions of Brittany and Provence, to Panama and Martinique, and finally to Tahiti and the Marquesas in the South Pacific. This stately portrait of Gauguin's young Tahitian *vahine* (lover), Tehamana, is perhaps a farewell, since it was painted shortly before the artist left the island, returning to France for two years. Elaborately dressed, her hair decorated with flowers, Tehamana is seated in front of a mysterious painted background reminiscent of a frieze on the wall of an ancient palace or temple. Two ripe mangoes—perhaps an offering or symbol of fertility—rest beside her hip. She points a fan, an emblem of beauty, toward the similarly frontal figure of a goddess, who also wears a red flower in her hair. The fan, flowers, fruit, and even Tehamana's glance suggest not only the strong, enigmatic bond between these two figures but also the connections between the present and the past, the corporeal and the spiritual, and the living and the dead.

CLAUDE MONET French, 1840–1926
Water Lilies, 1906
Oil on canvas; 89.9 × 94.1 cm (35 3/8 × 37 1/16 in.)
Mr. and Mrs. Martin A. Ryerson Collection, 1933.1157

"One instant, one aspect of nature contains it all," said Claude Monet, referring to his late masterpieces, the water landscapes that he produced at his home in Giverny between 1897 and his death in 1926. These works replaced the varied contemporary subjects he had painted from the 1870s through the 1890s (see p. 191) with a single, timeless motif—water lilies. The focal point of these paintings was the artist's beloved flower garden, which featured a water garden and a smaller pond spanned by a Japanese footbridge. In his first water-lily series (1897–99), Monet painted the pond environment, with its plants, bridge, and trees neatly divided by a fixed horizon. Over time, the artist became less and less concerned with conventional pictorial space. By the time he painted *Water Lilies,* which comes from his third group of these works, he had dispensed with the horizon line altogether. In this spatially ambiguous canvas, the artist looked down, focusing solely on the surface of the pond, with its cluster of vegetation floating amid the reflection of sky and trees. Monet thus created the image of a horizontal surface on a vertical one.

MODERN AND CONTEMPORARY ART

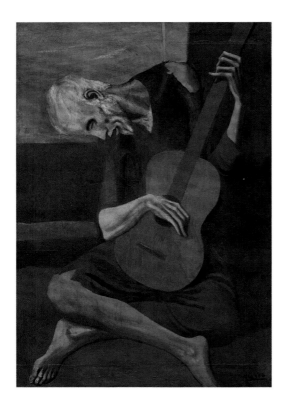

PABLO PICASSO Spanish, 1881–1973
The Old Guitarist, 1903–4
Oil on panel; 122.9 × 82.6 cm (48 ³/₈ × 32 ¹/₂ in.)
Helen Birch Bartlett Memorial Collection, 1926.253

Pablo Picasso produced *The Old Guitarist*, one of his most haunting images, while
working in Barcelona. In the paintings of his Blue Period (1901–4), of which this is
a prime example, Picasso restricted himself to a cold, monochromatic blue palette;
flattened forms; and the emotional, psychological themes of human misery and alienation, which are related to the Symbolist movement and the work of such artists as
Edvard Munch (see p. 318). Picasso presented *The Old Guitarist* as a timeless expression of human suffering. The bent and sightless man holds his large, round guitar
close to him; its brown body is the painting's only shift in color. The elongated, angular
figure of the blind musician relates to the artist's interest in the history of Spanish
art and, in particular, the great sixteenth-century artist El Greco (see p. 156). Most
personally, however, the image reflects the struggling twenty-two-year-old Picasso's
sympathy for the plight of the downtrodden; he knew what it was like to be poor,
having been nearly penniless during all of 1902. His works from this time depict the
miseries of the destitute, the ill, and the outcasts of society.

HENRI MATISSE French, 1869–1954
Still Life with Geranium, 1906
Oil on canvas; 100.3 × 81.5 cm (39 ½ × 32 ⅛ in.)
Joseph Winterbotham Collection, 1932.1342

Like his artistic hero, Paul Cézanne, Henri Matisse merged the traditional and the avant-garde. In *Still Life with Geranium,* he transformed a simple still life into a populated Arcadian landscape painting, rendered in the brilliant color, thick paint, and rapid brushwork characteristic of the group of painters known as the Fauves (French for "wild beasts"). Matisse was recognized by critics as the leader of this group.

This composition is one of contrasts—the pale palette and light brushwork in the upper half of the picture are juxtaposed with the darker colored, heavily painted lower half; the firmly planted pose of the female figure is contraposed with the almost-fleeing figure of the male; and the red vegetables grown near Paris are set near ceramic objects from exotic, faraway places. One of many still-life paintings in which Matisse incorporated his own figurative sculptures, here the artist challenged his viewers' expectations by rendering his modeled figures with minimal color and simple lines. Probably represented as plaster casts, these figures would later be made in bronze editions by the artist; versions of *Woman Leaning on Her Hands* (on the right of the geranium) and *Thorn Extractor* (on the left) are also in the collection of the Art Institute.

GEORGES BRAQUE French, 1882–1963

Little Harbor in Normandy, 1909

Oil on canvas; 81.1 × 80.5 cm (32 × 31 ³/₄ in.)

Samuel A. Marx Purchase Fund, 1970.98

In early 1908, Georges Braque began an artistic collaboration with Pablo Picasso. From 1909 until Braque was mobilized for World War I, they worked in creative dialogue, breaking down and reformulating the representation of objects and their structure. In doing so, they pioneered one of the most radical artistic revolutions of the twentieth century, Cubism. *Little Harbor in Normandy* is the first fully realized example of Braque's early Cubist style. He described the English Channel coast in severe geometries and a sober palette, reduced in range and intensity to pale shades of color. His compressed treatment of space and use of a shifting perspective seems to propel the two sailboats forward to the front edges of the picture. To further energize the scene, the artist added a fringe of whitecaps to the sea and dashes of clouds across the sky. His repetitive, striated modeling of form, inspired by his study of the art of Paul Cézanne, increased the rigid tension of this canvas. Documentation suggests that *Little Harbor in Normandy* was exhibited in Paris in March 1909 at the Salon des Indépendants, making this painting the first major Cubist work to be shown in such a prominent venue.

PABLO PICASSO Spanish, 1881–1973
Head of a Woman (Fernande), 1909
Bronze; 40.7 × 20.1 × 26.9 cm (16 1/8 × 9 7/8 × 10 9/16 in.)
Alfred Stieglitz Collection, 1949.584

This work is Pablo Picasso's first large Cubist sculpture and represents the distinctive physiognomy of Fernande Olivier, the artist's model and companion from 1905 until 1912. Before making the bust, Picasso produced countless drawings and gouaches to explore the specific form and structure of his subject's facial features—her dark almond-shaped eyes, sharp nose, peaked upper lip, fleshy chin, and braided topknot. He also looked to African and ancient Iberian sculpture to guide his translation of Fernande's profile into the geometric language of Cubism. Converting his studies to three dimensions, Picasso simultaneously built up and cut away the clay as he worked, giving the surface a unifying rhythm of light and shadow. The resulting bronze retains the basic shape of Fernande's head, though the surface and structure are broken up into faceted, fragmented forms.

The Art Institute's bronze is one of a small edition produced by the Parisian art dealer Ambroise Vollard in 1910. It was sold in 1912 to the photographer and dealer Alfred Stieglitz, who published his own photographs of the work in his journal *Camera Work*. A year later, he loaned it to the landmark Armory Show, for which the Art Institute was the only museum venue.

PABLO PICASSO Spanish, 1881–1973
Daniel-Henry Kahnweiler, 1910
Oil on canvas; 100.4 × 72.4 cm (39 ⁹/₁₆ × 28 ⁹/₁₆ in.)
Gift of Mrs. Gilbert W. Chapman in memory of Charles B. Goodspeed, 1948.561

The subject of this portrait is Daniel-Henry Kahnweiler (1884–1979), a German-born art dealer, writer, and publisher. Kahnweiler opened an art gallery in Paris in 1907 and in 1908 began representing Pablo Picasso, whom he introduced to Georges Braque. Kahnweiler was a great champion of the artists' revolutionary experiment with Cubism and purchased the majority of their paintings between 1908 and 1915. He also wrote an important book, *The Rise of Cubism*, in 1920, which offered a theoretical framework for the movement.

Kahnweiler sat as many as thirty times for this portrait. No longer seeking to create the illusion of true appearances, Picasso broke down and recombined the forms he saw. He described Kahnweiler with a network of shimmering, semitransparent surfaces that merge with the atmosphere around him. Forms are fractured into various planes and faceted shapes and presented from several points of view. Despite the portrait's highly abstract character, however, Picasso added attributes to direct the eye and focus the mind: a wave of hair, the knot of a tie, a watch chain. Out of the flickering passages of brown, gray, black, and white emerges a rather traditional portrait pose of a seated man, his hands clasped in his lap.

HENRI MATISSE French, 1869–1954
Bathers by a River, 1909–17
Oil on canvas; 260 × 392 cm (102 ½ × 154 ³/₁₆ in.)
Charles H. and Mary F. S. Worcester Collection, 1953.158

Henri Matisse considered *Bathers by a River* to be one of the five most "pivotal" works of his career, and with good reason: it facilitated the evolution of the artist's style over the course of nearly a decade. Originally, the work was related to a 1909 commission by the Russian collector Sergei Shchukin, who wanted two large canvases to decorate the staircase of his Moscow home. Matisse proposed three pastoral images, though Shchukin decided to purchase only two works, *Dance II* and *Music* (both State Hermitage Museum, Saint Petersburg).

Four years later, Matisse returned to this canvas, the rejected third image, altering the idyllic scene and changing the pastel palette to reflect his new interest in Cubism. He reordered the composition, making the figures more columnar, with faceless, ovoid heads. Over the next years, Matisse transformed the background into four vertical bands and turned the formerly blue river into a thick black vertical band. With its restricted palette and severely abstracted forms, *Bathers by a River* is far removed from *Dance II* and *Music,* which convey a graceful lyricism. The sobriety and hint of danger in *Bathers by a River* may in part reflect the artist's concerns during the terrible, war-torn period during which he completed it.

ROBERT DELAUNAY French, 1885–1941
Champs de Mars: The Red Tower, 1911/23
Oil on canvas; 160.7 × 128.6 cm (63 ¼ × 50 ⅝ in.)
Joseph Winterbotham Collection, 1959.1

Robert Delaunay was four years old when the Eiffel Tower was erected in Paris in the public green space known as the Champ de Mars. One of many artists to depict the landmark, Delaunay did a series of Eiffel Tower paintings, of which the Art Institute's example is among the best known. The artist infused the dynamism of modern life into this image by employing multiple viewpoints, rhythmic fragmentation of form, and strong color contrasts. Delaunay accented the structure's towering presence by framing it with tall buildings and placing smaller, shorter buildings, seen from above, at its base. The top of the tower seems to soar, its massive structure augmented by winglike clouds and patches of light-filled sky.

The artist first showed this painting in the winter of 1912, at the Galerie Barbazanges in Paris, where Guillaume Apollinaire described the work in a review as "unfinished, whether by design or accident." Although Delaunay's intent is not recorded, it is certain that by 1923, when this work was illustrated in the pages of the *Bulletin de l'effort moderne,* it looked as it does today: the artist had repainted portions of the canvas and filled areas of reserve with paint.

MARCEL DUCHAMP American, born France, 1887–1968
Bottle Rack, 1914/59, signed 1960
Galvanized iron; diam. at base: 59.1 × 36.8 cm (23 ¼ × 14 ¼ in.)
Through prior gifts of Mary and Leigh Block, Mr. and Mrs. Maurice E. Culberg, and Mr. and Mrs. James W. Alsdorf; Charles H. and Mary F. S. Worcester Collection Fund; through prior gift of Mary and Earle Ludgin Collection; Sheila Anne Morgenstern in memory of Dorothy O. Morgenstern and William V. Morgenstern; through prior bequests of Joseph Winterbotham and Mima de Manziarly Porter; Ada Turnbull Hertle and Modern Discretionary funds, 2017.422

Marcel Duchamp began his career as a painter of conventional portraits and nudes. By 1912, however, he set out to prove the end of "retinal art"—pictures created to delight the eye—in order to "put painting once again at the service of the mind." His answer was the "readymade," an ordinary object transformed into a work of art by virtue of the artist selecting it. Taken out of context, repositioned, and signed by the artist, the readymade upended tradition and artistic convention by revolutionizing the way we think about what an artwork is, how it is produced, and the ways in which it is exhibited.

In 1914 Duchamp purchased this mass-produced bottle rack at a department store. He felt free to acquire new versions for exhibitions and display after his sister accidentally discarded the "original." He selected the present version for the 1959 exhibition *Art and the Found Object in New York*. Artist Robert Rauschenberg acquired *Bottle Rack* and asked Duchamp to sign it. He obliged, writing in French, "Impossible for me to recall the original phrase M.D. / Marcel Duchamp /1960."

VASILY KANDINSKY French, born Russia, 1866–1944
Improvisation No. 30 (Cannons), 1913
Oil on canvas; 111 × 111.3 cm (43 ¹¹/₁₆ × 43 ¹³/₁₆ in.)
Arthur Jerome Eddy Memorial Collection, 1931.511

In his seminal 1912 text *Concerning the Spiritual in Art*, Vasily Kandinsky advocated an art that could move beyond imitation of the physical world, inspiring, as he put it, "vibrations in the soul." Pioneering abstraction as the richest, most musical form of artistic expression, Kandinsky believed that the physical properties of artworks could stir emotions, and he produced a revolutionary group of increasingly abstract canvases—with titles such as *Fugue*, *Impression*, and *Improvisation*—hoping to bring painting closer to music making.

Kandinsky's paintings are, in his words, "largely unconscious, spontaneous expressions of inner character, nonmaterial in nature." Although *Improvisation No. 30 (Cannons)* at first appears to be an almost random assortment of brilliant colors, shapes, and lines, the artist also included leaning buildings, a crowd of people, and a wheeled, smoking cannon. In a letter to the Chicago lawyer Arthur Jerome Eddy, who purchased the painting in 1913 and later bequeathed it to the Art Institute, Kandinsky explained that "the presence of the cannons in the picture could probably be explained by the constant war talk that has been going on throughout the year." Eventually, Kandinsky ceased making these references to the material world in his work and wholly devoted himself to pure abstraction.

FRANCIS PICABIA French, 1879–1953

Edtaonisl (Ecclesiastic), 1913

Oil on canvas; 300.4 × 300.7 cm (118 × 118 in.)

Gift of Mr. and Mrs. Armand Bartos, 1953.622

In 1911 Francis Picabia met Marcel Duchamp, who had devised a unique style of painting that combined Cubist elements with pseudodiagrams in humorous composi- tions. Stimulated by Duchamp's example, Picabia pioneered a new, colorful, and intellectual visual language, of which *Edtaonisl* is a prime example.

This picture relates to Picabia's experience aboard a transatlantic ship in 1913, on his way to the opening of the Armory Show, North America's first major exhibition of modern art. Picabia was amused by two fellow passengers—an exotic Polish dancer named Stacia Napierskowska and a Dominican priest who could not resist the temptation of watching her rehearse with her troupe. While the tumultuous shapes in this work suggest fragments of bodies and nautical architecture, the depiction of specific forms is less important than the effective expression of contrast and rocking motion, which evokes the sensations of dance and a ship moving through rolling seas. On the top right of the canvas, Picabia painted the word *Edtaonisl*—an acronym made by alternating the letters of the French words *étoile* (star) and *dans[e]* (dance), a process analogous to the artist's shattering and recombining of forms. He subtitled the work *Ecclesiastic*, hinting at the juxtaposition of the spiritual and the sensual.

GINO SEVERINI Italian, 1883–1966
Festival in Montmartre, 1913
Oil on canvas; 88.9 × 116.2 cm (35 × 45 ³/₄ in.)
Bequest of Richard S. Zeisler, 2007.281

Gino Severini was a member of the Futurists, a group of Italian artists that announced its existence with a manifesto published in 1909 on the front page of *Le Figaro*. The Futurists urged others to ignore the past and focus on the aesthetic power of modern life. Their paintings celebrate modernity—the speed, thrill, and especially the danger of factories, airplanes, automobiles, locomotives, and steamships. Their style blended Divisionism and Cubism to render "dynamic sensation" and the interpenetration of objects and their environment by superimposing different chromatic planes and lines of force.

Severini's work focused on Parisian entertainments, nightlife, and street activities. In *Festival in Montmartre,* he depicted the centrifugal motion of a carousel and the liberating, yet destabilizing, effects of color, speed, and sound. The artist presented this work in his first solo exhibition in 1913, writing in the catalogue, "My object has been to convey the sensation of a body, lighted by electric lamps and gyrating in the darkness of the boulevard. The shapes of the pink pigs and of the women seated on them are subordinate the whole, the rotary movement of which they follow while undergoing displacement from head to foot and vice versa."

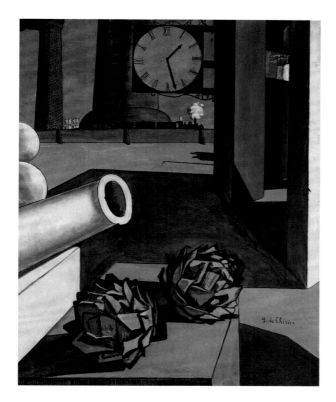

GIORGIO DE CHIRICO Italian, born Greece, 1888–1978
The Philosopher's Conquest, 1913/14
Oil on canvas; 125.1 × 99.1 cm (49 ¼ × 39 in.)
Joseph Winterbotham Collection, 1939.405

The work of Giorgio de Chirico represents an unexpected form of classicism in early avant-garde painting. This canvas, one of six in a series, combines a Mediterranean cityscape with still-life objects. Familiar elements appear in many of de Chirico's paintings like pieces of a mysterious puzzle: a classical arcade, oddly oversize artichokes, a cannon and cannonballs, a clock, an industrial brick chimney, a monumental tower, a running train, and a square-rigged sailing ship. Here the stage set for this extraordinary juxtaposition of objects is an Italian piazza, virtually deserted except for the menacing shadowy figures outside the edge of the scene.

De Chirico represented objects with a matter-of-fact, though intentionally crude, precision. He painted his scenes flatly, in bright colors, and illuminated them with a cold white light. Rendered in this clear style, works like *The Philosopher's Conquest* seem rife with meaning, though they remain resolutely enigmatic. Indeed, by juxtaposing incongruous objects, the artist sought to produce a metaphysical quality, what he called "art that in certain aspects resembles . . . the restlessness of myth." De Chirico's works would profoundly affect the Surrealists, who in the 1920s and 1930s attempted to portray dreams and images of the subconscious in their work.

AMEDEO MODIGLIANI Italian, 1884–1920
Jacques and Berthe Lipchitz, 1916
Oil on canvas; 81.3 × 54.3 cm (32 × 21 3/8 in.)
Helen Birch Bartlett Memorial Collection, 1926.221

After receiving his artistic training in Italy, the sculptor and painter Amedeo Modigliani moved to Paris in 1906. Three years later, he helped pioneer a general migration of artists to the neighborhood of Montparnasse, which remained the center of avant-gard activity in the city until World War II. Scores of artists lived there, and many of them shared a Jewish heritage—including Modigliani and his friend the Lithuanian-born sculptor Jacques Lipchitz.

Lipchitz commissioned Modigliani to paint this portrait on the occasion of his marriage to the Russian poet Berthe Kitrosser, as a way of helping his troubled friend financially. The double portrait is one of only three in the artist's oeuvre and, according to Lipchitz, took two days to paint. Modigliani made about twenty drawings on the first day; the next day, he declared the picture finished. At the modest price of what Lipchitz remembered as "ten francs per sitting and a little alcohol," however, he persuaded Modigliani to work on the portrait for another two weeks in an effort to provide more financial assistance to his friend. Despite Modigliani's exceptional talent, his work found a market only after his death in 1920, which was hastened by tuberculosis and his legendary bohemian lifestyle.

CONSTANTIN BRÂNCUSI

French, born Romania, 1876–1957
Golden Bird, 1919/20 (base c. 1922)
Bronze, stone, and wood; 217.8 × 29.9 × 29.9 cm
(86 × 11 ³/₄ × 11 ³/₄ in.)

Partial gift of the Arts Club of Chicago; restricted
gift of various donors; through prior bequest
of Arthur Rubloff; through prior restricted gift
of William E. Hartmann; through prior gifts of
Mr. and Mrs. Carter H. Harrison, Mr. and Mrs.
Arnold H. Maremont through the Kate Maremont
Foundation, Woodruff J. Parker, Mrs. Clive
Runnells, Mr. and Mrs. Martin A. Ryerson, and
various donors, 1990.88

Trained in both folk and academic traditions, Constantin Brâncusi sought
his own path for sculpture around 1907.
Breaking with the currents of the time,
he adopted direct carving, combined different materials for single works, and
simplified form in his search for his subjects' essential characters. His works
have profoundly influenced the development of twentieth-century abstraction.

More than any other theme, Brâncusi's
series *Bird* summarizes his quest for a self-
sufficient form. "All my life, I have sought
to render the essence of flight," the artist
once said. He began the first of twenty-
seven *Bird* sculptures around 1910 and
completed the last in the 1940s. He called
the earliest variations *Maiastra,* referring
to a bird in Romanian folklore that
leads a prince to his princess. In the Art
Institute's *Golden Bird*, details such
as feet, a tail, and an upturned crowing
beak are only suggested in an elegant,
streamlined silhouette. Brâncusi perched
this refined shape on a rough-hewn,
geometric base, contrasting the disem-
bodied, light-reflective surface with
an earthbound mass. The central polyhedron was cut from the middle of a
tree trunk, and its circles (indicating the
tree's age) rotate like a sun, as if radiating
light over the bird.

PIERRE BONNARD French, 1867–1947
Earthly Paradise, 1916–20
Oil on canvas; 130 × 160 cm (51 ¼ × 63 in.)
Estate of Joanne Toor Cummings; Bette and Neison Harris and Searle Family Trust endowments;
through prior gifts of Mrs. Henry C. Woods, 1996.47

Following a period spent producing Parisian scenes in the style of Édouard Vuillard
and Henri de Toulouse-Lautrec, Pierre Bonnard virtually reinvented his art around
1905. The artist's new emphasis on large-scale compositions, bold forms, and brilliant colors shows his awareness of the work of his contemporaries Henri Matisse
and Pablo Picasso, as does his focus on Arcadian landscapes, a theme he had not
previously explored. Part of a series of four canvases painted for his dealers, Josse
and Gaston Bernheim, between 1916 and 1920, *Earthly Paradise* demonstrates Bonnard's new, daring investigations of light, color, and space. Here the artist used
foliage to create a proscenium-like arch for a drama involving a brooding Adam
and recumbent Eve. The contrast Bonnard established between the figures seems to
follow a tradition in which the female, presented as essentially sexual, is connected
with nature, while the male, essentially intellectual, is able to transcend the earthly.
Heightening the image's ambiguity is an array of animals, including birds, a monkey, rabbits, and a serpent (here reduced to a garden snake). This less-than-Edenic
paradise may reflect the artist's response to the destruction of Europe during World
War I, which was still raging when he began the painting.

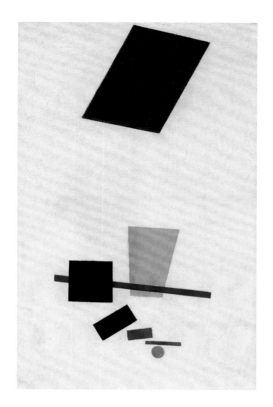

KAZIMIR MALEVICH Russian, born Ukraine, 1878–1935
Painterly Realism of a Football Player—Color Masses in the 4th Dimension, 1915
Oil on canvas; present size: 70.2 × 44.1 cm (27 ⅝ × 17 ⁵/₁₆ in.)
Through prior gifts of Charles H. and Mary F. S. Worcester Collection; Mrs. Albert D. Lasker in memory
of her husband, Albert D. Lasker; and Mr. and Mrs. Lewis Larned Coburn Memorial Collection, 2011.1

During the summer and fall of 1915, Kazimir Malevich secluded himself to prepare
for the groundbreaking exhibition *0.10 (Zero-Ten) The Last Futurist Exhibition
of Paintings*. Seeking to push the formal discoveries of Cubism and Futurism to their
limits, to find the most essential core—the "zero"—of painting, Malevich produced
a series of completely abstract works that he declared constituted an entirely new
system of art. Suprematism, as he called the new style, eradicated all references to
the natural world and focused instead on the inherent relationships between colored
geometric shapes against the void of a subtly textured white background. In the
exhibition catalogue he warned, "In naming some of the paintings I do not wish
to point out what form to seek in them, but I wish to indicate that real forms were
approached in many cases as the ground for formless painterly masses from which a
painterly picture was created, quite unrelated to nature." belongs to this very first
group of Suprematist works. The subtitle refers to the mathematical theory of fourth
dimensional space, a concept appropriated by many early twentieth-century artists to
justify their representation of truths beyond immediate sensory perception.

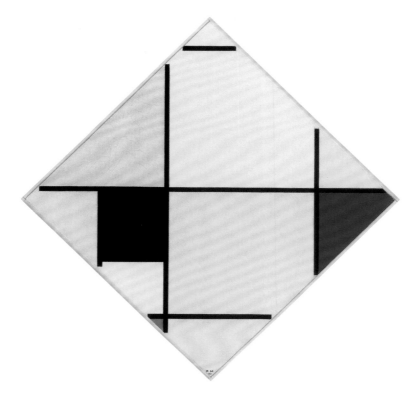

PIET MONDRIAN Dutch, 1872–1944
Lozenge Composition with Yellow, Black, Blue, Red, and Gray, 1921
Oil on canvas; 60 × 60 cm (23 ⅝ × 23 ⅝ in.)
Gift of Edgar Kaufmann, Jr., 1957.307

Although Piet Mondrian's abstractions may seem far removed from nature, his basic
vision was rooted in landscape, especially the flat geography of his native Holland.
Beginning with his early naturalistic landscapes, he reduced natural forms to their
simplest linear and colored equivalents to suggest their unity and order. Eventually
he eliminated such forms altogether, developing a pure visual language of verticals,
horizontals, and primary colors that he believed expressed universal forces.

In *Lozenge Composition with Yellow, Black, Blue, Red, and Gray* Mondrian
rotated a square canvas to create a dynamic relationship between the rectilinear composition and the diagonal lines of the edges of the canvas. Deceptively simple, his
works are the result of constant adjustment to achieve absolute balance and harmony,
and they reveal an exacting attention to the subtle relations between lines, shapes,
and colors. The artist hoped that his paintings would point the way to a utopian
future. This goal was first formulated in Holland around 1916–17 by Mondrian and
a small group of like-minded artists and architects who collectively referred to their
aesthetic as De Stijl (The Style). Their ideas have been extraordinarily influential for
all aspects of modern design, from architecture and fashion to household objects.

FERNAND LÉGER French, 1881–1955
Reclining Woman, 1922
Oil on canvas; 64.5 × 92 cm (25 ¹/₂ × 36 ¹/₄ in.)
A Millennium Gift of Sara Lee Corporation, 1999.369

Fernand Léger first saw the work of the Cubists Georges Braque and Pablo Picasso
at the Paris gallery of Daniel-Henry Kahnweiler. Around 1909 Léger began to experiment with geometric shapes, complementary colors, and strong outlines, although
his paintings remained largely nonrepresentational until after World War I. His involvement in the war had a profound impact on his work. In the years following, he
introduced volumetric forms that resembled pistons and pipes into his compositions,
joining others in the Parisian vanguard in charting a more sober, conservative course
that placed renewed emphasis on objective observation. Substituting hard metallic
tubes for pliant flesh and flat patterned disks for soft and dense pillows, the artist
updated the classical figure of the odalisque (a female slave or concubine often pictured in the history of art as a reclining nude) with his particular blend of Cubism
and machine aesthetics. *Reclining Woman* demonstrates Léger's interest in producing
"everyday poetic images": paintings in which the manufactured object is the "principal personage," shown as precisely as possible to reveal an absolute sculptural value
rather than sentimental associations. This work exemplifies the Purist style, a kind
of industrial classicism that focused on utilitarian objects. Léger hoped that through
such paintings, art would become accessible to the whole of modern society rather
than to just a privileged few.

PABLO PICASSO Spanish, 1881–1973

Mother and Child, 1921

Oil on canvas; 142.9 × 172.7 cm (56 ¼ × 68 in.)

Restricted gift of Maymar Corporation, Mrs. Maurice L. Rothschild, and Mr. and Mrs. Chauncey McCormick; Mary and Leigh Block Fund; Ada Turnbull Hertle Endowment; through prior gift of Mr. and Mrs. Edwin E. Hokin, 1954.270

In 1917 Picasso traveled to Rome to design sets and costumes for Sergei Diaghilev's famed Ballets Russes. Deeply impressed by the ancient and Renaissance art of that city, he began painting monumental figures inspired by antiquity. His new classical style was influenced by the finely modeled odalisques of Jean-Auguste-Dominique Ingres and the late, oddly proportioned female nudes of Pierre-Auguste Renoir. *Mother and Child* was also inspired by Picasso's own life. Just three years earlier he had married Russian dancer Olga Khokhlova, and in 1921 their son Paolo was born. Between 1921 and 1923 he produced at least twelve works on the subject of mothers and children, returning to a theme that he had explored during his Blue Period. But whereas those figures are frail and anguished, his classical-period figures, with their sculptural modeling and solidity, are majestic in proportion and feeling. Here an infant sits on the mother's lap and reaches up to touch her. The woman, dressed in a Grecian gown, gazes intently at her child. Behind them stretches a simplified background of sand, water, and sky. Picasso's treatment of the pair is not sentimental, but the relationship expresses a serenity and stability that characterized his own life at this time.

HENRI MATISSE French, 1869–1954
Woman before an Aquarium, 1921/23
Oil on canvas; 80.7 × 100 cm (31 ³/₄ × 39 ³/₈ in.)
Helen Birch Bartlett Memorial Collection, 1926.220

Henri Matisse was fascinated by the cultures of North Africa and the Middle East. In 1903 he visited an Islamic art exhibition at the Musée des Arts Décoratifs, Paris; in 1910 he traveled to Munich for a major display of Islamic objects and then to Spain to see Moorish architecture. He also collected brilliantly colored and richly ornamented textiles, pottery, and tiles. It was, however, the physical experience of these lands that proved to have the greatest impact on Matisse's vision and creativity. In May 1906 and for long periods between January 1912 and February 1913, he traveled to North Africa. There, he came to understand the unique quality of light and its effect on the perception of color and space.

Even a decade later, while Matisse lived in the southern French city of Nice, these experiences would continue to transform his work. In *Woman before an Aquarium,* the paneled screen and goldfish are pictorial elements drawn from Matisse's Moroccan journeys. Moreover, the artist's own transformation—the "new rhythm" of his inner vision that resulted from his travels—was responsible for the particular luminosity, cool palette, and intimate effect of this canvas. Matisse was entranced by the golden light and sea-soaked atmosphere of Nice, and his paintings from this period demonstrate his newfound interest in an impressionistic naturalism that was not a rejection of his earlier work but rather an effort to infuse his previous style with a "human element."

CLAUDE CAHUN French, 1894–1954
Object, 1936
Wood, paint, and hair; 13.7 × 16.2 × 10.2 cm (5 ³/₈ × 6 ³/₈ × 4 in.)
Through prior gift of Mrs. Gilbert W. Chapman, 2007.30

Claude Cahun, born Lucy Schwob, was closely associated with the Paris Surrealists of the 1930s. Attracted to the group's desire to transform society through the
exploration of the unconscious, she challenged traditional ideas about gender and
sexuality through her intimate photographic self-portraits, collages, and sculptures.
For *Object*, Cahun altered a number of seemingly unrelated components—a doll's
hand, a cloud-shaped piece of wood, and a tennis ball painted with a wide-open
eye—to produce a startling psychological resonance. The eye, in particular, a key
Surrealist symbol of inner perception, also suggests female anatomy. On the base
of the work, Cahun added the French phrase, "The Marseillaise is a revolutionary
song, the law punishes counterfeiters with forced labor." Much like the rest of the
work, the inscription is a juxtaposition of disparate elements: the first, a well-known
slogan from France's antifascist coalition, the left-wing Popular Front, and the other,
a phrase from Belgian currency. In combining these phrases, Cahun seems to point
an accusatory finger at the supposed "revolutionary" leaders of France—a rare direct
reference to politics in a Surrealist artwork. Her assemblages were typically ephemeral and made to be photographed; *Object* is the only sculptural work by the artist
known to still exist in its original form.

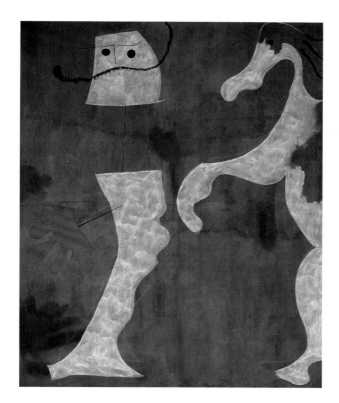

JOAN MIRÓ Spanish, 1893–1983
The Policeman, 1925
Oil on canvas; 248 × 194.9 cm (97 ⁵/₈ × 76 ³/₄ in.)
Bequest of Claire Zeisler, 1991.1499

Soon after Joan Miró moved to Paris from his native Barcelona in 1920, he met a group of avant-garde painters and writers who advocated merging the everyday rational world with that of dreams and the unconscious in order to produce an absolute reality, or surreality. To release images of this higher realm, the Surrealists embraced automatism, a spontaneous working method much like free association. Miró experimented with automatism: "Even a few casual wipes in cleaning my brush," he said, "may suggest the beginning of a picture." Between 1925 and 1927, his experiments unleashed a revolutionary series of works called the "dream paintings," which straddle abstraction and representation in freely moving, calligraphic compositions. In *The Policeman*, a large canvas from this group, two biomorphic shapes spring to life as a policeman and a horse, their forms defined by thinly applied white paint against a neutral ocher ground. The form on the left has sprouted five buds that act as fingers, and both forms extrude curves that suggest torsos or mouths. With graffiti-like dots and squiggles added to their heads to make eyes and a mustache, Miró's shapes come to life in a liquid space as animated equivalents of a policeman and his horse.

GEORGES VANTONGERLOO Belgian, 1886–1965
Interrelation of Volumes from the Ellipsoid, 1926
Plaster; 40 × 47 × 26 cm (15 $^3/_4$ × 18 $^1/_2$ × 10 $^1/_4$ in.)
Through prior gift of Lucille E. and Joseph L. Block; partial gift in memory of Lillian Florsheim,
2004.245

Near the end of World War I, Georges Vantongerloo felt the need to break with the
past. He came in contact with a group of artists, including Theo van Doesburg and
Piet Mondrian, who saw abstraction as an almost spiritual vehicle for the reconstruction of art and society. Their approach, known as De Stijl (The Style), was marked by
fundamentals: geometry combined with asymmetry; pure primary colors with black
and white; and positive and negative elements. Motivated by his belief in this utopian
aesthetic, Vantongerloo joined the De Stijl group in 1917, its founding year.

In 1919 he embarked on a series of sculptures based on the interrelation of masses.
Interrelation of Volumes from the Ellipsoid, the fifth in the group, explores the inter-
sections of a parallel-faced polyhedron within an ovoid volume. To produce this work,
the artist mapped the intersecting volumes of forms from different views in order to
reveal core geometric units and planes. While this sculpture was inspired by mathematical principles, it is not a sterile, scientific object but, in its realized form, suggests an
element of human invention in the mold marks and alterations that Vantongerloo
considered part of the artistic process.

ALBERTO GIACOMETTI Swiss, 1901–1966
Spoon Woman, 1926/27 (cast 1954)
Bronze; 146 × 52 × 25.4 cm (57 ¹/₂ × 20 ¹/₂ × 10 in.)
Gift of Florene May Schoenborn, 1971.880

After studying at the École des Beaux-Arts and the École d'Arts et Métiers in Geneva, Alberto Giacometti traveled throughout Italy and finally settled in Paris in 1923. Two years later, despite his formal training in drawing and painting, he began to focus solely on sculpture. During these early years, he forged a path based on a variety of influences, including the formal simplicity of Constantin Brâncusi's sculpture, aspects of Cubism, and the totemic quality of African art. *Spoon Woman* was inspired by a type of anthropomorphic spoon carved by the Dan people of West Africa; such works were exhibited frequently in Paris during the 1920s and were the subject of great fascination for artists, including Giacometti. Drawing on the frontality and cultural significance of these implements, he presented his female figure as a symbol of fertility. Topped by a set of simple blocks to suggest her torso and head, the woman's wide, curving womb is represented by the concave section of the spoon. Giacometti's interest in female totems extended beyond the art of the Dan; in the 1920s he studied and sketched prehistoric female figures—symbols of fertility and mystery—that were in the collections of many museums.

MAX ERNST French, born Germany, 1891–1976
Forest and Sun, 1927
Oil on canvas; 66 × 82.5 cm (26 × 32 ½ in.)
Bequest of Richard S. Zeisler, 2007.276

Among his many recollections of childhood, Max Ernst often recounted his fear and fascination with the forest that surrounded his home. He wrote of feeling "delight and oppression and what the Romantics called 'emotion in the face of Nature.'" By expressing his thoughts in these terms, Ernst linked himself with the spiritual landscape tradition of Romanticism, which conceived of an invisible realm at work in the natural world.

This dark and mysterious forest scene dates to one of the most creative periods of Ernst's career. Spurred by the Surrealist leader André Breton's proclamation of "pure psychic automatism" as an artistic ideal, he developed the innovative technique of frottage, his term for the method of reproducing a relief design (like the surface of a piece of wood) by laying paper or canvas over it and rubbing it with a pencil, charcoal, or another medium. In *Forest and Sun* Ernst used this technique to create a petrified forest, which he imbued with a sense of primordial otherworldliness. By scraping away almost-dry paint on the canvas (a process he called grattage), the artist produced the encircled sun at the center of the composition. Ernst painted six variations of the forest and sun theme. As in the other five canvases, the tree trunks suggest a letter in the artist's name: in this case, a capital M.

YVES TANGUY American, born France, 1900–1955
Untitled, 1928
Oil on eight joined panels; each: 200 × 59.7 cm (78 3/4 × 23 1/2 in.), installed
Joseph Winterbotham Collection, 1988.434

The largely self-taught Yves Tanguy decided to become an artist around 1923, when he was inspired by a painting by Giorgio de Chirico that he saw in a shop window. Tanguy became interested in Surrealism a year later, after reading the periodical *La révolution surréaliste*. André Breton welcomed him into the Surrealist group in 1925. Inspired by the metaphysical qualities of de Chirico's work, as well as the biomorphic forms of Jean Arp, Max Ernst, and Joan Miró, Tanguy quickly developed his own fantastic vocabulary of organic, amoeba-like shapes that populate mysterious, dreamlike settings.

Tanguy painted this primordial landscape on a hinged wooden screen. Little information exists about the circumstances of the work's making, but the artist probably intended it for a patron's home, since many Surrealists were interested in the decorative arts and produced folding screens, furniture, and other domestic objects. In this unusual example, although the screen retains the potential to close off the private sphere, it simultaneously opens up more intimate dreams and fantasies to the outside world.

PAUL KLEE German, born Switzerland, 1879–1940
Sunset, 1930
Oil on canvas; 46.1 × 70.5 cm (18 ⅛ × 27 ¾ in.)
Gift of Mary and Leigh B. Block, 1981.13

Paul Klee was an artist and teacher at the Bauhaus for most of that famed school's existence. Initially head of the bookbinding department, Klee made his greatest contribution as a lecturer on the theory of form in art for the basic design course. There, he developed his ideas about the "polyphony" of painting—the simultaneous effect of formal elements that produces "a transformed beholder of art."

Klee was also a trained musician and shared with many artists of the early twentieth century the idea that music was the key to producing a new, abstract art. He was interested in the temporal character of music and its possible translation into forms of art. Works like *Sunset* reflect the principles of rhythm: linear structures, forms, and tonal values are orchestrated into a measured, vibrating image. To produce such a harmonious effect, Klee layered an intricate pattern of dots over a neutral background. Abstract, geometric, and overlapping shapes balance with recognizable forms, such as the schematic face in the upper left and the red sun and arrow in the lower right. The resulting composition—balancing stillness and movement, shallowness and depth—relates to Klee's larger project of looking to music to produce an art that "does not reproduce the visible, but makes visible."

PABLO PICASSO Spanish, 1881–1973
The Red Armchair, 1931
Oil and Ripolin on panel; 131.1 × 98.7 cm (51 5/8 × 38 7/8 in.)
Gift of Mr. and Mrs. Daniel Saidenberg, 1957.72

Pablo Picasso painted numerous portraits of the many women in his life. Often the circumstances surrounding his relationships or the distinct personalities of his sitters seem to have precipitated stylistic changes in his work. Marie-Thérèse Walter came into the artist's life around 1925. Though twenty-eight years older and married, the smitten artist began to furtively reference her blond hair, broad features, and voluptuous body in his work. Perhaps acknowledging the double life they were leading, he devised a new motif: a face that encompasses both frontal and profile views.

Picasso experimented beyond form and style, exploring different materials—including found objects such as newspaper, wallpaper, and even studio scraps—in his work. *The Red Armchair* demonstrates the artist's innovative use of Ripolin, an industrial house paint that he first employed as early as 1912 for its brilliant colors as well as for its ability to provide an almost brushless finish if used straight from the can. In preparation for an exhibition of his work at the Galeries Georges Petit in 1931, Picasso began a series of large paintings of Walter, of which *The Red Armchair* was the first. Here he mixed Ripolin with oil to produce a wide range of surface effects—from the crisp brush marks in the yellow background to the thick but leveled look of the white face and the smooth black outlines of the figure.

SALVADOR DALÍ
Spanish, 1904–1989
Venus de Milo with Drawers, 1936
Painted plaster with metal pulls and mink
pompons; 98 × 32.5 × 34 cm (38 ⅝ ×
12 ¾ × 13 ⅜ in.)
Through prior gift of Mrs. Gilbert W. Chapman,
2005.424

Among Salvador Dalí's many memorable works, perhaps none is more deeply embedded in the popular imagination than *Venus de Milo with Drawers*, a half-size plaster reproduction of the famous marble statue (130/120 BC; Musée du Louvre, Paris), altered with pompon-decorated drawers in the figure's forehead, breasts, stomach, abdomen, and left knee. The combination of cool painted plaster and silky mink tufts illustrates the Surrealist interest in uniting different elements to spark a new reality. For the Surrealists, the best means of provoking this revolution of consciousness was a special kind of sculpture that, as Dalí explained in a 1931 essay, was "absolutely useless . . . and created wholly for the purpose of materializing in a fetishistic way, with maximum tangible reality, ideas and fantasies of a delirious character." Dalí's essay, which drew upon the ideas of Marcel Duchamp's readymades, inaugurated object making as an integral part of Surrealist activities.

Influenced by the work of Sigmund Freud, Dalí envisioned the idea of a cabinet transformed into a female figure, which he called an "anthropomorphic cabinet." *Venus de Milo with Drawers* is the culmination of his explorations into the deep, psychological mysteries of sexual desire, which are symbolized in the figure of the ancient goddess of love.

MAX BECKMANN

German, 1884–1950

Self-Portrait, 1937

Oil on canvas; 192.5 × 89 cm (75 ¾ × 35 in.)

Gift of Lotta Hess Ackerman and Philip E. Ringer, 1955.822

Max Beckmann was one of the Weimar Republic's most honored artists and one of those most vilified by the Nazis. This self-portrait was perhaps the last painting the artist completed in Berlin before he and his wife fled to the Netherlands on July 20, 1937. Their flight occurred just two days after Adolf Hitler delivered a speech condemning modern art and one day after the opening of the exhibition *Degenerate Art*, the Nazis' official denigration of the avant-garde, which included twenty-two of Beckmann's works. The artist departed Germany just in time: in 1937 more than five hundred of his works were confiscated from public collections.

The most brilliantly colored and aggressive of all of Beckmann's self-portraits (he painted over eighty), this powerful work depicts the artist, near life size, on the staircase of a hotel lobby, separated from two figures in the background on the right. Beckmann steps to the left, while his dark-rimmed gaze and the entire picture plane—curtains, flowers, staircase, and banisters—seem to slide off to the right. His large hands hang down, limp, against his black tuxedo.

SALVADOR DALÍ Spanish, 1904–1989
Inventions of the Monsters, 1937
Oil on canvas; 51.4 × 78.4 cm (20 ¼ × 30 ⅞ in.)
Joseph Winterbotham Collection, 1943.798

Salvador Dalí, Surrealism's most publicized practitioner, created monstrous visions of a world turned inside out, which he made even more compelling through his extraordinary technical skills. When the Art Institute acquired *Inventions of the Monsters* in 1943, the artist wrote his congratulations and explained:

> According to Nostradamus the apparition of monsters presages the outbreak of war. The canvas was painted in the Semmering mountains near Vienna a few months before the Anschluss [the 1938 political union of Austria and Germany] and has a prophetic character. Horse women equal maternal river monsters. Flaming giraffe equals masculine apocalyptic monster. Cat angel equals divine heterosexual monster. Hourglass equals metaphysical monster. Gala and Dalí equal sentimental monster. The little blue dog is not a true monster.

Inventions of the Monsters has an ominous mood. It is rife with threats of danger, from the menacing fire in the distance to the sibylline figure in the foreground with an hourglass and a butterfly, both symbols of the inevitability of death. Next to this figure sit Dalí and his wife and muse, Gala. With his native Catalonia embroiled in the Spanish Civil War, the artist surely felt great anxiety over a world without a safe haven, a world that indeed had allowed for the invention of monsters.

MARC CHAGALL French, born Russia (now Belarus), 1887–1985
White Crucifixion, 1938
Oil on canvas; 154.6 × 140 cm (60 ⅞ × 55 ¹/₁₆ in.)
Gift of Alfred S. Alschuler, 1946.925

The 1938 painting *White Crucifixion* represents a critical turning point for the artist Marc Chagall: it was the first of an important series of compositions that feature the image of Christ as a Jewish martyr and dramatically call attention to the persecution and suffering of European Jews in the 1930s.

In *White Crucifixion*, his first and largest work on the subject, Chagall stressed the Jewish identity of Jesus in several ways: he replaced the loincloth with a prayer shawl, his crown of thorns with a headcloth, and the mourning angels that customarily surround him with three biblical patriarchs and a matriarch, clad in traditional Jewish garb. At either side of the cross, Chagall illustrated the devastation of pogroms. On the left, a village is pillaged and burned, forcing refugees to flee by boat and the three bearded figures at bottom left—one of whom clutches a Torah—to escape on foot. On the right, a synagogue and its Torah ark go up in flames, while below a mother comforts her child. By linking the martyred Jesus with the persecuted Jews and the Crucifixion with contemporary events, Chagall's painting passionately identifies the Nazis with Christ's tormentors and warns of the moral implications of their actions.

RENÉ MAGRITTE Belgian, 1898–1967
Time Transfixed, 1938
Oil on canvas; 147 × 98.7 cm (57 ⁷/₈ × 38 ⁷/₈ in.)
Joseph Winterbotham Collection, 1970.426

Impressed by René Magritte's submissions to the 1936 International Surrealist Exhibition, the collector Edward James invited the artist to paint canvases for the ballroom of his London home. In response, Magritte conceived *On the Threshold of Liberty* (in the collection of the Art Institute) and his now-famous *Time Transfixed*. The artist later explained this picture: "I decided to paint the image of a locomotive. . . . In order for its mystery to be evoked, another *immediately* familiar image without mystery—the image of a dining room fireplace—was joined." The surprising juxtaposition and scale of unrelated elements, heightened by Magritte's precise realism, gives the picture its perplexity and allure. The artist transformed the stovepipe of a coal-burning stove into a charging locomotive, situating the train in a fireplace vent so that it appears to be emerging from a railway tunnel. Magritte was unhappy with the English translation of the original French, *La durée poignardé*, which literally means "ongoing time stabbed by a dagger." He hoped that the painting would be installed at the bottom of the collector's staircase so that the train would "stab" guests on their way up to the ballroom. Ironically, James installed it over his fireplace instead.

PAUL DELVAUX Belgian, 1897–1994
The Awakening of the Forest, 1939
Oil on canvas; 170.2 × 225.4 cm (67 × 88 ³/₄ in.)
Joseph Winterbotham Collection, 1991.290

Paul Delvaux painted *The Awakening of the Forest* in the late 1930s, after having adopted Surrealism as a visual language to give form to his inner world—one populated
with childhood memories and fantasy. For this monumental painting, the artist
transformed an episode from Jules Verne's *Journey to the Center of the Earth* (1864),
in which Professor Otto Lidenbrock and his nephew Axel discover a prehistoric forest
deep inside the earth. Delvaux showed the professor at left, examining a rock or
fossil; behind him stands Axel, who bears a striking resemblance to the artist himself.
Under a full moon, a group of women in the background appear like automatons. In
the foreground, several figures combine human and vegetal elements; these ambiguous
figures seem to embody a primordial, as yet undifferentiated, state. A woman in the
right foreground and another in the left middle ground, both in Victorian dress, hold
lamps and try in a vain to shed light on the unyielding mystery of the scene. Despite
the multitude of naked figures and their detailed description, *The Awakening of the Forest* retains a detachment that adds to its strange and mysterious effect.

BALTHUS (BALTUSZ KLOSSOWSKI DE ROLA) French, 1908–2001
Solitaire, 1943
Oil on canvas; 161.3 × 163.5 cm (63 ¹/₂ × 64 ³/₈ in.)
Joseph Winterbotham Collection, 1964.177

Balthus was born into an educated and artistic, but impoverished, family of Polish aristocrats who had fled political and economic turmoil to settle in Paris. As a young man, he traveled to Italy to study such Old Masters as Piero della Francesca. Aside from this direct experience, Balthus received little formal schooling; this permitted him to develop his own unique artistic vision. In 1933 he began painting the erotically charged images for which he is best known—enigmatic scenes of young girls lost in reverie that often place the viewer in the position of voyeur.

Balthus spent most of World War II in Switzerland, where in 1943 he painted *Solitaire*. The striking posture of the girl, deep in thought as she considers the cards on the table, is one the artist used in a number of earlier works. The insistent verticals of the patterned wallpaper create a counterpoint to the diagonal of the girl's back; the mysterious expression of her shadowed face contrasts with the strong, raking light that defines her delicate, long fingers. These details suggest how carefully Balthus orchestrated the painting's unsettling emotional tenor.

JOSEPH CORNELL American, 1903–1972
Untitled (Butterfly Habitat), c. 1940
Stained wood box with glass front, paper, screws, colored-paper butterflies, string, wood shavings,
hollowed reeds, plaster fragments, and paint; 30.5 × 23.2 × 7.9 cm (12 × 9 ⅛ × 3 ⅛ in.)
Lindy and Edwin Bergman Joseph Cornell Collection, 1982.1845

For approximately thirty years, Joseph Cornell worked in relative obscurity in the
basement of his home in Queens, New York, creating a multitude of wondrous
miniature worlds within his boxed constructions. Poetic mélanges of found objects
and materials, his deeply personal and elusive work (which also includes many
collages on paper) combines the enthusiasms of his childhood—butterflies, marbles,
seashells, sky charts, stamps—with adult fascinations such as ballerinas, empty
cages, and movie stars. Cornell's boxes often prompt a dizzying series of associations;
in *Untitled (Butterfly Habitat)*, these include Christmas decorations, collector's
cabinets for specimens, microscopes, natural history displays, sailor's boxes, and
windows. Some of these references are contradictory, reinforcing the work's ambiguity. Ideas linked to flight, voyages, and the exotic are countered by the rigid and
symmetrical organization of the display. The butterflies are not, however, pinned
as they would be on a specimen board. Each pane of paint-spattered glass encloses
a small compartment with white wood walls in which a cutout of a paper butterfly
is suspended with string, allowing for some movement as the box is handled.

ARSHILE GORKY American, born Turkish Armenia (now Turkey), 1904–1948
The Plough and the Song, 1946–47
Oil on canvas; 134.2 × 155.7 cm (51 ⁷/₈ × 61 ³/₈ in.)
Mr. and Mrs. Lewis Larned Coburn Fund, 1963.208

Born in Turkish Armenia, Arshile Gorky immigrated to the United States in the 1920s and became an influential member of the New York art scene. Profoundly interested in avant-garde European art, he experimented with a variety of styles. Young artists working in New York were particularly stimulated by the European Surrealists, many of whom moved to the city before and during World War II and whose circle Gorky joined. The 1940s, especially the years 1944–47, marked the creation of his most important work, produced in a kind of stream of consciousness or "automatic" manner of painting. *The Plough and the Song* reflects the artist's indebtedness to the lyrical Surrealism of Joan Miró, but the sketchy handling of paint, translucent color, and tumbling pile of shapes are hallmarks of Gorky's mature work. A delicate contour line delineates the biomorphic forms in the center of the composition, in marked contrast to the loose brushwork that defines the background. The title signals Gorky's nostalgia for his heritage, as the artist wrote in 1944: "You cannot imagine the fertility of forms that leap from our Armenian plows. . . . And the songs, our ancient songs of the Armenian people, our suffering people. . . . So many shapes, so many shapes and ideas, happily a secret treasure to which I have been entrusted the key." Deeply earthbound and poetic, *The Plough and the Song* is at once a still life, a landscape, and a fantasy.

BARNETT NEWMAN American, 1905–1970
The Beginning, 1946
Oil on canvas; 101.6 × 75.6 cm (40 × 29 ³/₄ in.)
Through prior gift of Mr. and Mrs. Carter H. Harrison, 1989.2

A key figure in the Abstract Expressionist movement, Barnett Newman is widely considered one of the most innovative and influential painters of the twentieth century. A brilliant colorist and a master of expansive spatial effects, he pioneered a new pictorial language that was at once emphatically abstract and powerfully emotive. For Newman, the spiritual content of abstract art was of paramount importance. Although his works seem largely focused on the formal qualities of painting, he insisted that they possessed symbolic meaning. This meaning was never explicit, but he often alluded to it in the titles of his works, as with *The Beginning*. In the mid-1940s Newman became preoccupied with the Old Testament story of Creation and began selecting titles in reference to the book of Genesis. In this painting, the bands of paint that emerge from the base of the canvas interrupt a richly variegated field of color, a sort of primordial fog. The artist created these three stripes with the aid of masking tape, which he applied to the canvas as a guideline before adding the surrounding color. This work is an important precursor to Newman's mature paintings, which are characterized by a single vertical band, or "zip," that divides the composition.

JASPER JOHNS American, born 1930
Target, 1961
Encaustic and newspaper on canvas; 167.6 × 167.6 cm (66 × 66 in.)
Gift of Edlis|Neeson Collection, 2015.119

In the mid-1950s Jasper Johns was searching for a way to move beyond Abstract Expressionism. He took the radical step of destroying his previous work and began painting a set of motifs that included numbers, the American flag, and the alphabet. These instantly recognizable images allowed him to reintroduce subject matter into his work, freeing him to explore other painterly concerns. One of the found images that Johns employed was the target, and from 1955 to 1961 the artist produced several dozen paintings and drawings that explored this device.

Initially, Johns chose a palette of primary colors, a preexisting schema as found as the image itself. The artist's use of oil and encaustic (pigment mixed with hot wax) created a quick-drying medium that recorded each drag and drip of the brush in almost sculptural terms. Indeed, these gestural nods to his Abstract predecessors allowed him to investigate the subtle nuances between form and material. There also exists a tension between the idea of the representational (a target) and the notion of the abstract (the geometry of concentric circles).

ROBERT RAUSCHENBERG American, 1925–2008

Untitled, c. 1955

Oil, house paint, paper, fabric, and printed reproductions, with sock and parachute, on canvas; 172.7 × 139.7 cm (68 × 55 in.)

Gift of Edlis|Neeson Collection, 2015.122

Robert Rauschenberg's fascination with methods and materials led to numerous experiments that pushed the boundaries of a wide range of media, including painting, sculpture, photography, printmaking, and drawing. Along with fellow artist Jasper Johns, Rauschenberg charted a viable path out of Abstract Expressionism, the predominant artistic practice when he emerged during the 1950s.

Rauschenberg is best known for the Combine, a painting-sculpture hybrid that integrated humble objects, ephemeral materials, and found images into works that bridge what he called "the gap between art and life." *Untitled* is an early work from this seminal series. A sock, a postcard, and an army-flare parachute are among the used and discarded remnants of everyday life held in balance by the expressive brush-strokes and spatters of paint. Echoing this application, the strings of the parachute drip like paint from the canvas, forming a catenary, the curve imposed by the force of gravity on a string suspended freely from two points. With this rupture of the picture plane, the fictive space of the artwork's surface engages the actual space occupied by the viewer.

WILLEM DE KOONING American, born Netherlands, 1904–1997

Excavation, 1950

Oil on canvas; 205.7 × 254.6 cm (81 × 101 ¼ in.)

Mr. and Mrs. Frank G. Logan Purchase Prize Fund; restricted gift of Edgar J. Kaufmann, Jr., and Mr. and Mrs. Noah Goldowsky, 1952.1

Willem de Kooning was a central figure in Abstract Expressionism, an art movement that espoused the painterly actions of the artist as a sign of his or her emotions. De Kooning completed *Excavation* in June 1950, just in time for it to be exhibited in the twenty-fifth Venice Biennale. His largest painting up to that date, the work exemplifies the Dutch-born innovator's style, with its expressive brushwork and distinctive organization of space into sliding planes with open contours. According to the artist, the point of departure for the painting was an image of women working in a rice field in *Bitter Rice*, a 1949 Neorealist film by Italian director Giuseppe de Santis. The mobile structure of hooked calligraphic lines defines anatomical parts—bird and fish shapes, human noses, eyes, teeth, necks, and jaws—that seem to dance across the painted surface, revealing the particular tension between abstraction and figuration that is inherent in de Kooning's work. The original white pigment has yellowed over the years, diluting somewhat the flashes of red, blue, yellow, and pink that punctuate the composition. Aptly titled, the painting reflects de Kooning's technically masterful painting process: an intensive building up of the surface and scraping down of its paint layers, often for months, until the desired effect was achieved.

JACKSON POLLOCK American, 1912–1956
Greyed Rainbow, 1953
Oil on linen; 182.9 × 244.2 cm (72 × 96 ⅛ in.)
Gift of Society for Contemporary American Art, 1955.494

In the late 1940s Jackson Pollock developed a revolutionary form of Abstract Expressionism by dripping, pouring, and splashing paint onto large-scale canvases. Pollock emphasized the expressive power of the artist's gestures, materials, and tools, often applying paint with sticks, trowels, and palette knives instead of brushes. He also challenged the concept of easel painting by working on canvases placed either on the floor or fixed to a wall. With no apparent beginning or end, top or bottom, his paintings imply an extension of his art beyond the edges of the canvas, engulfing the viewer. Among the last great purely abstract paintings Pollock made before his untimely death in 1956, *Greyed Rainbow* is a quintessential example of action painting. The paint application ranges from thick chunks squeezed directly from a tube to thin, meandering lines poured from a container with a small hole or squirted from a baster. The work is predominantly black, white, gray, and silver; in the bottom third of the canvas, however, Pollock thinly concealed orange, yellow, green, blue, and violet. The title of the work presumably refers to these grayed sections of hidden color.

ELLSWORTH KELLY American, 1923–2015
Red Yellow Blue White and Black, 1953
Oil on seven joined canvases; 99.1 × 350.2 cm (39 × 138 in.)
Gift of Anstiss and Ronald Krueck, 2001.157

Emphasizing the basics of line, shape, and color, Ellsworth Kelly's exquisitely spare paintings and sculpture influenced the development of Minimalist art and affected the course of color-field painting, hard-edge painting, and postpainterly abstraction. Among the Art Institute's rich holdings of Kelly's works, *Red Yellow Blue White and Black* stands apart: with startling clarity, this painting marks the moment at mid-century when Kelly's pure abstraction emerged in its mature form. After serving in World War II, the artist returned to Europe in 1948, living and working in France for the following six years. While abroad, Kelly expanded his practice of direct observation of nature and architectural forms into an experimental, rigorous study of abstraction. He made *Red Yellow Blue White and Black* in 1953 while still in France, creating it just as he was beginning to uncover the nearly infinite possibilities of monochrome, color spectrum, chance ordering, and multipanel composition. In the painting, Kelly centered the black panel so that it both divides and joins the three panels on either side of it, while the white panels simultaneously separate colors and pair them off. The blue panels at either end close and unify the sequence. Kelly's multipanel monochromes rely on the edges where sections meet, instead of handmade marks, to express their form. This seven-panel painting is the largest in a sequence of Paris-based works widely considered to be the artist's finest and most influential early statements on canvas.

MARK ROTHKO (MARCUS ROTHKOWITZ) American, born Russia (now Latvia), 1903–1970
Untitled (Painting), 1953–54
Oil on canvas; 265.1 × 298.1 cm (104 ³/₈ × 117 ³/₈ in.)
Friends of American Art Collection, 1954.1308

Known for an impassioned form of painting predicated on the poetics of color, Mark Rothko was one of the leading proponents of color-field painting, a type of nongestural Abstract Expressionism that entailed large canvases distinguished by monumental expanses of form and tone. The canvas of *Untitled (Painting)* burns with subtle variations of orange and yellow hues. The painting follows the characteristic format of Rothko's mature work, according to which stacked rectangles of color appear to float within the boundaries of the canvas. By directly staining the fabric of the canvas with many thin washes of pigment and by paying particular attention to the edges where the fields interact, he achieved the effect of light radiating from the image itself. This technique suited his metaphysical aims: to offer painting as a doorway into purely spiritual realms, making it as immaterial and evocative as music, and to communicate directly the most essential, rawest forms of human emotion. Rothko described his art as the "elimination of all obstacles between the painter and the idea, between the idea and the observer." In place of overt symbolism, he used color, overwhelming scale, and surface luminosity to elicit an emotive, profound response from the viewer.

JOAN MITCHELL American, 1925–1992
City Landscape, 1955
Oil on linen; 203.2 × 203.2 cm (80 × 80 in.)
Gift of Society for Contemporary American Art, 1958.193

Joan Mitchell's large, vibrant paintings have always been anchored in the particularities of place. The artist moved to New York City in 1950 and became an active member of the first generation of Abstract Expressionists. The gestural brushwork of Willem de Kooning (see p. 236) particularly impressed her. Soon Mitchell was painting big, light-filled abstractions, animated by loosely applied skeins of bright color, infused with the energy and excitement of a large metropolis. In *City Landscape*, a tangle of pale pink, scarlet, mustard, sienna, and black hues threatens to coagulate or erupt. The painting's title suggests that this ganglia of pigments evokes the nerves or arteries of a city. Stabilizing this energized center are the roughly rectangular white forms of fore- and background, modulated with touches of gray and violet. The sense of spontaneity conveyed in *City Landscape* belies Mitchell's painting methods. Unlike many of her contemporaries, who were dubbed "action painters," Mitchell worked slowly and deliberately. "I paint a little," she said. "Then I sit and look at the painting, sometimes for hours. Eventually, the painting tells me what to do."

CLYFFORD STILL American, 1904–1980
Untitled, 1958
Oil on canvas; 290.2 × 406.4 cm (114 ¹/₄ × 160 in.)
Mr. and Mrs. Frank G. Logan Purchase Prize Fund; Roy J. and Frances R. Friedman Endowment;
through prior gift of Mrs. Henry C. Woods; gift of Lannan Foundation, 1997.164

In the late 1940s Clyfford Still, along with Barnett Newman and Mark Rothko, originated the type of Abstract Expressionism known as color-field painting, a term
used to describe very large canvases dominated by monumental expanses of intense,
homogeneous color. Like most of Still's mature work, *Untitled* is a sheer wall of
paint, imposing and self-sustaining, that makes no concessions to conventional notions
of beauty or pictorial illusionism. This painting's textural effects give it an insistent,
complex materiality. Dominated by blacks applied with both a trowel and brushes,
the surface is by turns reflective and chalky, granular and smooth, feathery and
leaden. These variegated black surfaces are even more emphatic because their continu-
ity is broken by areas of blank canvas and white paint. Like veins in igneous rock,
streaks of orange, yellow, and green paint are embedded in the black voids. Mediating between the light and dark masses are areas of crimson, heightened at the edges,
as if inflamed, by bright orange.

FRANCIS BACON English, born Ireland, 1909–1992
Figure with Meat, 1954
Oil on canvas; 129.9 × 121.9 cm (51 ⅛ × 48 in.)
Harriott A. Fox Fund, 1956.1201

Permeated by anguished visions of humanity, Francis Bacon's paintings embody the existential ethos of the postwar era. In his powerful, nihilistic works, tormented and deformed figures become players in dark, unresolved dramas. Bacon often referred in his paintings to the history of art, interpreting borrowed images through his own bleak mentality. *Figure with Meat* is part of a now-famous series he devoted to Diego Velázquez's *Portrait of Pope Innocent X* (c. 1650; Galleria Doria-Pamphilj, Rome). Here he transformed the Spanish Baroque artist's iconic portrayal of papal authority into a nightmarish image, in which the blurred figure of the pope, seen as if through a veil, seems trapped in a glass-box torture chamber, his mouth open in a silent scream. Instead of the noble drapery that frames Velázquez's pope, Bacon is flanked by two sides of beef, quoting the work of seventeenth-century Dutch artist Rembrandt van Rijn and twentieth-century Russian artist Chaim Soutine, both of whom painted brutal and haunting images of raw meat. Framed by the carcass, Bacon's pope can be seen alternately as a depraved butcher, or as much a victim as the slaughtered animal hanging behind him.

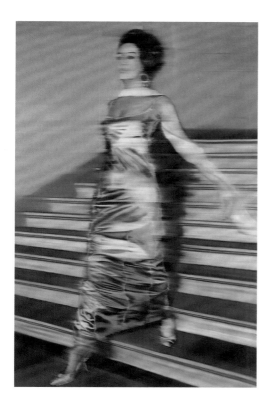

GERHARD RICHTER German, born 1932
Woman Descending the Staircase, 1965
Oil on canvas; 198 × 128 cm (79 × 51 in.)
Roy J. and Frances R. Friedman Endowment; gift of Lannan Foundation, 1997.176

Throughout his career, Gerhard Richter has alternated between figuration and abstraction. *Woman Descending the Staircase* is one of Richter's photo paintings, figurative works in which the artist transferred found photographs, such as personal snapshots or media images, onto canvas and then dragged a dry brush through the wet pigment, thus blurring the image and rendering the forms elusive. Here, the slightly out-of-focus quality reinforces the motion of an unknown, glamorously dressed woman descending a set of stairs. The work's silver-blue brushwork suits the elegance of the subject with her glistening evening gown and diaphanous scarf. The composition's subject and title evoke Marcel Duchamp's famous work *Nude Descending a Staircase* (1912; Philadelphia Museum of Art). When it was exhibited in the United States at the 1913 Armory Show, Duchamp's painting shocked Americans for its radical abstraction. Rather than honoring this modernist icon, Richter protested it, stating that he "could never accept that it had put [an end], once and for all, to a certain kind of painting." Indeed, in the Art Institute's work, Richter produced a hauntingly sophisticated image that floats between reality and illusion.

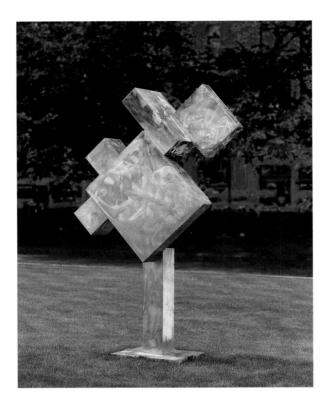

DAVID SMITH American, 1906–1965
Cubi VII, 1963
Stainless steel; 281.9 × 175.3 × 58.4 cm (111 × 69 × 23 in.)
Grant J. Pick Purchase Fund, 1964.1141

David Smith was among the first American artists to master the use of steel and other industrial materials. After many years of working metal into evocative linear compositions, he forged a new, formal language for sculpture through increased focus on shape, volume, surface, and structure. *Cubi VII* is part of a series executed in the four years that preceded his untimely death in 1965; the twenty-eight sculptures are most known for their use of industrial stainless steel. While the spare, sleek forms of the *Cubi* series relate them to Minimalist sculpture of the 1960s, the works also reflect the artist's connection to Abstract Expressionism in the gestural quality of their wire-brushed surfaces and their attendant emotive power. Its abstract qualities intact, *Cubi VII* also seems to allude to the human figure. Indeed, the large, central form and adjacent shapes evoke a torso with limbs. Yet when one walks around the sculpture, it becomes less a symbol of the human form than a vehicle for exploring the relationship between architectonic volumes and the space surrounding them. Despite its solidity, the piece appears to have no fixed center, and its elements seem precariously positioned, challenging accepted notions of balance. The reflective, burnished surfaces of *Cubi VII* pick up the shifting light of its outdoor site—the Art Institute's north garden on Michigan Avenue.

MARISA MERZ Italian, born 1926
Living Sculpture, 1966
Aluminum and paint; 351.2 × 264.2 × 180.3 cm (138 ¼ × 104 × 71 in.)
Through prior gifts of Adeline Yates and Fowler McCormick; Wilson L. Mead Fund, 2011.52

In the late 1960s the term *Arte Povera* was coined to describe the radical style of a group of Italian artists who began to engage everyday materials. Marisa Merz was included in the important *Arte Povera + Azioni Povere* exhibition in 1968 as one of the movement's leading practitioners. She spent the majority of her career, however, retreating from the public sphere, creating works in intimate settings such as her home. Merz has in fact stated, "There has never been any division between my life and my work." This three-part work belongs to the larger series *Untitled (Living Sculptures)*, begun in 1965. These extraordinary objects, crafted from thin folds of pliant, layered sheet metal, were made to hang from the ceiling of her Turin apartment. Her living and working spaces became, to varying degrees, a forest, a hive, a cave, and a womb. Merz's process turned simple industrial materials into fluid, organic forms. Removed from any social or narrative context, her abstract, formal inventions operate within their own temporal logic, reflecting the artist's belief in the enduring effect of each artwork beyond its material realization and the constraints of time and place.

CY TWOMBLY American, 1928–2011
Untitled, 1969
Oil-based house paint, wax crayon, and graphite on canvas; 199.4 × 240 cm (78 ½ × 94 ½ in.)
Gift of Edlis|Neeson, 2015.139

Cy Twombly is best known for a synthesis of drawing, painting, and writing that balances abstract with suggestively pictorial impulses. His inimitable scribbles and scrawls are at once intuitive and sublime, casual or even crude and refined. Twombly made the dynamic, brooding *Untitled* as one in a suite of fourteen large-scale paintings during the summer of 1969 while ensconced at Palazzo del Drago on the shores of Lake Bolsena in central Italy. Against a rich, creamy ground, he elaborated on the cascades of planar and tubular shapes that had emerged in his painting the year before, using diagram-like forms to imbue the canvas with a sense of spatiotemporal flow, as well as a certain airiness. On the other hand, the white field—darkened here and there by passages of erasure—also takes on the aspect of a heavily revised mathematical worksheet. Twombly was immersed both in his work and in his particular location, titling these paintings with the place-name Bolsena. But while typically he might find inspiration in the history of his ancient rural retreat, in this case he was as attuned to that summer's defining moment: the *Apollo II* moon landing. Such context enhances our reading of the painting's enigmatic visual language of measurement, drift, and direction.

EVA HESSE American, born Germany, 1936–1970
Hang Up, 1966
Acrylic on cloth over wood; and acrylic on cord over steel tube; 182.9 × 213.4 × 198.1 cm
(72 × 84 × 78 in.)
Through prior gifts of Arthur Keating and Mr. and Mrs. Edward Morris, 1988.130

Eva Hesse produced an extraordinarily original, influential body of work in her short
career, pioneering the use of eccentric materials and idiosyncratic sculptural forms.
Hesse considered *Hang Up* among her most important works because it was the first
to achieve the level of "absurdity or extreme feeling" she intended. Produced at the
height of Minimalism and the Pop Art movement but belonging to neither, the piece
was fabricated by her friend the artist Sol LeWitt, and her husband, Tom Doyle, who
wrapped the wood stretcher with bed sheets and attached the cord-covered steel tubing. Sealed with acrylic, the object is subtly shaded from pale to dark ash gray. It is
an ironic sculpture about painting, privileging the medium's marginal features: the
frame and its hanging device, represented by the cord that protrudes awkwardly into
the gallery. The title might be understood as a humorous instruction for the sculpture's
display but also acts on a more psychological level. Collapsing the space between
the viewer and the artwork, *Hang Up* creates a sense of disorientation and toys with
our ability to discern a clear demarcation between painting and sculpture.

JIM NUTT American, born 1938
Miss E. Knows, 1967
Acrylic on Plexiglas with aluminum and rubber, in artist's painted frame; 192.1 × 131.1 cm
(75 5/8 × 51 5/8 in.)
Twentieth-Century Purchase Fund, 1970.1014

Jim Nutt is a principal member of the Hairy Who, an irreverent group of artists that emerged in Chicago during the late 1960s. Exhibiting Surrealist-inspired work aimed at subverting artistic conventions and standards of taste, these artists became part of the Chicago Imagist movement. Although each member developed a distinct style, collectively they shared an emphasis on intuition and spontaneity and an affection for wordplay and humor. In his earliest paintings, Nutt referenced popular culture, particularly painted store windows and pinball machines, through his choice of medium and support—acrylic paint on Plexiglas. In addition, many elements of his early style relate to the comic strip: hard, crisp forms stand out boldly against simple backgrounds. In *Miss E. Knows* he also appropriated a sequential format, incorporating small, framed images in the upper-left corner of the painting. The work depicts a grotesquely imagined, highly sexualized female figure—Nutt's satire of ideal beauty. The artist included the cartoonish light beam across her eyes as a reference to the cinema. By attaching objects such as rubber tubing and a coat hook to its surface, Nutt heightened the Surrealist effect of this image.

ED PASCHKE American, 1939–2004
Minnie, 1974
Oil on linen; 128 × 96.5 cm (50 ³⁄₈ × 38 in.)
Gift of the Robert A. Lewis Fund in memory of William and Polly Levey, 1982.397

Ed Paschke is celebrated as one of the leading figures of the Chicago Imagist Movement, a group of late-1960s artists whose expressive style of figurative painting was
rooted in outsider art, popular culture, and Surrealism. Drawing inspiration from New
York–based Pop Art, Paschke often culled his subjects from newspapers, tabloid
magazines, and television, producing work that taps into the movement's kitsch aesthetic. Although his paintings depict representational imagery, they play heavily upon
expressionist distortion, particularly in his use of psychedelic, inharmonious colors.
Paschke's love of urban subcultures and his interest in the underbelly of American
society translated into a penchant for sensational subject matter. In his early works,
Paschke painted circus freaks and other marginal figures, in marked contrast to,
for example, Andy Warhol's (see pp. 250, 256) overriding concern with mainstream
celebrity. *Minnie,* which depicts a now-anonymous individual silhouetted against a
background of emanating light, is typical of his artistic production from this period.
With her theatrical costume, elaborate hairdo, and bizarre makeup, this larger-than-
life figure becomes a grotesque. By painting a flamboyant, overtly sexualized under-
world character in a peculiar mixture of electric hues, Paschke added heat to Pop
Art's cool aesthetic.

ANDY WARHOL American, 1928–1987

Twelve Jackies, 1964

Silkscreen ink on twelve joined canvases; 152.4 × 162.6 cm (60 × 64 in.)

Gift of Edlis|Neeson Collection, 2015.124

Pop artist Andy Warhol's fascination with fame and his complicated veneration of
popular culture permeated every aspect of his career. Early on he adopted the commercial printing process of photoemulsion silk screen applied to canvas as a means
of reproducing the same image, over and over, quickly and efficiently. His studio
became known as the Factory, a reference to his preference for mass production. He
embraced both household goods and Hollywood personalities, rendering Campbell's
Soup cans and Coca-Cola bottles as stars, Marilyn Monroe and Elizabeth Taylor as
products, and vice versa. He also recognized that notoriety could be found even in
tragedy. *Twelve Jackies* comes from a body of work created shortly after the 1963
assassination of President John F. Kennedy. As was his practice, Warhol worked from
existing imagery; in this case, press photography from the slain president's funeral.
By cropping and enlarging the selected image of the veiled former First Lady, Warhol
focuses attention on his "star" much like a director using a close-up lens. The effect is
a chilling glamorization of the tragic. Warhol's use of repetition not only emphasizes
the feeling of mourning and loss but also imports a cinematic quality to the work.
This emphasis parallels the artist's interest in the language of film as well as his growing involvement at this time in the world of underground cinema.

DAVID HOCKNEY English, born 1937
American Collectors (Fred and Marcia Weisman), 1968
Acrylic on canvas; 213.4 × 304.8 cm (83 ⅞ × 120 in.)
Restricted gift of Mr. and Mrs. Frederic G. Pick, 1984.182

One of England's most versatile and inventive artists of the postwar era, the painter, printmaker, set designer, and photographer David Hockney settled in Los Angeles in 1964. His work since then has often reflected, with wit and incision, the sun-washed flatness of the Southern California environment. Perhaps the most iconic example from a group of double portraits of friends and associates from the 1960s, this large painting depicts contemporary-art collectors Fred and Marcia Weisman in the sculpture garden of their Los Angeles home. As Hockney said, "The portrait wasn't just in the faces, it was in the whole setting." As relentlessly stiff and still as the objects surrounding them, the couple stands apart, his stance echoed in the totem pole to the right, hers in the figurative sculpture behind her. Mrs. Weisman's distorted mouth also mirrors that of the totem pole. Mr. Weisman's shadow falls possessively over the abstract sculpture at his feet. His hand is clenched so tightly it seems as if he were squeezing paint out of his fist (Hockney deliberately left the drips). Brilliant, raking light flattens and abstracts the scene. This pervasive aridity is reinforced by the segregation of living, green foliage, including the lonely potted tree, to the edges of the painting. Unsurprisingly, the Weismans did not favor Hockney's harsh portrayal and did not keep the painting.

ROY LICHTENSTEIN American, 1923–1997
Mirror #3 (Six Panels), 1971
Oil and Magna on two sets of three joined canvases; 305 × 335 cm (120 × 132 in.)
Anstiss and Ronald Krueck Fund for Contemporary Art, facilitated by the Roy Lichtenstein
Foundation, 2005.18

Roy Lichtenstein was perhaps the most consistently inventive artist among the
group of individuals who rose to prominence as the progenitors of American Pop Art
in the early 1960s. Throughout his career, he explored the functional simplicity
and visual clichés that characterize processes of mechanical reproduction. Initially
preoccupied with the visual immediacy of cartoons, Lichtenstein embraced the
technical constraints of graphic illustration, applying them to painting. *Mirror #3
(Six Panels)* is among the most ambitious, summarizing canvases in the artist's *Mirror*
series (1969–72). Like his famous cartoon images, these paintings were inspired by
popular culture sources. Studying illustrations from furniture and glass-company
catalogues, Lichtenstein familiarized himself with pictorial conventions used to represent reflection. The work also references the long tradition of rendering mirrors in
art, a theme that was explored by artists from Diego Velázquez to Pablo Picasso.
Lichtenstein was perhaps most invested, however, in broadly generic questions of
surface and support. Only stylized gleam and shadow are reflected in his mirror;
thus, the puzzling, fragmented, even conceptual abstraction becomes the real subject
of the work.

BRICE MARDEN American, born 1938
Rodeo, 1971
Oil and wax on two joined canvases; 243.8 × 243.8 cm (96 × 96 in.)
Ada S. Garrett Prize Fund; estate of Katharine Kuh; through prior gift of Mrs. Henry C. Woods; gift of
Lannan Foundation, 1997.160

During the past four decades, Brice Marden has played a key role in maintaining
the vitality of abstract painting. *Rodeo*, a work of imposing scale and stark presence,
represents a high point of his early career. Two rectangular canvas panels—one yellow,
the other gray—are joined to form an eight-foot square. Each canvas is pulled across
a deep (two and one-eighth-inch) stretcher and painted with a combination of oil and
beeswax. The stretchers and thick, opaque pigment give *Rodeo* a sense of weight and
a sculptural presence. Like all of Marden's paintings, *Rodeo* is insistently handmade.
The artist laid multiple layers of the medium over his canvas panels, adding an extraordinary sense of tactility to this relatively simple composition. The line joining the
two panels may suggest a horizon line, and thus a landscape. The juxtaposition of two
rectangular fields also recalls the work of Mark Rothko (see p. 239). In contrast to
Rothko's luminous, floating fields of color, Marden's twin panels seem determinedly
earthbound, presented as physical facts rather than as expressions of spiritual aspiration.

ROBERT SMITHSON American, 1938–1973
Chalk-Mirror Displacement, 1969
Sixteen mirrors and chalk; diam. approx. 3.1 m (10 ft.)
Through prior gift of Mr. and Mrs. Edward Morris, 1987.277

The painter, sculptor, theorist, filmmaker, and photographer Robert Smithson helped
pioneer the Earthwork Movement of the late 1960s and 1970s, which took as its
subject the artistic reordering of the American landscape in its many varied forms.
Chalk-Mirror Displacement belongs to a series of works, executed in 1968 and 1969,
that combine mirrors and organic materials. Eight double-sided mirrors radiate like
spokes from the center of a chalk pile located on the gallery floor. As they slice through
the pile, the mirrors separate the chalk into almost identical wedge-shaped compartments. The double reflection in each compartment preserves the illusion of the whole
pile, making the mirror dividers appear nearly invisible. This work is also one of
Smithson's *Site/Nonsite* pieces. The artist referred to the first stage of the work as a
"Site Incarnation," which he created for a particular outdoor location: in this case,
a chalk quarry in Oxted, York, England. After setting up and photographing the Site
piece, the artist then dismantled it. The materials were subsequently reinstalled in
the Nonsite location, the seminal 1969 exhibition *When Attitude Becomes Form* at
the Institute of Contemporary Arts in London. This process purposefully blurred
the boundaries between art and its environment, within and without gallery walls.

DONALD JUDD American, 1928–1994
Untitled, 1968

Stainless steel and amber Plexiglas; ten units; each unit: 15.2 × 68.6 × 61 cm (6 × 27 × 24 in.)
Through prior gifts of Mrs. Morton G. Schamberg and Mr. and Mrs. Edward E. Hokin; Charles H. and Mary
F. Worcester Collection Fund; through prior gifts and bequest of Solomon B. Smith, Dr. and Mrs. Irving
Forman, Mrs. Roy J. Friedman and Mr. and Mrs. Samuel A. Marx; Mary and Leigh B. Block Fund; through
prior purchase of the Twentieth-Century Discretionary Fund; Ada Turnbull Hertle and Frederick W.
Renshaw Acquisition funds; through prior gift of Florene May Marx and Samuel A. Marx; restricted gift of
Aaron Fleischman; Alyce and Edwin DeCosta and Walter E. Heller Foundation Fund; Wirt D. Walker Trust;
restricted gifts of Judith Neisser and Janet and Craig Duchossois; through prior gift of Joachim Jean
Aberbach and Julian J. Aberbach; Wilson L. Mead, Watson F. Blair Prize, Marian and Samuel Klasstorner,
and Gladys N. Anderson funds; through prior bequest of Marguerita S. Ritman; Mr. and Mrs. Frank G.
Logan Prize Fund; through prior gifts of Mrs. Leonard Haddad and an Anonymous Donor, 2014.5

An influential practitioner of what would come to be called—much to his chagrin—
Minimalism, Donald Judd preferred to describe his often sleek, industrially fabricated
works as "specific objects," neither painting nor sculpture as understood traditionally.
His primary form became the box—solid or hollow, enclosed or open—often in exacting, serial arrays. *Untitled* comprises Judd's seventh "stack," a compositional mode that
became the signature manifestation of his ideas. Every stack is installed like a spine or
column, not only cantilevered out from the wall but also connecting floor to ceiling.
Judd sought to banish symbolism from abstraction, intending his work to be experienced physically. This "stack" casts a lush orange glow against the wall around it; as a
result, negative space is as much a part of the work as the boxes themselves.

ANDY WARHOL American, 1928–1987

Mao, 1973

Synthetic polymer paint and silkscreen ink on canvas; 448.3 × 346.7 cm (176 ½ × 136 ½ in.)

Mr. and Mrs. Frank G. Logan Prize and Wilson L. Mead funds, 1974.230

The most influential of Pop artists, Andy Warhol cast a cool, ironic light on the pervasiveness of commercial culture and contemporary celebrity worship. Early in his career, he began to utilize the silk-screen process to transfer photographed images to canvas, creating multiple portraits of celebrities including Marilyn Monroe, Elvis Presley, and Jacqueline Kennedy, as well as duplicated images of mass-produced products such as Campbell's soup cans and Coca-Cola bottles. In this example from his *Mao* series, Warhol melded his signature style with the scale of totalitarian propaganda to address the cult of personality surrounding the Chinese ruler Mao Zedong (1893–1976). Nearly fifteen feet tall, this towering work mimics the representations of the political figure that were ubiquitously displayed throughout China. Warhol's looming portrait impresses us with the duality of its realistic qualities and its plastic artificiality. In contrast to the photographic nature of the image, garish colors are applied to Mao's face like makeup. The gestural handling of color in the portrait shows Warhol at his most painterly.

PHILIP GUSTON American, born Canada, 1913–1980
Couple in Bed, 1977
Oil on canvas; 206.2 × 240.3 cm (81 ⅛ × 94 ⅝ in.)
Through prior bequest of Frances W. Pick, and memorial gift from her daughter, Mary P. Hines,
1989.435

An established painter of some of the most poetic Abstract Expressionist work of
the late 1950s, Philip Guston gradually abandoned abstraction in the 1960s in favor
of seemingly crude, cartoonish images drawn from memory. For the artist, these new
paintings represented a return to his creative beginnings. From 1934 to 1940, he had
worked on Works Progress Administration murals in Los Angeles and New York,
bringing to bear upon these projects such wide-ranging interests as cartoons, Cubist
innovations, Italian Renaissance painting, and leftist politics. The radical stylistic
shift Guston recaptured in the final decade of his life is fully evident in *Couple in Bed*.
Here the artist employed gritty, graphic imagery to explore the ongoing conflicts
between his marriage and his all-consuming preoccupation with painting. In bed with
his wife, he wears work shoes and grasps three paintbrushes that point to her tawny
halo of hair. Missing its hands, and thus unable to track time, the artist's wristwatch
symbolizes the enduring nature of his and his wife's love for each another as well as
their ongoing conflict over his priorities. Head to head, they huddle under a pale gray
blanket in an inky-black cosmos that surrounds but does not envelop them.

TAKEN FROM HERE TO WHERE IT CAME FROM AND TAKEN TO A PLACE AND USED IN SUCH A MANNER THAT IT CAN ONLY REMAIN AS A REPRESENTATION OF WHAT IT WAS WHERE IT CAME FROM

LAWRENCE WEINER American, born 1942
TAKEN FROM HERE TO WHERE IT CAME FROM AND TAKEN TO A PLACE AND USED IN SUCH A MANNER THAT IT CAN ONLY REMAIN AS A REPRESENTATION OF WHAT IT WAS WHERE IT CAME FROM, 1980
Vinyl letters on wall; dimensions vary with installation
Gift of Coosje van Bruggen and Claes Oldenburg, 1982.402

Lawrence Weiner established himself as one of the leading figures in the Conceptual Art Movement during the late 1960s by creating works that challenge traditional assumptions about the nature of the art object. Using language as his medium, Weiner set out to question the conventional relationship between artist and viewer and to redefine standard systems of artistic display and distribution. In 1968 he issued a statement of intent, outlining the three conditions in which his works could exist: they could be built by him; fabricated by someone else; or not constructed at all. His works have the potential for being realized in countless ways and contexts; they may be shown outdoors as a public project, published in a book, printed on a matchbook cover, or simply spoken. He is best known, however, for written phrases presented on gallery or museum walls, typically in stenciled or vinyl lettering. Weiner felt the permanence and integrity of a linguistic construction, presented as a title in the form of a simple descriptive phrase on the wall, was less vulnerable to change over time than an actual sculpture. This work—which describes a physical act of displacement as a metaphor for representation—and its title are one and the same.

SIGMAR POLKE German, 1941–2010
Watchtower with Geese, 1987–88
Resin and acrylic on various fabrics; 290 × 290 cm (114 ¼ × 114 ¼ in.)
Restricted gift in memory of Marshall Frankel; Wilson L. Mead Fund, 1990.81

Sigmar Polke was born in Silesia, which, after World War II, became part of East
Germany. After moving to West Germany in the 1960s, he began to produce art
in response to life in his bifurcated, psychologically damaged country. Between 1984
and 1988, Polke executed five paintings featuring the central image of a watchtower.
The last in the series, the Art Institute's composition has a disjunctive quality, created
partly by the superimposition of multiple images on a surface covered with diverse
fabrics: a bright-pink quilted textile; striped awning material; and black cloth. The
title of the work indicates an elevated seat frequently used in the German countryside as a lookout for hunting fowl, a reference underscored by a gaggle of geese in
the painting's right-hand corner. The designs on the black fabric evoke the pleasures
of leisure time at a beach and provide an association to another kind of raised chair,
that of a lifeguard. More ominously, watchtowers are related to guard towers, prisons,
concentration camps, and walled countries. Polke is one of a number of German
artists who have confronted the collective trauma that characterizes the history of
their nation in the twentieth century.

LEON GOLUB American, 1922–2004
Interrogation II, 1981
Acrylic on canvas; 305 × 427 cm (120 × 168 in.)
Gift of Society for Contemporary Art, 1983.264

Leon Golub's often harrowing paintings express his commitment to the possibility that art can effect social and political change. In the 1960s and early 1970s Golub's political activism and his pursuit of a painterly, figurative style ran counter to the prevailing Pop Art and Minimalist movements. It was not until the 1980s that Golub's monumental canvases finally received widespread critical and popular attention. One of three depictions of brutal torture sessions that Golub painted in 1981, *Interrogation II* was inspired by human-rights violations in El Salvador and elsewhere in Central America. The work depicts four mercenaries and their naked, hooded victim, who is bound to a chair. A grayish black torture rack provides the only interruption to the intense, red-oxide color field, which creates a symbolically bloody backdrop for the heinous activity. The rawness of the scene is reinforced by Golub's technique of scraping the applied paint down to the tooth of the canvas. An image of cruel intensity, *Interrogation II* is made even more disturbing by the torturers' grinning faces and the direct eye contact they make with the viewer, drawing us into uncomfortable complicity with their terrible acts.

CINDY SHERMAN American, born 1954
Untitled #92, 1981
Chromographic print; 61 × 122 cm (24 × 48 in.)
Gift of Edlis|Neeson Collection, 2015.157

Cindy Sherman is a major figure in the contemporary revival of directed, or staged, photography. Her work explores the pervasive effects that mass-media images have upon the construction, assumption, and projection of individual identities. Since the late 1970s, the artist has served as both photographer and model for a large cast of fictional personalities created through changes in costume, hair (usually a wig), make-up, and lighting. Sherman first gained recognition for a series of black-and-white works that imitate the look and feel of stills from popular films of the 1950s and 1960s. In 1981 she began a series of large color photographs that mimic the horizontal format of a magazine centerfold. Though formally reminiscent of such glossy spreads, Sherman's representations are fraught with anxiety, vulnerability, and longing. In *Untitled #92*, she depicted herself in a moment of cinematic distress, crouched on the floor with wet hair. Her costume—white blouse and plaid skirt—evokes a school uniform, and her well-manicured hands offer evidence of some unknown struggle. An imposing darkness surrounds her but a bright light, suggestive of a flashlight or the headlights of a car, illuminates her blank expression.

BRUCE NAUMAN American, born 1941
Human Nature/Life Death, 1983
Neon tubing with clear glass tubing suspension frames; 182.9 × 182.9 × 10.2 cm (72 × 72 × 4 in.)
Acquired from City of Chicago Public Art Program Collection, through prior gifts of Florence S. McCormick and Emily Crane Chadbourne, 2004.151

Regarded as one of the most innovative artists of his generation, Bruce Nauman has produced an oeuvre of stunning diversity, encompassing works of film, installation, performance, photography, sculpture, and video. He creates profoundly aesthetic experiences that are often aimed at disrupting viewers' habits of perception. In the mid-1960s the artist adopted the medium of flashing neon in order to critically examine the role of language in visual art. Inspired by its hypnotic aura and non-art aesthetic, Nauman began using this quintessentially commercial medium in an ironic way, as a vehicle for wordplay, puns, and jokes. The artist created this neon sign for an invitational sculpture exhibition held in Chicago in 1985. Three pairs of words, antithetical in their connotations, line the six-foot circumference: *life* and *death*, *love* and *hate*, and *pleasure* and *pain*. In the center, *human*, *animal*, and *nature* are repeated in stacked sets of two. Each word blinks independently, ordered so that over several minutes all possible permutations are displayed. Juxtapositions of colors produce optical illusions that create a jarring, visceral effect. This work ultimately insists on language's inability to deliver a fixed or stable set of meanings, conveying a deep suspicion about what constitutes truth, especially in the public realm.

BRUCE NAUMAN American, born 1941

Clown Torture, 1987

Four channel video with sound (two projections, four monitors); approx. 60-minute loop

Watson F. Blair Prize, Wilson L. Mead, and Twentieth-Century Purchase funds; through prior gift of Joseph Winterbotham; gift of Lannan Foundation, 1997.162

Bruce Nauman's wildly influential, relentlessly imitated work explores the poetics of confusion, anxiety, boredom, entrapment, and failure. One of the artist's most spectacular achievements to date, *Clown Torture* consists of two rectangular pedestals, each supporting two pairs of stacked color monitors; two large color-video projections on two facing walls; and sound from all six video displays. The monitors play four narrative sequences in perpetual loops, each chronicling an absurd misadventure of a clown (played to brilliant effect by the actor Walter Stevens). In "No, No, No, No (Walter)," the clown incessantly screams the word *no* while jumping, kicking, or lying down; in "Clown with Goldfish," the clown struggles to balance a fish bowl on the ceiling with the handle of a broom; in "Clown with Water Bucket," the clown repeatedly opens a door booby-trapped with a bucket of water that falls on his head; and finally, in "Pete and Repeat," the clown succumbs to the terror of a seemingly inescapable nursery rhyme. The simultaneous presentation and the relentless repetition creates an almost painful sensory overload. With both clown and viewer locked in an endless loop of failure and degradation, the humor soon turns to horror.

MARTIN PURYEAR American, born 1941
Lever #1, 1988/89

Red cedar, cypress, poplar, and ash; 429.3 × 340.4 × 45 cm (169 × 134 × 17 ³/₄ in.)

A. James Speyer Memorial, UNR Industries in honor of James W. Alsdorf, and Barbara Neff Smith and Solomon Byron Smith funds, 1989.385

Martin Puryear has produced an expertly handcrafted body of sculpture characterized by extreme elegance of form and organic simplicity. Influenced by his travels through Africa, Asia, Europe, and the United States, Puryear fuses modern traditions—his work pays homage to Constantin Brâncuşi, Jean Arp, and Scandinavian furniture designers—with non-Western architecture, sculpture, and craft. Consisting of a tall, narrow, wood vessel and a dramatically arched top flap that seems poised to slam down upon it, *Lever #1* exemplifies the artist's ongoing exploration of the relationship between interior space, form, and volume. The sculpture suggests an array of possible associations, including a deep-hulled boat, a coffin, or sexual themes. It also reflects some of the most celebrated methods of avant-garde art, notably Constructivism and assemblage. While the sculpture alludes to recognizable forms and subjects, Puryear intended for it to remain independent of specific interpretations. The surface is alive with the remnants of glue, staples, and other marks of construction; these residual effects serve as a reminder that, above all else, the work is about the process of making sculpture.

CHRISTOPHER WOOL American, born 1955
Maggie's Brain, 1995
Enamel on aluminum; 274.3 × 182.9 cm (108 × 72 in.)
Gift of Society for Contemporary Art, 1996.399

Equally concerned with process and picture making, Christopher Wool's works explore points of intersection between signage and language, pattern and decoration—typically by altering found, mass-producible imagery through techniques of layering, over-painting, and variations in register. Since the late 1980s, Wool has produced black-and-white text paintings consisting of single words and pointed phrases in allover compositions of stenciled block letters. He has also executed paintings based on decorative motifs such as vines, flowers, and polka dots. In 1995 Wool began using a spray gun to apply black paint in a drawing-like manner onto both paper and aluminum surfaces. Later he employed the spray gun in conjunction with more conventional silk-screen and painting techniques. In *Maggie's Brain*, a silk-screened surface is overpainted with white, then silk-screened again and topped with an explosive, floral-like spray in the center. Here Wool's critical engagement with the history of painting has resulted in hybrid approaches that combine the emphasis on gesture and touch of Abstract Expressionism with the cool, mediated remove of Pop Art.

JEFF WALL Canadian, born 1946
The Flooded Grave, 1998–2000
Transparency in light box; 228.6 × 282 cm (90 × 111 in.)
Promised gift of Pamela J. and Michael N. Alper; Claire and Gordon Prussian Fund for Contemporary
Art; Harold L. Stuart Endowment; through prior acquisitions of the Mary and Leigh Block Collection,
2001.161

Jeff Wall uses state-of-the-art photographic and computer technology to create images
that evoke the composition, scale, and ambitions of the grandest history paintings.
His works frequently have the formal clarity of documentary photography or photo-
journalism, but he often relies on staged or constructed artifices. This image is the
result of two years of work, during which the artist fused countless photographs of
both documentary and fabricated scenes into a single, surreal whole. After taking
pictures in two Vancouver cemeteries over the course of several months, Wall built
an aquatic system in his studio, crafting the tank from a plaster cast of an actual
grave. With the aid of marine-life specialists, the artist cultivated a living, underwater
ecosystem identical to one found off the coast of Vancouver. In the finished product,
the two worlds are married through a technical process that presents the illusion of
a water-filled grave. *The Flooded Grave* therefore challenges the notion of the photograph as the record of a single moment in time; instead, it is an elaborate fantasy
on the subconscious life of the image it projects.

DIANA THATER American, born 1962
Delphine, 1999
Five-channel digital color video, sound (projection) with nine-monitor cube, light filters, and existing architecture
Howard and Donna Stone New Media Fund, 2005.93

Widely recognized as a pioneer of video art as installation, California-based artist Diana Thater is best known for work featuring images of animals such as bees, horses, and wolves. In *Delphine*, which takes as its primary subject wild dolphins interacting with humans, the artist worked for the very first time with untrained animals in their natural habitat. Complex spatial thinking is key to Thater's projects; she understands installation art as a dialogue between sculpture and architecture. Projected on a large scale—onto entire ceilings, walls, and floors—her work thoroughly transforms the physical realities of the spaces it inhabits. This generic and spatial fluidity blurs conventional boundaries between the work and the viewer. The artist also insists on revealing how her images are made. Shot in both digital video and film, *Delphine* was edited without regard for separating the different media. Clarity and grain flow together as the immediacy and flatness of video gives way to the depth of film. These self-conscious production methods are mirrored by Thater's particular aesthetic of presentation: she always leaves her equipment in full view inside the installation. This transparent approach, the artist insisted, "does not, as some people might have us believe, preclude transcendence. This is ultimately my point—that neither magic nor superficial beauty is required to approach the sublime."

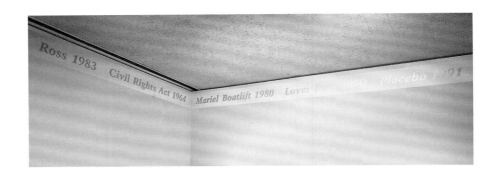

FELIX GONZALEZ-TORRES American, born Cuba, 1957–1996
"Untitled," 1989

Paint on wall; dimensions vary with installation

The Art Institute of Chicago, bequest of Carolyn Spiegel; Watson Blair Prize, Muriel Kallis Newman, Sara Szold, and Modern and Contemporary Discretionary funds; Samuel and Sarah Deson Fund, established by Marianne Deson-Herstein in their memory; Oscar Gerber Memorial endowments; and San Francisco Museum of Modern Art, Accessions Committee Fund Purchase: gift of Jean and James E. Douglas, Jr., Carla Emil and Rich Silverstein, Collectors Forum, Doris and Don Fisher, Niko and Steve Mayer, Elaine McKeon, and Danielle and Brooks Walker, Jr., 2002.80

Felix Gonzalez-Torres's work is consistently characterized by a sense of quiet elegy. One of the defining moments in his widely influential career, *"Untitled"* can be considered a self-portrait in the form of words and dates. First realized in 1989, the work expanded with subsequent installations until the artist's premature death in 1996, and can continue to shift in ongoing manifestations. The portrait joins historical events and enigmatic personal milestones into a running text placed close to the ceiling. Such an installation is reminiscent of traditional friezes carved on the faces of public architecture, including the facade of the Art Institute's 1893 Allerton Building, which includes artists' names chiseled into a horizontal band. By offering clues to a personal history in a commemorative form normally dedicated to institutional use, Gonzalez-Torres undercuts the public and official in favor of the private and subjective, reminding us that an individual's identity is not always reducible to an image captured on canvas or etched in marble. *"Untitled"* can change each time it is installed and may be presented in an infinite variety of ways. Its owner is obliged to consider adding (or subtracting) events, including ones subsequent to the artist's death, ensuring that it remains relevant and dynamic.

ROBERT GOBER American, born 1954
Untitled, 1989

Silk satin, muslin, linen, tulle, welded steel, hand-printed silkscreen on paper, cast hydrostone plaster, vinyl acrylic paint, ink, and graphite; approx. 74 sq. m. (800 sq. ft.), installed

Restricted gift of Stefan T. Edlis and H. Gael Neeson Foundation; through prior gifts of Mr. and Mrs. Joel Starrels and Fowler McCormick, 2008.174

Robert Gober's insistently handmade, deceptively modest sculptures are re-creations of familiar things—body parts and everyday objects such as children's furniture, sinks, and urinals. As imitations of the originals, Gober's works have an uncanny effect, triggering disquieting thoughts about the most commonplace aspects of daily life. At the Paula Cooper Gallery in New York in 1989, Gober constructed two three-sided rooms defined by temporary sheetrock walls. The room seen here was outfitted with wallpaper depicting alternating images of a sleeping white man and a lynched black man hanging from a tree. At the literal center of the installation, the figure of a bride is strongly conjured by a wedding dress supported by a welded steel armature. The delicate dress stands rigid and empty, waiting to be filled. Gober himself has speculated that the relationship between the bride and the sleeping man in the wallpaper is that of husband and wife. Eight hand-painted plaster bags of cat litter line the walls of the room. A material that absorbs or hides waste, the litter serves as a symbolic remedy for the figurative mess of the bride, groom, and murdered black man. More to the point, however, it speaks to the lasting obligations and intimacy of committed love. On the whole, the room—and the veiled story of the imaginary couple it contains—can be considered a meditation on gender, race, romance, and terrible violence in contemporary American life.

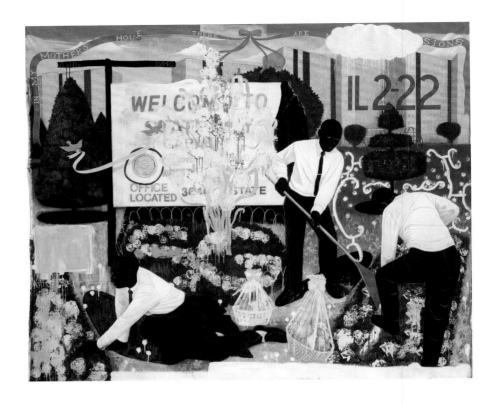

KERRY JAMES MARSHALL American, born 1955
Many Mansions, 1994
Acrylic on paper mounted on canvas; 289.6 × 342.9 cm (114 × 135 in.)
Max V. Kohnstamm Fund, 1995.147

Inspired by the names of urban housing projects, Kerry James Marshall explored
the triumphs and failures of these much-maligned developments in a series entitled
Garden Project. With these works, the Chicago-based-artist—who once lived in
public housing in Birmingham, Alabama, and in Los Angeles—hoped to expose and
challenge stereotypes. "These pictures," Marshall remarked, "are meant to represent
what is complicated about life in the projects. We think of projects as places of utter
despair . . . but [there] is also a great deal of hopefulness, joy, pleasure, and fun."
Set in Stateway Gardens, an immense public housing project on Chicago's South
Side (demolished in 2007), *Many Mansions* depicts three men tending a surprisingly
elaborate garden. Negating misperceptions of the black male, the dark-skinned trio—
attired in white dress shirts and ties—enterprisingly beautify their harsh surroundings. Two bluebirds on the left hold aloft a banner proclaiming "Bless Our Happy
Home," while the sun seems ready to dispel an ominous cloud. The red ribbon in the
background bears the message "In My Mother's House There Are Many Mansions";
this feminist gloss on a famous biblical phrase (John 14:2) expresses an inclusive
understanding of the idea of home.

LUCIAN FREUD English, born Germany, 1922–2011
Sunny Morning—Eight Legs, 1997
Oil on canvas; 234 × 132.1 cm (92 1/8 × 52 in.)
Joseph Winterbotham Collection, 1997.561

Lucian Freud subjected the human face and figure to uncompromising scrutiny for
over fifty years. The monumental *Sunny Morning—Eight Legs* confronts us with
three models arranged on top of and under a sheet-draped bed in the artist's London studio. With his head thrown back, his upper torso twisted, and his bent legs
stretched awkwardly, the male nude is a study in tension and discomfort, in contrast to
the easy tenderness with which he holds a sleeping dog. The legs that emerge from
beneath the bed are the reverse of those of the reclining man; the inclusion of the
lower pair, without a body, imparts a tone of perversion or even violence. Employing a
mostly neutral palette, Freud used thick strokes of paint to create his forms, molding
his subject's flesh similar to the way a sculptor works with clay. The model's exposed
genitals and almost pleading expression; the downward angle of the floor, accentu-
ated by the second pair of legs; the heavy, falling linen; and the dog's delicate frame as
it nestles against the man combine to present a disturbing image of vulnerability.

VIJA CELMINS American, born Latvia 1938
Night Sky #2, 1991
Alkyd on canvas mounted on aluminum; 45.7 × 54.6 cm (18 × 21 ½ in.)
Ada S. Garrett Fund, 1995.240

In the mid-1960s Vija Celmins began using photographs from books, magazines, and newspapers that she found in secondhand stores and at yard sales as the point of departure for her paintings. While she produced work in the wake of Pop Art, her interest in the quotidian had nothing to do with issues of commerce or the media but rather with the illusionistic process of image making itself. Since the early 1970s, the artist has created exacting depictions of such expansive subjects as desert floors, ocean waves, the surface of the moon, and star-studded night skies—the latter derived from satellite photographs. To create her smooth, velvety compositions, Celmins often applies multiple layers of pigment to her canvases, sanding each down before she adds the next. Each work is further modulated through the use of a wide range of black, white, and silvery-gray tones. With its jewel-like imagery and suggestion of vastness, *Night Sky #2* is at once romantic and unsettling. Lacking the anchor of a horizon, a humanly scaled reference point, or a recognizable landmark, viewers may have difficulty determining their relationship to the image. The enormity of the subject presented on a relatively small scale (the work is less than two feet wide) furthers this sense of disorientation.

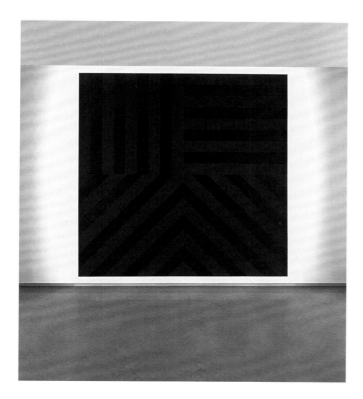

SOL LEWITT American, 1928–2007

Wall Drawing #821: A black square divided horizontally and vertically into four equal parts, each with a different direction of alternating flat and glossy bands, 1997

Acrylic paint; 3.45 × 3.45 m (12 × 12 ft.) (variable)

Through prior gifts of Judith Neisser and Mary and Leigh Block; Norman Waite Harris Purchase Fund, 2006.168

Over nearly four decades, Sol LeWitt's work—equal parts conceptual and visual—introduced new ways of making and thinking about art. The artist posited his influential ideas most clearly in over 1,200 wall drawings, which he conceived between 1968 and his death in 2007. LeWitt shared the creation of his work with other makers—trained draftsman and, in most cases, assistants hired from local art schools or institutions—extending the collaborative possibilities of his artwork indefinitely. Through the 1980s, the artist used only traditional drawing media such as crayon, ink, and pencil. In the following decade, however, acrylic paint became his dominant medium. *Wall Drawing #821* depicts a signature motif with monumental solemnity. The work comprises a grid of horizontal, vertical, and opposing diagonal lines, which were LeWitt's most fundamental geometric and linear building blocks. The artist usually rendered this motif graphically; in this work, however, the figure-ground relationship is articulated solely through the juxtaposition of subtly differentiated matte and gloss paints.

THOMAS SCHÜTTE German, born 1954
Urns (Set of 8), 1999
Terra-cotta and porcelain; 165 × 177.8 × 188 cm (64 × 70 × 74 in.), installed
Gift of Michael N. Alper in memory of Pamela J. Alper, 2004.247.1–8

Avoiding any signature style, Thomas Schütte has produced an oeuvre of perplexing diversity, including architectural models, photographs, sculpture, and watercolor drawings. His decidedly unimposing, antiheroic works explore the cultural, economic, historical, and social conditions of his native Germany with a detached, often humorous, sensibility. Much of Schütte's work addresses the almost existential difficulty postwar German artists encounter in attempting to create monuments and memorials. As such, it evidences an ongoing preoccupation with themes of death, mourning, and collective memory. This is true of *Urns,* an installation comprising eight ceramic vessels glazed in a palette of solid colors marked by streaks, drips, and other surface effects. Ranging from three to five feet in height, these fragile containers at once imply living bodies and oversize repositories for their ashes. The vessels are intended to be grouped together, like a family. Displayed closed, these mysterious containers prompt speculation about what might be contained inside. One of the urns, however, lacks a top and bottom; viewing the installation from above reveals that it is empty.

KATHARINA FRITSCH German, born 1956
Monk, 1997/99
Polyester and paint; 193 × 58.4 × 43.1 cm (76 × 23 × 17 in.)
Anstiss and Ronald Krueck Fund for Contemporary Art, 2000.49

Born in 1956 in the heart of Germany's industrial Ruhr district, Katharina Fritsch roots her work in personal memories and folklore. Her iconic sculptures—meticulously crafted transformations of recognizable objects—also engage broader aspects of German history, drawing on both high art and mass culture. Through experimentation with scale, surface, and color, Fritsch provides new forms for old symbols, creating a strange tension between the familiar and the uncanny. *Monk* is a life-size representation of a man in a monk's habit; his stiff posture and closed eyes signal intense contemplation. With a uniform matte-black surface, the looming figure seemingly absorbs light like a black hole in space. By painting the sculpture black, a color associated with evil, Fritsch asks the viewer to reconsider the spiritual purity and goodness associated with the religious figure. The work draws on the artist's fascination with Christian rituals and the medieval towns, such as Nuremberg and Bamberg, that she visited during her youth. It also recalls an important art-historical antecedent, Caspar David Friedrich's *Monk by the Sea* (1809–10; Nationalgalerie, Berlin). This exemplar of German Romantic painting depicts the monk as an embodiment of the sublime, standing on the shore, gazing at the unknowable void before him.

STEVE MCQUEEN British, born 1969
Caribs' Leap/Western Deep, 2002

Caribs' Leap: 8 mm and 35 mm color film, sound, transferred to two-channel digital color video (projection), 28:53 min. loop, and 12:06 min. loop; edition 2 of 3; *Western Deep*: 8 mm color film, sound, transferred to digital video (projection), 24:12 min. loop

Marilynn Alsdorf Discretionary, Annabelle Decker, Wilson L. Mead, and Modern and Contemporary Discretionary funds; Robert and Marlene Baumgarten Endowment, 2003.86

British artist Steve McQueen's projected video and film installations are rich in cinematic tradition and compelling in content. His earliest works—black-and-white silent films—are indebted to 1960s structural filmmaking, wherein the mechanics of shooting and projection become essential components of the film's subject. His more recent work explores the relation between the medium and the spectator. At once confrontational and seductive, these colossally scaled works transform a purely visual experience into a visceral event. Presented as a single installation, *Caribs' Leap* and *Western Deep* are linked by the theme of descent. The dual-screen projection *Caribs' Leap* juxtaposes luminous scenes of the beachfront on the island of Grenada— the birthplace of McQueen's parents—with irregular images of tiny figures falling through a vast sky. The latter pay homage to the island's indigenous Caribs, who in 1651 leapt to their death rather than surrender to the invading French. In *Western Deep*, the viewer takes a nightmarish journey into the hot, noisy depths of a South African goldmine. Presented and considered together, these two films suggestively liken modern mining conditions to a historical act of genocide.

PETER DOIG Scottish, born 1959
Gasthof zur Muldentalsperre, 2000/2002
Oil on canvas; 196 × 296 cm (77 ⅛ × 116 ½ in.)
Gift of Nancy Lauter McDougal and Alfred L. McDougal, 2003.433

Peter Doig creates dreamlike, psychologically charged landscapes that display a peculiar
blend of abstraction and representation. Combining a hallucinatory palette with
expressionist brushwork, his paintings have a mysterious, often melancholic air. Doig
works exclusively from found images, drawing inspiration from film stills, newspaper
clippings, personal photo albums, record album covers, and the work of earlier artists
such as Edvard Munch (see p. 318) and Ernst Ludwig Kirchner (see p. 322). The image
of the two men in *Gasthof zur Muldentalsperre* derives from a photograph taken when
the artist was working as a dresser at the London Coliseum. One night, after a production
of Igor Stravinsky's burlesque ballet *Petrouchka* (1911), Doig and a friend donned
costumes from the performance and comically posed for a snapshot. The artist initially
used the photo as the basis for a figure study; he then superimposed the two figures
on a landscape he borrowed from an antique postcard, which depicts the vista from
an old German tavern, Gasthof zur Muldentalsperre. In Doig's version, the view has
undergone strange chromatic shifts, resulting in a fantastical, nocturnal scene that
resembles a theatrical backdrop. The men at the gate are an otherworldly presence;
the winding path behind them seems to lead to another realm beyond the edge of
the painting.

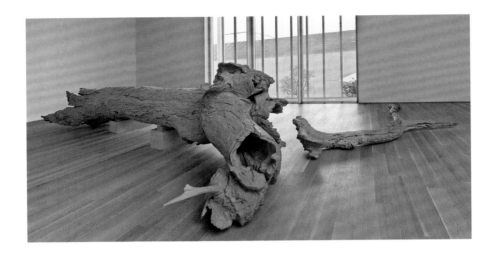

CHARLES RAY American, born 1953
Hinoki, 2007
Cypress; three elements: 172.7 × 762 × 233.7 cm (68 × 300 × 92 in.); 63.5 × 426.7 × 208.3 cm
(25 × 168 × 82 in.); approx. 60.5 × 400 × 200 cm (25 × 150 × 78 in.)
Through prior gifts of Mary and Leigh Block, Mr. and Mrs. Joel Starrels, Mrs. Gilbert W. Chapman, and Mr. and Mrs. Roy J. Friedman; restricted gift of Donna and Howard Stone, 2007.771

The work of Chicago-born sculptor Charles Ray is based on a complex interplay between realism and artifice. Possessed by the idea to make a sculpture of a felled tree, Ray spent several years searching for a model. In 1998, while walking in the woods of central California, he encountered the source for *Hinoki*, a coastal oak that had fallen decades earlier. The artist was drawn to the complexity of the tree's surfaces; over time, gravity, weather, bugs, and the sun's rays had done considerable damage, and it was partially sunken into the ground. Aided by several assistants, Ray transported the tree—hacked apart by a chainsaw—back to his Los Angeles studio. Silicone molds were taken, and a fiberglass version of the log was reconstructed. The fiberglass version was then cut into five sections and sent to Osaka, Japan, where master woodcarvers, working by eye from the model, painstakingly rendered an actual-size replica out of *hinoki* (Japanese cypress). The use of this pristine, sturdy wood to create a sculpture of an already partially collapsed and rotted oak tree is pointed: Ray both re-created and extended the tree's life cycle. Inevitably, *Hinoki* will change over time; its patina will darken, it will begin to rot, and, in hundreds of years, it will eventually decay, albeit more slowly than the original form.

TAKASHI MURAKAMI Japanese, born 1962
Mr. Pointy, 2011
Acrylic on canvas; 350.5 × 247.6 cm (138 × 97 ½ in.)
Gift of Edlis | Neeson Collection, 2015.147

Rising to prominence in the 1990s, Takashi Murakami skillfully mixes Japanese pop culture, animé, and cartoon aesthetics into a new form of global pop art. At once an artist and a businessman, his large-scale paintings and sculptures are as well known as his mass-produced trinkets and collaborations with Louis Vuitton. However, both practices disclose his persistent and tempered engagement with art-historical precedents set by Pop Art. In 2000 Murakami coined the term "superflat" to describe not only his art practice and that of his Japanese contemporaries but also a larger cultural shift toward the "extremely two-dimensional." While this sensibility is most present in Japanese animé, Murakami asserts it is a worldwide phenomenon. According to Murakami's own "Superflat Manifesto," the phrase accounts for the way in which different layers of culture, especially high and low, "fuse into one." *Mr. Pointy* embodies the concept of superflat. The character combines religious iconography taken from sources as diverse as Mayan culture, Tibetan Buddhism, and the Thousand-Armed Buddha (*Kannon* in Japanese) with a cartoon style. *Mr. Pointy* was devised by Murakami in 2003 and has since been repeatedly rendered in paintings, mass-market prints, and sculptures.

JASPER JOHNS American, born 1930
Near the Lagoon, 2002
Encaustic on canvas and wooden boards with objects; 300 × 198.1–214.6 (variable) × 10 cm
(118 × 78–84 ½ [variable] × 4 in.)
Through prior gift of Muriel Kallis Newman in memory of Albert Hardy Newman, 2004.146

In his artistic practice, Jasper Johns repeatedly revisits certain images, motifs, and themes, as he did in his *Catenary* series (1997–2003). The term *catenary* describes the curve assumed by a cord suspended freely from two fixed points. The artist has often affixed objects to the surfaces of his paintings in an ongoing search for non-illusionistic ways of mediating between the flat plane of the picture and a fully dimensional world. Johns formed his catenaries by tacking ordinary household string to the canvas or its supports. The string activates and engages the abstract, collaged field of multitonal gray behind it in several ways, both literally and figuratively. It casts an actual shadow on the canvas, in addition to painted ones that Johns rendered by hand; it also appears as a rut, where the artist embedded it in and later pulled it out of the encaustic. The catenaries are also Johns's playful attempt to show a work's front, side, and back from a single vantage point, as the cord strongly suggests a picture's hanging device. Epic and elegant, *Near the Lagoon* is the largest and last work to be completed in the *Catenary* series.

PHOTOGRAPHY

WILLIAM HENRY FOX TALBOT English, 1800–1877
Two Plant Specimens, 1839
Photogenic drawing; 22.1 × 18 cm (8 ¹¹/₁₆ × 7 ¹/₈ in.)
Edward E. Ayer Endowment in memory of Charles L. Hutchinson, 1972.325

Contained within this haunting and poetic image is the seed of photography: the possibility of creating a negative from which an unlimited number of positives can be made. William Henry Fox Talbot produced this image by placing botanical specimens on sensitized paper and exposing them to light. He made this groundbreaking discovery after his 1833 honeymoon on the shores of Lake Como, in Lombardy, Italy. Frustrated by his inability to draw his Italian surroundings accurately, Talbot recalled the fleeting images of external objects that appeared within a camera lucida (an optical prism that creates a superimposed image on an artist's drawing surface) and wondered how he could make them "imprint themselves durably, and remain fixed upon the paper." What resulted, two years later, were the first camera negatives. Unveiled in 1839 and called photogenic drawing, Talbot's process was perfected two years later into the calotype (from the Greek word *kalos*, meaning "beautiful"). By the end of his life, Talbot—whose far-ranging interests included mathematics, botany, etymology, and ancient Assyria—had also discovered the basis of halftone printing, obtained twelve patents, and authored seven books, including one of the first photographically illustrated books, *The Pencil of Nature* (1844).

SAMUEL J. MILLER American, 1822–1888
Frederick Douglass, 1847–52

Daguerreotype; plate: 14 × 10.6 cm (5 $\frac{1}{2}$ × 4 $\frac{1}{8}$ in.); mat opening: 12.1 × 8.8 cm (4 $\frac{3}{4}$ × 3 $\frac{1}{2}$ in.); plate in closed case: 15.2 × 12 × 1.4 cm (6 × 4 $\frac{3}{4}$ × $\frac{1}{2}$ in.); plate in open case: 15.2 × 24 × 2 cm (6 × 9 $\frac{1}{2}$ × $\frac{3}{4}$ in.)
Major Acquisitions Centennial Endowment, 1996.433

In 1839 Louis-Jacques-Mandé Daguerre announced the perfection of the daguerreo-type, a photographic process that employed a silver-coated copperplate sensitive to light. This new artistic process was celebrated for its remarkably sharp detail and praised as a "democratic art" that brought portraiture into reach for the masses. Within a few years, thousands of daguerrean portrait studios had sprung up all over the United States, among them the one that Samuel J. Miller owned in Akron, Ohio. Although most of the likenesses made in commercial studios were formulaic and not very revealing of the subject's character, this portrait of Frederick Douglass—an escaped slave who had become a lauded speaker, writer, and abolitionist agitator— is a striking exception. Northeastern Ohio was a center of abolitionism prior to the Civil War, and Douglass knew that this picture, one of an astonishing number that he commissioned or posed for, would be seen by ardent supporters of his campaign to end slavery. Douglass was an intelligent manager of his public image and likely guided Miller in projecting his intensity and sheer force of character. As a result, this portrait demonstrates that Douglass truly appeared "majestic in his wrath," as the nineteenth-century feminist Elizabeth Cady Stanton observed.

CARLETON WATKINS American, 1829–1916
Big River from the Rancherie, Mendocino, California, 1863
Albumen print; image/paper: 40 × 52.5 cm (15 ³/₄ × 20 ¹¹/₁₆ in.)
Gift of the Auxiliary Board, 1981.649

Like the vast and untapped landscape of the American West, Carleton Watkins's photographic images are grand in spirit and in size. Using a giant wet-plate camera whose thick glass negatives—coated with a sensitized emulsion called collodion and exposed while still wet—were often as large as the average easel painting of the time, Watkins here fused a sense of the picturesque with a Romantic expression of nature's timelessness, immensity, and silence. The trees are sharply defined, still, and majestic. Depicted with equal clarity is the river, which winds into the receding hills. This technical and aesthetic perfection was all the more remarkable considering the difficulty of the wet-plate process for a frontier photographer. In the field, Watkins had to transport (with the aid of several pack mules) mammoth cameras, dark tents, chemicals, and as many as four hundred glass plates. He also had to contend with constant packing and unpacking, the lack of pure water, and the tendency of dust to adhere to the sticky collodion. Photographs such as *Big River* and Watkins's famous views of Yosemite (which helped persuade the US Congress to pass legislation protecting the valley's wilderness) provided the world with some of the first glimpses of the American West.

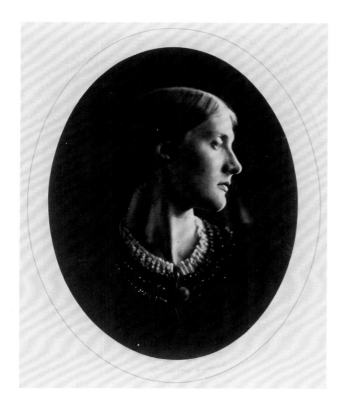

JULIA MARGARET CAMERON English, 1815–1879
Mrs. Herbert Duckworth, April 1867
Albumen print; 34.2 × 26.3 cm (13 ¹/₂ × 10 ³/₈ in.)
Mary and Leigh Block Endowment Fund, 2001.59

Julia Margaret Cameron began photographing at age forty-eight, after receiving a camera as a gift from her daughter and son-in-law. She soon became obsessed with photography, reveling in its messy magic and focusing more on the overall effects of her pictures than on technical perfection. Although she made portraits of some of the most important men of her day, Cameron's female subjects helped her to explore the realm of mythology and imagination in highly allegorical and literary pictures. She delighted in dressing and posing friends, relatives, and servants as the Virgin Mary, Queen Esther, or Shakespeare's faithful Cordelia. Julia Jackson, Cameron's niece, was one of the few female sitters who posed for the photographer as herself. Known as a great beauty throughout her life, she was a favorite subject for Cameron, who took dozens of photographs of her over the course of ten years. In April 1867, shortly before Jackson's wedding to her first husband, Herbert Duckworth, Cameron made a series of head-on portraits of the young bride-to-be that alternately reveal Jackson as noble, tender, and vulnerable. In this photograph, made after the wedding, Cameron captured Jackson's mature beauty and extraordinary strength.

LEWIS WICKES HINE American, 1874–1940
Newsies at Skeeter Branch, St. Louis, Missouri, 11:00 a.m., May 9, 1910
Gelatin silver print; image: 8.9 × 11.5 cm (3 ½ × 4 ⁹/₁₆ in.)
Restricted gift of Charles and Ruth Levy Foundation, 1974.216

Beginning in 1906, Lewis Hine was employed by the National Child Labor Committee to photograph and investigate scenes of child labor across the country. He
produced some five thousand images of deplorable working and living conditions
for children—some just four or five years old—in coal mines, cotton mills, canneries,
and farms, sometimes posing as a fire inspector or postcard salesman to gain access.
Hine composed his images to elicit sympathy from viewers, adding captions noting
his subjects' ages, heights, or work histories. Interested in art as a means to enhance
persuasion and critical thinking rather than to create things of rarefied beauty, Hine
distributed his photographs in reformist or popular magazines; they were also made
into graphic posters and employed as lantern slides in lectures. It was relatively hard
to inspire compassion for those in the "street trades," especially newspaper delivery
boys (newsies), whom contemporary literature both valorized and sentimentalized.
The committee, however, demonstrated that in no other occupation were children so
unsupervised and that the harsh city environment exposed them to physical danger
and adult vices. The young boys seen here, smoking like their elders, seem prema-
turely hardened to life on the street.

ALFRED STIEGLITZ American, 1864–1946
Georgia O'Keeffe—Hands and Thimble, 1919
Palladium print; image: 24.4 × 19.4 cm (9 ⅝ × 7 ⅝ in.); paper: 25.1 × 20.3 cm (9 ⅞ × 8 in.)
Alfred Stieglitz Collection, 1949.745

Alfred Stieglitz campaigned throughout the first half of the twentieth century to legitimize photography and modern art. He founded an exhibiting organization, the Photo-Secession, then the periodical *Camera Work*, and finally a series of galleries. The most influential of these, the gallery known simply as 291, operating from 1908 until 1917, introduced the work of such leaders of the European avant-garde as Paul Cézanne, Henri Matisse, and Pablo Picasso. Georgia O'Keeffe, who became Stieglitz's wife in 1924, was among the progressive American artists whose work he also exhibited at 291. In a search for objective truth and pure form, the innovative photographer took some five hundred photographs of O'Keeffe between 1917 and 1937. The essence of O'Keeffe, he felt, was not confined to her head and face alone; equally expressive were her torso, feet, and especially her hands, as seen here. What resulted is a "composite portrait" of the painter, in which each photograph, revealing her intrinsic nature at a particular moment, can stand alone as an independently expressive form. When these serial images are viewed as a whole, they portray the essence of O'Keeffe's many different "selves."

EL LISSITZKY (LAZAR MARKOVICH LISSITZKY) Russian, 1890–1941
Untitled, 1923
Gelatin silver photogram; image/paper: 17.6 × 23.7 cm (6 ¹⁵/₁₆ × 9 ⁵/₁₆ in.)
Mary L. and Leigh B. Block Collection, 1992.100

A painter, architect, and designer as well as a photographer, El Lissitzky believed that avant-garde art could transform daily life. One of the key figures to integrate artistic developments in Russia with those in Western Europe, he began experimenting with photography seriously in Germany in 1923. Lissitzky was fascinated by the possibilities of photograms, multiple exposures, and what he called *fotopis*—loosely translatable as "photo-writing"—and he eventually abandoned painting to focus on combined photographic and architectural projects.

Photograms (images made by placing objects directly on photographic paper and exposing them to light, rather than with a camera) were taken up in Dada and Constructivist circles in different countries between 1919 and 1923. The primitive technology, which dispensed with lenses, permitted a merger of touch and sight that Lissitzky thematized in this picture by having himself (at left) and fellow painter and designer Vilmos Huszár appear to be the twinned pupil of a ghostly eyeball—at once pictured and the embodied agent of picturing.

JEAN-EUGÈNE-AUGUSTE ATGET French, 1857–1927
Fête du trône, 1925
Gelatin silver printing out paper print; image/paper: 18 × 22.6 cm (7 ¹/₁₆ × 8 ⁷/₈ in.)
Julien Levy Collection; Special Photography Acquisition Fund, 1979.56

For almost three decades, Eugène Atget, an actor turned documentary photographer, organized views of Paris into an elaborately ordered archive that mapped the city in its details and registered a broad complaint against its transformation from a world of artisans and individuals into a capital of spectacle. Usually early in the morning, Atget hauled a large view camera, a wood tripod, and heavy glass plates around the city to do his work. In *Fête du trône*, the photographer captured a curious window display featuring articles associated with a giant and a midget, a sort of ready-made Surrealism. In 1925, the year this photograph was taken, Atget was discovered by the expatriate American artist and photographer Man Ray, who was part of the Surrealist circle of poets and artists in Paris. With Man Ray's support, Atget's work began to be published and recognized as more than just a visual history of Paris. Upon Atget's death, Man Ray's assistant, the photographer Berenice Abbott, acquired the more than eight thousand prints found in his studio and devoted decades to promoting his vast and remarkable oeuvre. The funds for Abbott's purchase were supplied by Julien Levy, a prominent dealer of photography and Surrealism, the core of whose photographic collection is held at the Art Institute.

ANDRÉ KERTÉSZ American, born Hungary, 1894–1985
Satyric Dancer, Paris, 1926, 1926
Gelatin silver print; 9 × 7.8 cm (3 ½ × 3 ¹/₁₆ in.)
Gift of Nicholas and Susan Pritzker, 2009.646

In 1915 André Kertész began submitting pictures to newspaper and exhibition competitions in his native Hungary. He arrived in Paris one decade later greatly attuned
to the possibilities of photographs as both unique display objects and mass-media
images. This gorgeously printed view of the dancer Magda Förstner posing in the
Montparnasse studio of sculptor Etienne (István) Beöthy (who, like the photographer
and dancer, was also a Hungarian émigré) is a variant of one published by the Berlin
leisure magazine *Die Dame* in 1927 to illustrate a parable of marital infidelity. Clad
in a short halter dress with a ruff around her neck, Förstner perches alluringly on a
couch, her lower legs swiveled outward as if in imitation of a Charleston step. Beöthy
was pursuing an abstracted figural language in sculpture, just as Kertész was in photography, and his statue *Direct Action*, which appears in a corner next to the sofa,
serves as a foil for the latter's camera work. Interestingly, the published photograph
became an icon, and possibly gained its current title only in the 1960s, when Kertész
recovered the negative and reprinted it multiple times. The Art Institute's version,
meanwhile, is believed to be unique.

LÁSZLÓ MOHOLY-NAGY American, born Hungary, 1895–1946
Berlin Radio Tower, 1928
Gelatin silver print; 36 × 25.5 cm (14 ³/₁₆ × 10 in.)
Julien Levy Collection, Special Photography Acquisition Fund, 1979.84

Over the winter and spring of 1927–28, Bauhaus professor László Moholy-Nagy took a series of perhaps nine views looking down from the Berlin Radio Tower, one of the most exciting new constructions in the German capital. Moholy had already photographed the Eiffel Tower in Paris from below, looking up through the tower's soaring girders. In Berlin, however, Moholy turned his camera around and pointed it straight down at the ground. This plunging perspective showed off the spectacular narrowness of the Radio Tower, finished in 1926, which rose vertiginously to a height of 450 feet from a base seven times smaller than that of its Parisian predecessor (which opened in 1889). Moholy attached exceptional importance to this, his boldest image: he hung it just above his name in a room devoted to his work at the Berlin showing of *Film und Foto*, a mammoth traveling exhibition that he had helped to prepare. Moholy also chose this view and one other to offer Julien Levy, the pioneering art dealer, when Levy visited him in Berlin in 1930. The following year the pictures went on view at the Levy Gallery in New York, in Moholy's first solo exhibition of photographs.

MANUEL ALVAREZ BRAVO Mexican, 1902–2002
Wineskins, 1932
Gelatin silver print; image/paper: 15.9 × 23.9 cm (6 ¼ × 9 ⅜ in.)
Julien Levy Collection, gift of Jean Levy and the Estate of Julien Levy, 1988.157.9

During and following the Mexican Revolution (1910–20), art entered politics, and
the handicrafts of indigenous peoples were celebrated as expressions of a new
national culture and identity. Manuel Alvarez Bravo, who embraced nativist iconography from a distinctly modernist vantage beginning in the later 1920s, flourished
in this Mexican renaissance. He fostered relationships with Mexican muralists as
well as with European and American artists who traveled to Mexico, including such
figures as Surrealist leader André Breton and photographers Henri Cartier-Bresson
and Edward Weston. Julien Levy exhibited this print and other photographs by Bravo
alongside works by Cartier-Bresson and Walker Evans in the 1935 show *Documentary
and Anti-Graphic Photographs*. In his press release for the show, Levy explained
"anti-graphic" as something that defies or eschews generally accepted criteria for good
photography and remains "in many ways the more dynamic, startling, and inimitable"
on that account. Bravo's image of Mexican goatskin vessels—a traditional means
of transporting wine—suggests an intoxicating ambiguity between inanimate and
animal creations in the spirit of the Surrealist movement.

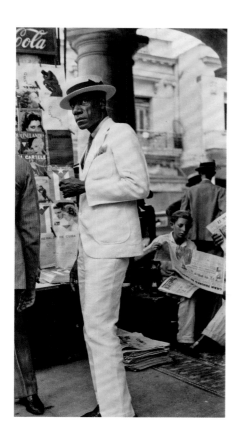

WALKER EVANS

American, 1903–1975

Citizen in Downtown Havana, Cuba,
1932/33, printed c. 1962

Gelatin silver print; image/paper: 22.2 × 11.7 cm
(8 ³/₄ × 4 ⁵/₈ in.)

Restricted gift of Mrs. James Ward Thorne,
1962.162

Walker Evans is perhaps best known
for his dispassionate photographs of
the American South during the Depres-
sion. It was during a 1933 assignment
in Havana, Cuba, however, that he truly
honed his eye as a social documentar-
ian. Evans was hired by Carlton Beals to
illustrate his book *The Crime of Cuba*,
a polemical work that criticized American capitalists for their contribution
to the island's economic and political
collapse. In the three weeks Evans spent
in Havana, he was dismayed by the
cultural crisis and police repression but
visually delighted by the urban crowds,
street grids, advertisements, and cinema
posters. "It's still a frontier town, and
half savage, forgetful and unsafe," he
noted. "I have been drunk with this new
city for days." This photograph of a
Cuban man—nonchalantly dapper in
a white suit and skimmer hat, calling
to mind the "dandy" figure praised
by nineteenth-century critic and poet
Charles Baudelaire—suggests Havana
streets that were overwhelmingly male
but racially diverse. Although omitted
from Beals's book, this image became
one of Evans's favorites, and he featured
it in his landmark 1938 Museum of
Modern Art exhibition and book,
American Photographs.

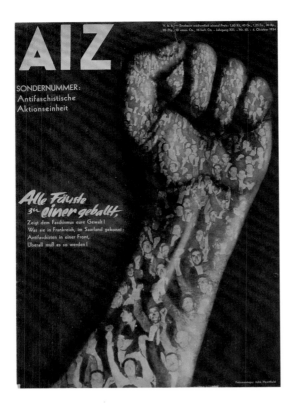

JOHN HEARTFIELD German, 1891–1968

All Fists Clenched As One, 1934

Cover for *AIZ (Arbeiter-Illustrierte-Zeitung)*, 12, no. 40 (Oct. 4, 1934)

Photolithograph of photomontage; 38.1 × 28 cm (15 × 11 in.)

Wirt D. Walker Trust, 2009.488

In 1929, following ten years of activity in photomontage and publishing, John Heartfield began working for the left-wing periodical *Workers' Illustrated Magazine* (*Arbeiter-Illustrierte-Zeitung* [*AIZ*]). The weekly magazine, founded to popularize news and images from a working-class viewpoint, served from the first as a major organ of opposition to the rising National Socialist Party. When Hitler took power in early 1933, Heartfield and the *AIZ* editorial office fled to Prague; many of Heartfield's best-known covers for the magazine were made in the Czech capital. Among them is this iconic picture of a monumental fist that contains a multitude of arms raised in solidarity. The composition, exceptional for Heartfield in that it shows a picture of inspiration rather than acerbic critique, was undoubtedly influenced by the work of Soviet photomontage artist Gustav Klutsis, particularly a 1932 election poster for which Klutsis repeated the image of his own raised palm numerous times to evoke a crowd acting as one. In 2009 the Art Institute acquired a premier collection of Central and Eastern European photography in print that includes 163 issues of *AIZ*—one of the largest such holdings in the United States—and many other books, periodicals, and posters by both Heartfield and Klutsis.

HARRY CALLAHAN American, 1912–1999
Chicago, 1950
Gelatin silver print; image/print: 19.2 × 24.2 cm (7 ⁹/₁₆ × 9 ½ in.)
Mary and Leigh Block Endowment Fund, 1983.65

One of the most important figures in modern American photography, Harry Callahan was a humble and intuitive artist. He was largely self-taught, and as a teacher at Chicago's Institute of Design (1946–61), he continued to learn by assigning photographic problems to students and then solving them himself. Influenced by both the classicism of Ansel Adams and the experimentalism of László Moholy-Nagy, Callahan fused formal precision and exploration with personal subjectivity. He photographed a wide range of subjects—female pedestrians lost in thought on Chicago's streets; architectural facades; his wife, Eleanor; and weeds and grasses in snow. *Chicago,* one of his best-known pictures, shows trees covered in snow along Chicago's Lake Shore Drive. Although Callahan captured all of the detail available in the bark and snow in his negative, he purposely printed this image in high contrast to emphasize the black-and-white forms of the trees against the stark backdrop. With a graphic sensibility typical of the Institute of Design, Callahan reminds the viewer that a photograph is first and foremost an arrangement of tones and shapes on a piece of paper.

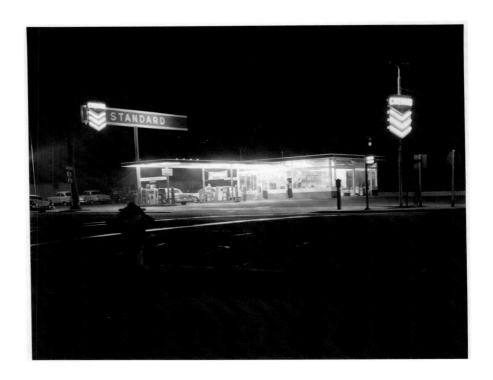

ED RUSCHA American, born 1937
Standard—Figueroa St., from *Twentysix Gasoline Stations*, 1962
Gelatin silver print; image: 19.1 × 24 cm (7 ½ × 9 ⁷/₁₆ in.)
Photography Gala Fund and restricted gift of Martin and Danielle Zimmerman and the Comer
Foundation, 2012.118

Ed Ruscha radically changed the basis for art with his photobooks, the earliest of
which appeared in 1963 with the matter-of-fact title *Twentysix Gasoline Stations*.
Photographed on Route 66 between Los Angeles, where Ruscha still lives and works,
and his hometown of Oklahoma City, the book heralded fundamentally influential
turns in contemporary art: to vernacular corporate architecture and the branding of
public space; to critical and creative possibilities found on the interstate highway; and
to the impersonal, banal, and random as sources of inspiration. Ruscha interspersed
pictures of industry giants such as Standard, Shell, or Texaco with others of mom-
and-pop stations. He never showed the photographs but instead presented the coolly
designed books (eighteen in all, recently acquired by the Art Institute along with a
selection of the original photographs) in galleries, where the asking price of a few
dollars apiece confounded purchasers of his paintings and drawings; and at book-
stores, where they failed equally to attract buyers for many years. Yet, by equating an
artist's book with a dime novel, Ruscha achieved his desire to "be the Henry Ford of
book making."

DIANE ARBUS American, 1923–1971
Identical Twins, Roselle, N.J., 1966, 1966
Gelatin silver print; image: 38 × 37 cm (14 ⅞ × 14 ⁹⁄₁₆ in.)
Gift of Richard Avedon, 1986.2976

Two years before she received her first camera, Diane Arbus wrote: "There are and have been and will be an infinite number of things on Earth. Individuals all different, all wanting different things, all knowing different things, all loving different things, all looking different. . . . That is what I love: the differentness." Arbus's appreciation for the unusual, eccentric, and extraordinary led her to photograph a range of subjects over the thirty years of her career—transvestites, giants, art philanthropists, nudists, and, as here, identical twins. No one knows how Arbus learned about a small-town Christmas party in 1967 being held for local twins and triplets, but it is in keeping with her interest in how people are who they are. Isolating these seven-year-old girls against the wall of the Knights of Columbus hall in Roselle, New Jersey, and photographing them in her typically straightforward manner, Arbus ensured close attention would be paid to the details: the matching homemade dresses (which were green but appear black), the lace stockings bunched below the knees, and the barely discernible difference in each girl's presentation before the camera. Such details variously belie and reinforce the uncanny suggestion of two thoroughly identical individuals.

JOEL STERNFELD American, born 1944
After a Flash Flood, Rancho Mirage, California, July 1979, printed September 1987
Chromogenic print; image: 40.6 × 50.8 cm (16 × 20 in.)
Gift of Ralph and Nancy Segall, 1993.410

Just as color photography was coming into its own as a medium for art, Joel Sternfeld
started his career dedicated to using color film. In the late 1960s he made a major
aesthetic shift by transitioning from images of life on the streets captured with a hand-
held camera to studies of the American landscape taken with a large-format view
camera. In 1978 a Guggenheim grant allowed Sternfeld to embark on a nearly decade-
long project that began as a drive across the United States. His photographic *Wan-
derjahr*, which echoed those of Walker Evans in the 1930s and Robert Frank in the
1950s, yielded the 1987 publication *American Prospects*, the contents of which the
Art Institute owns in its entirety. *After a Flash Flood, Rancho Mirage, California, July
1979* is typical of photographs in that book, many replete with details that take time
to register fully, such as the comparison between a more visible car that sits calmly
parked and another, destroyed, that lies overturned and embedded in the underside
of a largely beige-to-brown landscape. Sternfeld uses color here and often to add layers of emotional complexity to seemingly straightforward images.

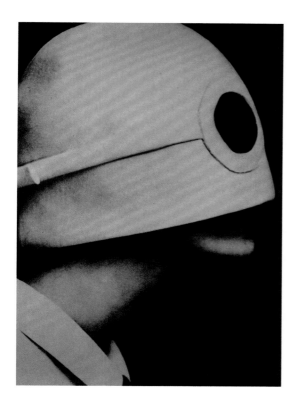

RICHARD PRINCE American, born 1949
Untitled (Fashion Helmet), 1982
Chromogenic print; image: 59.6 × 40.9 cm (23 ⁷/₁₆ × 16 in.)
Gift of Boardroom, Inc., 1992.708

Around the time he made this piece, Richard Prince was watching lots of movies that he rented from a World of Video store. Asked by a store employee what he did for a living, Prince answered that he was a thief—a statement whose possible truth belied its apparent irony. From 1977 until 1984, Prince presented as his own work rephotographed advertisements from magazines. Liberated from their initial context, the images, or details of images, took on a fantastic quality, one that kept in play the aura of desire, money, and power fuelling all consumer culture while adding dimensions of instability and true freedom that consumerism is designed to repress. In this photograph fashion sheaths its wearer like a condom, making a man-part out of a woman while cloaking manliness in a feminine accoutrement. Copyright infringement, an act of thievery in legal terms, is the most obvious but not the greatest transgression accomplished by Prince's appropriation of publicly circulating photographs, an interest he retains to this day.

THOMAS STRUTH German, born 1954
Art Institute of Chicago II, Chicago, 1990
Chromogenic print mounted on acrylic; edition 3 of 10; 184.1 × 219 cm (72 × 86 in.)
Restricted gift of Susan and Lewis Manilow, 1991.28

As a student of the renowned photographers Bernd and Hilla Becher at the Kunst-akademie Düsseldorf in the 1970s, Thomas Struth absorbed their objective, methodical style of making pictures, often emphasizing the camera's single-point perspective. To his varied subject matter—city streets, rainforests, family portraits—Struth brings an acute awareness of the act of observation. His use of relatively great depth of field allows him to lead the viewer's eye to certain details and gloss over other ones.

Struth's celebrated *Museum Photographs* series is composed of monumental images of museum visitors in various stages of observation, captivation, and even distraction. As part of this series, *Art Institute of Chicago II* depicts a woman pushing a stroller facing Gustave Caillebotte's famous *Paris Street; Rainy Day* (p. 180), while another woman reads the label. The women's clothing harmonizes remarkably with the palette of the painting, and the gallery's marble floor seems transformed into a continuation of the wet cobblestones rendered so believably by Caillebotte's paintbrush. As historian Hans Belting concluded of this work, "One no longer knows what is inside the painting and what is in front of it. . . . We feel like rubbing our eyes when the space in front of the painting transforms itself into a picture that is not separated from the painting."

DAWOUD BEY American, born 1953
Candida and Her Mother, Celia, II, 1994
Internal dye diffusion transfer prints (six); each panel: 76.5 × 56 cm (30 ⅛ × 22 ¹/₁₆ in.)
Gladys N. Anderson Endowment, 2002.554.1–6

In the dispiriting years just after World War I, the Irish poet William Butler Yeats wrote the famous line: "Things fall apart; the centre cannot hold." We have since gotten used to living with pieces—pieces of time, heritage, even morality. Although Dawoud Bey sometimes seeks a solitary moment or a single point of view in his photographs, he knows that the essence of what lives before the camera often eludes such an approach. Thus, in *Candida and Her Mother, Celia, II*, he emphasized the complexities of mother-daughter relationships. The grid format of his composition includes frames in which the mother's and daughter's faces and hands are captured together, as well as separate frames in which they gaze back at the artist. In the wholesome beauty of this loving family bond, Bey constructed a cohesive sanctuary apart from the horrors and ambiguities of our time.

NAN GOLDIN American, born 1953
The Ballad of Sexual Dependency, 1979/2001
Multimedia installation (720 color slides and programmed soundtrack); edition 7 of 10; running time: 43 min.
Through prior bequest of Marguerita Ritman; restricted gift of Dorie Sternberg, the Photography Associates, Mary L. and Leigh B. Block Endowment, Robert and Joan Feitler, Anstiss and Ronald Krueck, Karen and Jim Frank, and Martin and Danielle Zimmerman, 2006.158

For thirty-five years Nan Goldin has obsessively recorded her life experiences, and her slide installation *The Ballad of Sexual Dependency* represents the zenith of this endeavor. A hybrid of photography, film, and installation art, the work projects hundreds of Goldin's photographs in a unique sequence, accompanied by a specified soundtrack. Images representing couples, gender roles, dependency, and alienation are paired with evocative songs such as Dean Martin's "Memories Are Made of This." It is appropriate that images of her subjects' fantasies and sorrows should be realized as short-lived projections. The slide projector was adopted as an artistic vehicle in the 1960s and 1970s for public performance-based work, and *The Ballad* codifies more performative presentations by the artist in the clubs and cinemas of 1980s New York's artistic demimonde.

Goldin's pictures, like images of family vacations or holidays, embrace photography's potential for immediacy, emotion, and anecdote. Unlike such snapshots, however, they capture Goldin, her friends, and her family in moments of intimacy—lovemaking, violence, addiction, hospitalization—and depict the rollercoaster of human emotions that accompanies these moments. In this way, *The Ballad* offers a more exposed, and potentially more honest, version of the traditional domestic slideshow.

MASTER OF THE HOUSEBOOK German, active c. 1470–1500
The Road to Calvary, 1475/80
Drypoint in black on ivory laid paper; sheet trimmed within plate mark: 13 × 19.4 cm (5 ⅛ × 7 ⅝ in.)
Clarence Buckingham Collection, 1958.299

This dramatic depiction of Christ's suffering on his way to the Crucifixion is one of the first examples of drypoint by the anonymous master who invented this method of engraving. In drypoint the image is drawn directly on a metal plate with a sharp instrument, a process that preserves the artist's personal "handwriting" and imparts to the print a characteristically velvety line. Here the printmaker skillfully exploited the soft, atmospheric effects, silvery shadows, and sense of delicate, luminous distances that are attainable in drypoint. The forest of lances that juts up behind the hills in the background also creates the illusion of depth. The central motif is Christ's ordeal at the hands of three soldiers who force him and Simon of Cyrene, an innocent bystander, onward to the Mount of Calvary. On the left, the grieving figure of Mary, supported by the apostle John, is strikingly juxtaposed with the utterly indifferent soldier on the right, who has turned his back on the whole scene. This impression of *The Road to Calvary* is one of only three versions of this print. The Rijksprentenkabinet in Amsterdam owns eighty of the approximately ninety surviving prints by his hand.

ALBRECHT DÜRER German, 1471–1528
Young Steer, c. 1496
Pen and black ink on ivory laid paper; 17.5 × 14 cm (6 ⅞ × 5 ½ in.)
Clarence Buckingham Collection, 1965.408

From an early age, Albrecht Dürer displayed an inquisitive mind and exceptional talent as a draftsman. He was born in Nuremberg and first trained as a goldsmith in his father's shop before apprenticing with the painter Michael Wolgemut. One of his earliest animal drawings, *Young Steer* shows its subject grazing in an unseen field. The artist's sure strokes and adept cross-hatching delineate the steer's sculptural form, with taut skin stretched over a strong yet bony frame. Dürer's precise drafts-manship recalls the drawings and prints of the celebrated German master Martin Schongauer, whom he greatly admired. This work was probably a study from nature; sketchy lines around the animal's right hind foot, back, muzzle, and horns reveal that the artist originally drew the steer in a slightly different position, with his mouth open. A masterful engraver who would elevate printmaking to an expressive art form over the course of his career, Dürer employed the steer's hindquarters for the barnyard scene in his engraving *The Prodigal Son amid the Swine* (1494/96), an impression of which is in the Art Institute.

GIOVANNI BENEDETTO CASTIGLIONE Italian, 1609–1664

The Creation of Adam, c. 1642

Monotype (dark manner) on ivory laid paper; 30.3 × 20.3 cm (11 ¹⁵/₁₆ × 8 in.)

Gift of an anonymous donor; restricted gifts of Dr. William D. and Sara R. Shorey, and Mr. and Mrs. George B. Young, 1985.1113

Considered one of the most original and innovative Italian artists of the Baroque period, Giovanni Benedetto Castiglione literally separated light from darkness, creating form out of chaos in this work, his earliest known monotype. In a perfect match of medium and message, Castiglione, the Genoese artist credited with inventing the technique, used this new method to portray the central act of Genesis: the creation of man. He produced this electrifying image by subtracting the design from the inked surface of a copperplate with a blunt instrument, such as a stick or paintbrush handle, and then printing directly on a sheet of paper. Broad, angular strokes of white depict God emerging from a cloud, while thin, fluid lines extract the languid body of Adam from velvety blackness. Castiglione's monotypes employ both this dark-ground technique, which naturally lends itself to dramatic and mysterious imagery, and the light-ground manner, in which the design is drawn in ink directly on a clean plate. Both processes yield only one fine impression. It was not until the nineteenth century that such versatile artists as Edgar Degas (see p. 316) explored the monotype's full potential.

CLAUDE LORRAIN (CLAUDE GELLÉE) French, 1600–1682
Panorama from the Sasso, 1649/55

Pen and brown ink, with brush and brown wash, heightened with white gouache and traces of white chalk, over black chalk, and graphite, on cream laid paper; 16.2 × 40.2 cm (6 ³/₈ × 15 ⁷/₈ in.)
Helen Regenstein Collection, 1980.190

For Claude Lorrain, one of the most important aspects of his adopted city of Rome was its surrounding countryside, the Campagna, which the artist studied, sketched, and painted all his life. His evocative classical landscapes were sought after by papal patrons as well as by aristocrats and royalty throughout Europe. For nearly a century after his death, travelers on the grand tour of European capitals judged real scenery according to his standards. In Claude's landscapes, as in this superb drawing, order and tranquility prevail; men perform no labor but rather exist peacefully in beautiful pastoral settings blessed by the warm Roman light. Depicted here is the region around the Sasso, a large rock ten miles south of Civitavecchia, Rome's modern seaport. Evidently made at the site of the rock itself, the drawing is remarkable in its mastery of subtle ink washes that evocatively suggest, rather than describe, the landscape and sea. Individual trees stand out as nearly geometric forms against the unifying light. The drawing's horizontal format enhances the idyllic landscape's panoramic sweep, which the viewer savors along with the solitary shepherd.

REMBRANDT HARMENSZ. VAN RIJN Dutch, 1606–1669

Seated Female Nude, 1660/62

Pen and brown ink, and brush and brown wash, on ivory laid paper; laid down on cream laid card;

21.2 × 17.4 cm (8 ¼ × 6 ⅞ in.)

Clarence Buckingham Collection, 1953.38

For Rembrandt van Rijn, simple honesty of vision and sureness of line were far more important than the classical glorification of the nude. He focused on this subject only during certain phases of his career, and very few of the resulting studies, which he used to prepare biblical or mythological representations, survive today. This strong form is a late work, and one of only four extant drawings of the female nude attributed to Rembrandt with certainty. Unlike the almost scientific realism of his earlier nudes, his late studies are less detailed and more painterly. He attained a maximum of expression with a minimum of means. Rendered with a swift treatment by brush and the blunt reed pen favored by the artist in his late years, this ample figure projects a forceful presence. Her face is generalized, and her feelings are suggested through her contemplative pose. Her simple shape and external immobility seem to increase the viewer's sense of her inner vitality. In *Seated Female Nude*, Rembrandt's penstrokes and brushwork are integrated with the utmost lightness and perfection; the pen stresses structural features, while the brush provides a transparent, atmospheric tone linking figure and space.

JEAN-ANTOINE WATTEAU French, 1684–1721

The Old Savoyard, c. 1715

Red and black chalk, with stumping, on buff laid paper, laid down on cream wove card, laid down on cream board; 35.9 × 22.1 cm (14 ⅛ × 8 ¹¹/₁₆ in.)

Helen Regenstein Collection, 1964.74

The Flemish-born artist Jean-Antoine Watteau deviated from his acclaimed scenes of courtly figures in park-like settings (called *fêtes galantes*) with this arresting and naturalistic chalk drawing of a humble Savoyard. This elderly vagabond from the Savoy region of France was one of many peasants who, around the turn of the eighteenth century, flocked to Paris, where they tried to eke out livings as chimney sweeps, scavengers, or street entertainers. This old entertainer's props accompany him: a large box of curiosities is on his back, and under his arm is a smaller case probably containing his constant companion and coperformer, a furry marmot. Using only two colors of chalk, Watteau depicted the Savoyard's shrewd, humorous face, his tattered clothing, and his bulky paraphernalia with remarkable precision, sensitivity, and humanity. Of the ten extant studies of Savoyards by Watteau, four appear to portray the same salty character seen here. The drawing's broad, free execution points to the accomplished late works of this gifted artist.

ROSALBA CARRIERA Italian, 1675–1757
A Young Lady with a Parrot, c. 1730
Pastel on blue laid paper; 60 × 50 cm (23 ⅝ × 19 ⅝ in.)
Regenstein Collection, 1985.40

Rosalba Carriera is renowned for the distinction she brought to pastel portraiture
in Italy and France during the first half of the eighteenth century. No female artist
enjoyed greater success or exerted more influence on the art of her era than Rosalba,
as she is known. The artist's work in pastel divides itself into two categories: portraits and allegories. A shrewd judge of character, she enhanced but never obscured
the actual appearance of the sitters in her portraits. In contrast, her allegorical types
are often so generalized that they can seem repetitive, bland, and undistinguished.
A Young Lady with a Parrot is an intriguing combination of both genres. The colorful parrot is a witty conceit that subtly transfers the provocative gesture of baring
one's breast from the young woman to a mischievous bird, whose beak pulls back the
gauzy fabric that edges the sitter's bodice. With its rich colorism and vaporous effects,
A Young Lady with a Parrot is a mature work, exhibiting the assurance of Rosalba's
finest and most famous portraits. The pastel may depict a young Englishwoman,
perhaps one of the daughters of Lord Manchester. Whoever the model, this image's aura
of grace and seduction was to characterize the arts of much of the century, marking
Rosalba as one of the originators of the Rococo style in Italy and France.

JOSEPH WRIGHT OF DERBY English, 1734–1797
Self-Portrait in a Fur Cap, 1765/68
Monochrome pastel (grisaille) on blue-gray laid paper; 42.5 × 29.5 cm (16 ³/₄ × 11 ⁵/₈ in.)
Clarence Buckingham Collection, 1990.141

Joseph Wright, a leading artist of the eighteenth century, spent most of his life in the central Midlands town of Derby, where he ran a successful portrait-painting practice. His best work in this vein portrays solid middle-class citizens, much like himself, with a keen perceptiveness of both character and physical appearance. Throughout his career, Wright was preoccupied with the evocative effects of light, specifically those produced by a single light source such as a candle, and the resulting play of shadows. Influenced by the powerful chiaroscuro of the superb mezzotints of Thomas Frye, a contemporary printmaker, Wright produced a number of dramatically lit self-portraits in oil, charcoal, and black-and-white pastel during the mid-1760s. Depicting himself in nocturnal lighting, wearing an exotic black hat, the artist evoked a time-honored tradition in portraiture: the deeply pensive artist who confronts himself and the viewer with a quiet challenge. Wright later ventured into landscape and genre subjects, the most original of which are concerned with the exploration of light phenomena. Portrait commissions continued to be a reliable source of income throughout his career.

JEAN-SIMÉON CHARDIN French, 1699–1779
Self-Portrait with a Visor, c. 1776
Pastel on blue laid paper, mounted on canvas; 45.7 × 37.4 cm (18 × 14 ¹³/₁₆ in.)
Clarence Buckingham Collection; and the Harold Joachim Memorial Fund, 1984.61

Over a century after its creation, the French novelist Marcel Proust said of Jean-Siméon Chardin's audacious self-portrait, "This old oddity is so intelligent, so crazy . . . above all, so much of an artist." In a fitting finale to a long, successful career as a painter of still lifes and genre scenes, Chardin turned in his last decade to a new medium, pastel, and to a new subject matter, portraits (primarily self-portraits). Eye problems arising from lead-based oil paint poisoning were the partial cause of this dramatic change. Of his thirteen extant pastel self-portraits, the most famous are versions of the example seen here, with the casually dressed, aging artist in his studio. A virtuoso colorist, the septuagenarian here revealed a joyously free stroke and palette. Nonetheless, the construction of the figure is solid and rigorous, adding to his powerful presence. This composition was created at the same time as a portrait of the artist's wife for the 1775 Salon (Musée du Louvre, Paris). A year later, Chardin—with greater daring—replicated the pair. These later portraits were separated for almost two hundred years, until they were reunited in the collection of the Art Institute.

JEAN-HONORÉ FRAGONARD French, 1732–1806
The Letter, or The Spanish Conversation, c. 1778
Brush and brown ink and brush and brown wash, with graphite, on ivory laid paper; 39.9 × 29 cm
(15 ¹¹/₁₆ × 11 ⁷/₁₆ in.)
Margaret Day Blake Collection, 1945.32

Jean-Honoré Fragonard's highly personal, powerful style emerged after periods of study with both François Boucher and Jean-Siméon Chardin, and over five years at the Académie de France in Rome. Entitled *The Letter, or The Spanish Conversation* (because of the man's elegant attire—with a doublet of full sleeves and a wide, stiff neck ruff—a costume that was "in the Spanish mode"), this lively sheet depicts with wit and teasing ambiguity an intimate incident in an upper-class drawing room. The artist's rapid, virtuoso draftsmanship evokes forms with what seems like a minimum of effort, and his powerful handling of brush and wash reflects his ability to capture the effects of light. The interplay between the drawing's broad, free underdrawing and its shimmering veils of wash lend this work its charm and vivacity. The woman in this drawing is said to be Fragonard's sister-in-law, the artist Marguerite Gérard.

CASPAR DAVID FRIEDRICH German, 1774–1840
Statue of the Madonna in the Mountains, 1804
Brush and black ink and gray wash, with graphite, on cream wove paper; 24.4 × 38.2 cm (9 ⅝ × 15 ¹⁄₁₆ in.)
Margaret Day Blake Collection, 1976.22

This vast landscape by one of the central figures of German Romanticism dates from Caspar David Friedrich's early years in Dresden, where he settled after studying in Copenhagen (then considered the artistic center of northern Europe). Subtly graded shades of gray wash evoke the gloomy, overcast days so common in Germany in November, when this image was created. The drawing also conveys, in the artist's words, "Not only what he sees before him, but also what he sees within him." In the center of the landscape, atop the highest peak, a tiny pilgrim kneels in prayer at the base of a statue of the Madonna. Nature—with its sheer, blank sky, stark hills, and mute firs—is depicted almost religiously. In this deeply spiritual image, humankind's experience of nature seems as overwhelming as the unfathomable mystery of our existence. Just as the infinitesimal pilgrim wanders in this faraway, expansive landscape, so too did the artist embark upon his own Romantic quest, a search for meaning in the natural world that reveals the sacred.

EUGÈNE DELACROIX French, 1798–1863
Crouching Woman, 1827

Black and red chalk, with pastel, heightened with white chalk, over wash, on tan wove paper; 24.6 × 31.4 cm (9 ¹¹/₁₆ × 12 ³/₈ in.)

Through prior bequest of Mr. and Mrs. Martin A. Ryerson Collection, 1990.226

Crouching Woman is one of five pastel studies for Eugène Delacroix's monumental painting *The Death of Sardanapalus* (1827; Musée du Louvre, Paris), which helped establish his reputation as the leader of the French Romantic movement. Of the few pastels that Delacroix produced, this is the only group that can be related to a single painting. Inspired by an 1821 play by the English Romantic poet Lord Byron, the canvas dramatically depicts the last king of the Assyrians. Reclining on his bed moments before his own suicide, the king gazes passively at his wives, concubines, and live-stock as they are slain by his order to prevent their slaughter by the enemy army that has just defeated them. In this expressive image of one of the concubines, Delacroix convincingly captured the horror of the moment. With a sure, sweeping line, he described the rhythmic, taut posture of a figure recoiling from a blow or the stab of a knife. Although this powerful figure is significantly truncated in the final painting, the pastel provides insight into Delacroix's creative process, and its sensual drama is representative of the Romantic period.

EDGAR DEGAS French, 1834–1917
Ballet at the Paris Opéra, 1877
Pastel over monotype on cream laid paper; sheet: 35.9 × 71.9 cm (14 ⅛ × 28 ¼ in.)
Gift of Mary and Leigh Block, 1981.12

One of the nineteenth century's most innovative artists, Edgar Degas often combined traditional techniques in unorthodox ways. In *Ballet at the Paris Opéra,* the artist creatively joined the monotype technique, rarely used in his time, with the fragile medium of pastel. Described as "the powder of butterfly wings," pastel was the perfect medium to illustrate the onstage metamorphosis of spindly young dancers into visions of beauty as perfect and short-lived as butterflies. This work, executed on one of the widest monotype plates ever used by the artist, bears Degas's characteristically cropped forms and odd vantage points, which effectively convey the immediacy of the scene. The view is from the orchestra pit, with the necks of the double basses intruding into the dancers' zone. The central dancer is in fifth position, *en pointe,* but the random placement of the corps de ballet, with the dancers' free-flowing hair, suggests a rehearsal rather than a performance. The Paris Opéra was the official school of the first state-supported ballet, the Académie Royale de Danse, created in 1661.

JAMES MCNEILL WHISTLER American, 1834–1903
Green and Blue: The Dancer, c. 1893
Transparent and opaque watercolor, over traces of black chalk, on brown wove paper, laid down
on card; 27.5 × 18.3 cm (10 $^{13}/_{16}$ × 7 $^{3}/_{16}$ in.)
Restricted gift of Dr. William D. Shorey; through prior acquisitions of the Charles Deering Collection
and through prior bequest of Mrs. Gordon Palmer, 1988.219

Inspired by Greek sculpture and Japanese prints, James McNeill Whistler became
entranced with portraying the female form clad in diaphanous drapery in the 1890s.
He developed this theme in all the media in which he worked, including transfer
lithography, oil, pastel, and watercolor. The artist usually provided garments for his
models to wear, often classical gossamer gowns with high waists and crossed bodices
paired with brightly colored kerchiefs. His models needed a certain degree of strength
and agility, as he sometimes asked them to dance about his studio until he found a
suitable pose. In *Green and Blue: The Dancer,* Whistler employed thin watercolor
washes to distill the graceful movements of his lissome young model. The brown
paper on which he painted lends opacity to the washes, thereby adding subtle weight
to the thin veils of fabric draping the figure.

EDVARD MUNCH Norwegian, 1863–1944
Printed by Auguste Clot (French, 1858–1936)
The Sick Child I, 1896
Transfer lithograph printed from two stones in pale-blue and black ink on ivory wove paper;
sheet: 48.3 × 63.5 cm (19 × 25 in.)
Major Acquisitions Fund, 2003.1

When Edvard Munch was thirteen years old, his sister Sophie died of tuberculosis.
Nine years later, he created the first of five painted versions of *The Sick Child*, all
representing Sophie just prior to her death. Munch later described the process of
painting these works as a form of technical and personal catharsis.

Due to the great success of the paintings and his own psychological preoccupations,
in 1894–96 Munch made three prints based on the motif, of which *The Sick Child I*
was the last. In 1896 the artist traveled to Paris to experiment with new print-making
processes and work with respected printers such as Auguste Clot, hoping to gain the
commercial success that had previously eluded him in the French capital. There he made
this, his first color lithograph, which features Sophie's head silhouetted against a pillow.
Munch printed the lithograph with several different stones and a variety of color
combinations: he made the keystone either black or red and added up to four other
color stones in combinations of blue, gray, red, yellow, reddish brown, and purple-blue.
Munch was keenly aware of the symbolic associations of various colors, and the icy
blue and stark black of this impression suggest the haunting pallor of death.

PABLO PICASSO Spanish, 1881–1973
Printed by Eugène Delâtre (French, 1864–1938)
The Frugal Meal, from *The Saltimbanques*, September 1904
Etching on zinc in blue-green on ivory laid paper (discolored to cream); 48 × 38 cm (18 ⁷/₈ × 15 in.)
Clarence Buckingham Collection, 1963.825

The remarkable artistic career of Pablo Picasso spanned more than seven decades and influenced nearly every major trend in the first half of the twentieth century. One of the last works of Picasso's Blue Period (1901–4), this large, hauntingly expressive etching was completed just after the artist settled permanently in France and moved into a dilapidated Montmartre tenement nicknamed the Bateau-Lavoir ("washerwoman's boat"). During this time, the struggling artist's palette and the mood of his particular cast of characters—the poor, ill, and outcast—were dominated by the color blue, then symbolically associated with melancholy. In this austere etching, two subjects that fascinated Picasso—couples in cafés and the solitude of the blind—are brought to refinement. The man's emaciated face is in profile, while the woman stares directly at the viewer, emphasizing the blindness of her companion. Their angular bodies and elongated fingers and the chalky, cold light recall works by El Greco. *The Frugal Meal*, which was only Picasso's second attempt at printmaking, reveals the artist's extraordinary gift for draftsmanship and his remarkable facility with new media and techniques.

WINSLOW HOMER American, 1836–1910
After the Hurricane, Bahamas, 1899
Transparent watercolor, with touches of opaque watercolor, rewetting, blotting, and scraping,
over graphite, on moderately thick, moderately textured (twill texture on verso) ivory wove paper;
38 × 54.3 cm (14 ¹⁵/₁₆ × 21 ³/₈ in.)
Mr. and Mrs. Martin A. Ryerson Collection, 1933.1235

Revered as America's master of watercolor, Winslow Homer did not begin working
in the medium until the mature age of thirty-seven. As a watercolorist, Homer adapted
his practice to the diverse locales he visited. His sojourns in the tropics took him to
the Bahamas, Bermuda, Cuba, and various locations in Florida. In each new environment, the self-taught artist pushed the flexible medium in new directions as he applied
his increasingly sophisticated understanding of color and light to a new set of atmospheric conditions. This compelling watercolor was painted during Homer's second
trip to the Bahamas in the winter of 1898–99. Depicting a luckless man washed up
on the beach, surrounded by fragments of his shattered craft, the work demonstrates
the artist's fascination with the rapid and dangerous weather changes of the region.
Here sunlight glints through gradually thinning storm clouds. Homer employed
thickly applied opaque red and yellow pigments for the seaweed tossed on the sand,
creating a contrast with the thin washes and fluid brushstrokes that he used to
render the receding waves.

ODILON REDON French, 1840–1916

Flower Clouds, c. 1903

Pastel, with touches of stumping, incising, and brushwork, on blue-gray wove paper with multi-colored fibers altered to tan; perimeter mounted to cardboard; 44.5 × 54.2 cm (17 ⁹/₁₆ × 21 ⁵/₁₆ in.)

Through prior bequest of the Mr. and Mrs. Martin A. Ryerson Collection, 1990.165

The evocative, symbolic art of Odilon Redon drew its inspiration from the internal world of his imagination. For years this student of Rodolphe Bresdin worked only in black and white, producing powerful and haunting charcoal drawings, lithographs, and etchings. Just as these black works, or *Noirs*, began to receive critical and public acclaim in the 1890s, Redon discovered the marvels of color through the use of pastel. His immersion in color and this new technique brought about a change in the artist's approach to his subject matter as well. *Flower Clouds* is one of a number of pastels executed around 1905 that are dominated by spiritual overtones. Here a sailboat bears two figures, perhaps two saintly women, on a timeless journey through a fantastic, phosphorescent sea and sky. The dreamlike skiff may reflect Redon's internal voyage, replacing the nocturnal turmoil of the earlier *Noirs* with a more hopeful vision. The luminous intensity of the pastels echoes the ardent spirituality of the theme.

ERNST LUDWIG KIRCHNER German, 1880–1938
Portrait of Otto Mueller, 1915
Color woodcut with charcoal on cream wove paper; image block: 27.3 × 54.6 cm (10 ³/₄ × 21 ¹/₂ in.)
Gift of Dr. Eugene Solow in honor of Paulette Solow, Judy Solow Kleckner, Bryan Kleckner, and
Gabrielle Kleckner, 1988.433

Ernst Ludwig Kirchner's *Portrait of Otto Mueller*—with its vibrant, modulated color
and penetrating psychological force—is emblematic of the artist's innovative approach
to technique and imagery. A pivotal figure of the German Expressionist movement,
Kirchner first met Mueller, also a painter-printmaker, in 1910. Mueller then joined
Die Brücke (The Bridge), the group Kirchner had helped found in 1905, which was
instrumental in promoting Expressionism. The period between 1915 and 1919 marked
Kirchner's most concentrated and productive phase of work with portrait prints,
which he made primarily as large-format woodcuts. In this depiction of Mueller, Kirchner
used a spare, planar composition and broad areas of undifferentiated color to depict
his subject's sharp features. He painted on a single block with a brush and varying
colors; thus, each print is unique. The cobalt-blue striated forms that emanate from
the figure's right and from the side of his head in this print are abstract representations
of the painted bands that decorated Kirchner's studio wall, against which Mueller
posed. These bands, which Kirchner painted himself, exemplify his adoption of motifs
and styles from Palauan art of the South Pacific and resonate with Mueller's own
fondness for African-inspired furniture and wall paintings. Indeed, his hieratic, frontal
position may suggest his interest in Egyptian art.

LOVIS CORINTH German, 1858–1925
Self-Portrait, 1924
Gouache, with possible additions in oil, on heavy ivory wove paper; 48.6 × 30.5 cm (19 ⅛ × 12 in.)
Clarence Buckingham Collection, 1987.280

"The times are not the same for us old folk anymore," reads a 1923 diary entry by
Lovis Corinth, who suffered a stroke in 1911 and never quite recovered. "We have lost
our way . . . so sad, so very sad." The following year, the artist created this tortured
self-image; he was sixty-five, with one year left to live. An inveterate self-portraitist,
Corinth produced more images of himself than almost any other artist except
Rembrandt van Rijn. In this haunting gouache, he gazes at the viewer in anguish. The
brooding palette portrays a deeply shadowed face—contorted, haggard, and sunk
into hunched shoulders. The pain that both the diary entry and this portrait convey is
curiously at odds with Corinth's professional life, which had, in fact, been successful.
Challenging traditional approaches to art, his early figure compositions, with their
overt sexuality and theatrical movements, made his reputation. Later he executed
intensely colored, windswept landscapes that became his most popular works. But
Corinth was a deeply patriotic man, and his personal accomplishments failed to
assuage the torment he experienced after Germany's humiliation in World War I
and his despair over the values of the Weimar Republic that followed.

ARSHILE GORKY American, born Turkish Armenia (now Turkey), 1904–1948
The Artist's Mother, 1926 or 1936
Charcoal on ivory laid paper; 63 × 48.5 cm (24 ⁷/₈ × 19 ³/₁₆ in.)
The Worcester Sketch Fund, 1965.510

"The eyes of the Armenian speak before the lips move and long after they cease to," Arshile Gorky once wrote. These words aptly describe this heroic portrait of the artist's mother, Shushan der Marderosian. Although of noble lineage, Shushan and her family were peasants who faced poverty and Turkish persecution and massacre; in 1919 she died from starvation. The following year, Gorky and one of his sisters immigrated to the United States. This tender, haunting image is based on a photograph of the artist with his mother taken in 1912. Clad in simple country clothes, Shushan is a gaunt, distant figure with remarkable and piercing eyes. Gorky depicted his mother with careful, classical simplicity, transforming her dark beauty into the perfect features of an Orthodox church icon. The same photograph served as the inspiration for two canvases entitled *The Artist and His Mother* (1926–c. 1936; Whitney Museum of American Art, New York; c. 1926–c. 1942; National Gallery of Art, Washington, DC), as well as numerous notebook sketches and other drawings, of which this is the most finished. From this early representational mode, Gorky's art underwent a complex evolution that led, in the 1940s, to his dynamic, biomorphic abstractions. Tragically, the artist did not escape hardship. After a series of personal disasters in the 1940s, Gorky took his own life.

PABLO PICASSO Spanish, 1881–1973
Printed by Roger Lacourière (French, 1892–1966)
Weeping Woman I, July 1, 1937

Drypoint, aquatint, and etching, with scraping on copper in black on ivory wove paper; sheet:
77.4 × 56.8 cm (30 ¹/₂ × 22 ³/₈ in.)

Through prior acquisition of the Martin A. Ryerson Collection with the assistance of the Noel
and Florence Rothman Family and the Margaret Fisher Endowment, 1994.707

A ferocious image of grief, *Weeping Woman I* is one of the most powerful works
that Pablo Picasso undertook in the wake of his seminal *Guernica* (1937; Museo
del Prado, Madrid). After completing *Guernica*, an expression of the horrors of war
and a critique of fascist tyranny, Picasso continued to be drawn to the subject of
agonized grief. Between June and December 1937, he undertook a series of drawings,
paintings, and prints known as *The Weeping Women*, in which he focused and eolabo-
rated on two figures first presented in *Guernica*. The figure in this print may also represent the artist's lover, the Surrealist photographer Dora Maar. In *Weeping Woman
I*, Picasso drew inspiration from contemporary events and sixteenth- and seventeenth-
century religious imagery. He modernized the traditional theme of the Virgin Mary
lamenting the death of her son. The importance Picasso accorded this etching is suggested not only by its size—it was the largest plate he had yet attempted—but also by
the energy he invested in it. He developed the finished print through seven independent
states. It seems that he felt the need to work and rework this image, perhaps in an effort to exorcise the demons of war and his difficult relationship with Maar.

WILLEM DE KOONING American, born Netherlands, 1904–1997
Two Women's Torsos, 1952
Pastel and charcoal on ivory wove paper; 47.9 × 61 cm (18 7/8 × 24 in.)
John H. Wrenn Memorial Collection, 1955.637

A pioneer of Abstract Expressionism, Willem de Kooning experimented with the human form throughout his career, which reached its apex in the early 1950s with his celebrated *Woman* series. *Two Women's Torsos* was created during an intense campaign in which the artist focused on drawings related to his *Woman* paintings, which were exhibited together with this and other drawings at the Sidney Janis Gallery, New York, in 1953.

De Kooning's drawings are admired for their number and variety as well as for the artist's expressive technique, exemplified here by his gestural use of pastel in concert with charcoal. This drawing's velvety texture and almost violently animated surface are characteristic of the approximately one hundred sheets that remain from his intense work on the woman theme in 1952 and 1953. Also typical of de Kooning's art is the way in which *Two Women's Torsos* references aspects of related paintings but stands alone as an independent work. As the artist tried to jettison traditional modes of composition, he used drawing as a primary vehicle for the sequential development of his most important early body of work.

CHARLES WHITE American, 1918–1979
Harvest Talk, 1953
Charcoal, Wolff's carbon drawing pencil, and graphite, with stumping and erasing, on ivory wood-pulp laminate board; 66.1 × 99.2 cm (26 × 39 in.)
Restricted gift of Mr. and Mrs. Robert S. Hartman, 1991.126

Charles White is recognized for the richness of his graphic work and his paintings, which typically depict aspects of the history, culture, and life of African Americans. A native of Chicago, White attended the School of the Art Institute, the Art Students League of New York, and later the Taller de Gráfica Popular in Mexico. Beginning in 1939, he was employed by the Federal Art Project of the Works Progress Administration.

White's father was a railroad and steel worker and his mother was a domestic worker; this inspired in White a deep respect for labor. *Harvest Talk*, one of six charcoal and carbon pencil drawings originally exhibited at ACA Galleries in New York in 1953, exemplifies the artist's mature drawing style. Here his strong, assured manner, coupled with the heroic proportions of the figures and the emphasis on the large scythe (an emblem often associated with the Soviet Union)—as well as the social realist sensibilities that prevail throughout his oeuvre, his travels to the Soviet Union, and his writings for and affiliation with left-wing publications such as *Masses and Mainstream*, *Freedomways*, and the *Daily Worker*—suggest that *Harvest Talk* was inspired by socialist ideals. Like many of White's works on paper, it conveys the power of a mural despite its relatively small format.

LEE KRASNER American, 1908–1984
Black and White, 1953
Oil paint, gouache, and cut and torn painted paper, with adhesive residue, on cream laid paper;
76.6 × 57.1 cm (30 ¹/₈ × 22 ¹/₂ in.)
Margaret Fisher Endowment, 1994.245

Lee Krasner's pictures from the 1940s on were informed by her understanding of the Abstract Expressionist ideal: to infuse abstract, painterly forms with mysterious and significant content. The substantial body of work she created shows her sustained development toward a refined expression of this concept. *Black and White* is one of Krasner's first and most important works in a group of early paper collages. The drawings that she disassembled to create these collages echo the work of her husband, Jackson Pollock, from the same period. According to the art historian Ellen Landau, however, it is difficult to determine who originated the strategy of cannibalizing previous works to create new ones. Throughout her career, Krasner employed the technique more consistently than Pollock.

In *Black and White*, Krasner not only appropriated her own discarded markings but also referred to Pollock's early-1940s tactic of quoting Pablo Picasso's studio subjects. She reversed the gender implications of Picasso's prototypes by showing, at right, a female figure who may be a painter contemplating her works of art, or perhaps a woman looking in a mirror. The artist's redeployment of studio scraps in a new context helped her, paradoxically, to mark out new aesthetic territory.

ROY LICHTENSTEIN American, 1923–1997

Alka Seltzer, 1966

Graphite and lithographic rubbing crayon pochoir, with scraping, on cream wove paper, fixed; 76.3 × 56.7 cm (30 × 22 in.)

Margaret Fisher Endowment, 1993.176

Roy Lichtenstein had been exhibiting in galleries for nearly ten years when, in 1961, he dramatically changed the course of his work. Prompted by the comic strips on his children's gum wrappers, he began to create paintings based on cartoon images. The reductive style that soon emerged became his particular contribution to the idiom known as Pop Art. From around 1961 until 1968, the artist created a group of highly finished black-and-white drawings that demonstrate his subversive use of commercial illustration techniques. In *Alka Seltzer*, Lichtenstein exploited everyday practices of visual representation and magnified them, indicating the gas bubbles rising over the glass by meticulously scraping away extra spaces from a field of imitation hand-stenciled Benday dots. To signify the reflective surface of the glass, he drew flat black graphite shapes—a parody, like the dots, of the reductive, linecut effect of pulp advertising. The artist's use of mechanical reproduction conventions served to unify his composition and produce movement and volume on a two-dimensional surface. *Alka Seltzer* is one of Lichtenstein's watershed works because it shows the artist summing up his early graphic techniques and introducing what would become his most significant formal preoccupations in the years that followed.

JASPER JOHNS American, born 1930

Perilous Night, 1982

Higgins ink on frosted Mylar; 85.3 × 109.8 cm (39 ⁹/₁₆ × 43 ¼ in.)

Through prior gift of Mary and Leigh Block; Harold L. Stuart Endowment, 1989.82

Jasper Johns began his career in the mid-1950s by re-creating, with great precision, such familiar images as targets, letters, numbers, and flags. Although his subject matter has become less commonplace, he continues to "borrow" from the public domain. *Perilous Night,* for instance, owes its title to a pivotal and expressive piece of music written by the American composer John Cage (1912–1992) in 1945. Both score and cover sheet are rendered on the right-hand side of the drawing with Johns's characteristically fluid handling of ink. On the sheet's left side is a freehand rendition—abstracted, reversed, and turned ninety degrees—of a single, terror-stricken soldier from the Resurrection panel of Matthias Grünewald's sixteenth-century masterwork the Isenheim Altarpiece (Unterlinden Museum, Colmar). Between the soldier and the musical score is a black imprint of Johns's right arm, evidence perhaps of the creative power that can merge two disparate images into a cogent statement. The overcome soldier witnessing the Resurrection of Christ and a piece of music marking a key transition in a composer's career both point to "perilous nights" that can change the course of a human life. Characteristically, Johns also explored the same subject in different media. This somberly colored drawing derives from a painting of the same name (1982; National Gallery of Art, Washington, DC).

FRAGMENT (HANGING)

Byzantine; Egypt, Roman period (30 BC/AD 641), 5th/6th century

Linen and wool, plain weave with uncut weft pile and embroidered linen pile formed by variations of back and stem stitches; 136.5 × 88.3 cm (53 ³/₄ × 34 ³/₄ in.)

Grace R. Smith Textile Endowment, 1982.1578

Because many textiles made by early Egyptians were preserved in arid tombs, a substantial number of these fabrics have survived in remarkably good condition. This striking portion of a wall hanging depicts a figure standing beneath a colonnaded, arched opening. With raised arms, which perhaps once held candelabrum, he wears a traditional tunic with clavic bands (the narrow strips extending down from the shoulders, on the front and back, to the waist or hem). This woven piece is distinguished by its large size, imposing composition, and brilliant, unfaded shades of red, green, blue, brown, and yellow. The figure's commanding frontality, solemn expression, and animated side glance, together with the composition's bold lines and vivid colors, relate this fragment to hauntingly realistic portrait icons. Also suggestive of icons is the three-dimensional appearance of the warrior's face and legs and the columns—an effect much easier to achieve in painting than in weaving. Woven of indigenous materials, this hanging is composed of linen warps and wool and linen wefts that create an uncut pile against a plain-weave foundation, a fabric surface less common in Byzantine textiles than the tapestry weave.

FRAGMENT (DRESS FABRIC)
China, Tang dynasty (618–906), late 8th/early 9th century

Silk, weft-float faced 1:2 'S' twill weave of complementary wefts and inner warps (samite); 61.6 × 90.2 cm (24 ¼ × 35 ½ in.)

Robert Allerton Endowment, 1998.3

This textile reflects the cosmopolitan richness and inventiveness of the Tang dynasty. During this period, caravans of merchants and Buddhist clerics traversed the vast network that modern scholars call the Silk Road, transporting China's luxurious silks westward across Asia and returning with exotic goods from empires extending to the Mediterranean Sea.

In this textile's jewel-like floral medallion, symmetrically curled and layered tendrils derived from the classical half palmette were adopted and refined by Chinese weavers from foreign sources. The stylized floral head seen from above, the blossoming stems in three-quarter view, and the half palmettes in profile merge naturalism and geometry by subtly varying perspective and color. This design pervaded East Asian decorative arts; similar floral medallions and scrolls embellish wall paintings, stone carvings, and vessels of ceramic and silver that Tang aristocrats commissioned for their tombs, Buddhist temples, and private treasuries. Architectural tiles from palace sites in Korea and, most notably, exquisite silk fabrics and carpets preserved in the Shosoin repository in Nara, Japan, attest to the transmission of these patterns throughout East Asia in the eighth century.

FRAGMENT OF A SACRED HEIRLOOM TEXTILE (MAWA' OR MA'A)

Gujarat, India, late 14th or 15th century

Cotton; block printed, resist and mordant dyed; 94 × 120 cm (37 × 47 in.)

Belle M. Borland Estate; Marie Walters Endowment Fund; Christa C. Mayer Thurman Textile Endowment Fund, 2011.271

Textiles were the primary Indian goods traded for southeast Asian spices ultimately destined for European markets. This fragment is among the oldest extant Indian textiles found in southeast Asia. Made in Gujarat for the Indonesian market, it has been radiocarbon-dated to between 1382 and 1502. The pattern features a block-printed image arranged horizontally along the textile's length, repeated without regard for vertical alignment in seven and a half rows. The repeat consists of a seated male figure with three attendant figures of lesser scale, the group is complemented by small geese and vegetal or perhaps architectural elements. The main figure may be a Jain sage, and indeed the three-quarter profile view and the so-called protruding eye do provide a link to the Jain painting tradition seen in Gujarati manuscripts dating from the fourteenth and fifteenth centuries.

Trade cloths such as this have not survived in India, where they may have originally functioned as ceremonial hangings or backdrops. In Indonesia such cloths were treasured as heirlooms, preserved and handed down for use as banners and architectural decoration during thanksgiving ceremonies.

FEATHERED TUNIC WITH FELINES, BIRDS, AND FISH
Chimú; south coast, possibly Nazca Valley, Peru, 1470/1532

Cotton, plain weave; embellished with feathers knotted and attached with cotton in overcast stitches; 85.1 × 86 cm (33 ½ × 33 ⅞ in.)

Kate S. Buckingham Endowment, 1955.1789

One of the most extraordinary works in the Art Institute's archaeological textile collection, this feathered tunic was created by Chimú weavers in northern Peru in 1470/1532. The knee-length, sleeveless garment is composed of a plain-weave cotton cloth completely concealed by thousands of brightly colored feathers. These coveted plumes were taken from macaws, parrots, toucans, cotingas, and tanagers from the tropical forests of South America. Because they were transported across the treacherous peaks of the Andes, the feathers were extremely rare and valuable and would only have been available to the most elite members of pre-Hispanic society. Thus, the feathered tunic—with its stylized felines, birds, and fish—would have been a sumptuous emblem of power, wealth, and prestige. Like many other pre-Hispanic textiles, it was buried with its owner in a subterranean tomb on the southern coast of Peru. The dark and arid conditions in these tombs protected the tunic, thereby allowing its vibrant colors and bold motifs to endure.

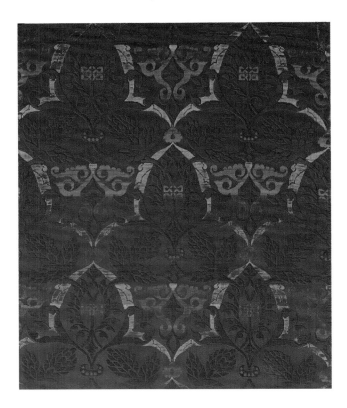

FRAGMENT (DETAIL)

Probably Granada, Spain, Nasrid dynasty (1230–1492), late 15th century

Silk, lampas technique; 60.8 × 30.5 cm (23 7/8 × 12 in.)

Restricted gift of the Textile Society; Mrs. Julian Armstrong Jr.; Barbara E. and Richard J. Franke Fund; and the Nicole Williams Contemporary Textile Fund, 2007.17

Highly sought after in Islamic Spain, silk textiles such as this one are remarkable for their wide variety of designs and vivid color combinations. The design of this fragment is vibrant and sophisticated, setting an intricate geometric pattern against a lustrous satin-weave ground. The pattern joins white trilobed arches with a repeat design of green hop blossoms, stylized vegetal motifs, and yellow scrolling ornaments that recall the lush interior settings of the Alhambra, an extensive royal complex overlooking the city of Granada. These elements are closely connected to architectural decoration—especially stuccowork and wall tiles—and they were shared by potters, stucco carvers, and weavers. In impressive condition, this textile presents a clear sense of the luxury and splendor of Nasrid palace interiors. Indeed, weaving establishments were often attached to palaces and formed an important part of royal households.

COPE

England, 1490/1517, with later restoration

Silk cut and voided velvet, linen appliqué, silk and gilt metallic thread embroidery, and metal spangles; 160.7 × 291.1 cm (64 ¼ × 114 ⅝ in.)

Grace R. Smith Textile Endowment, 1971.312a

The production of textiles for churches—hangings, altar frontals, and liturgical vestments—was a thriving industry in Europe from the twelfth century through the eighteenth century. Among the finest ecclesiastical vestments is this resplendent velvet cope, a semicircular cloak worn as an outer garment in processions or during special ceremonies by a priest or bishop. The elegant needlework was called *opus anglicanum* (English work). Surrounding the cope's central image of the Assumption of the Virgin, rendered in silk and gold threads, are seraphim standing on wheels, thistles, fleurs-de-lis, and double-headed eagles—all connected by tendrils animated by spangles. Old Testament prophets and New Testament saints with their attributes alternate on the orphrey band, which runs the full width of the work. Saint Paul is depicted on the hood, which rests on the back of the cope, while an image of God holding an orb decorates the morse, or closure. The brown-velvet ground is an unusual color for vestments of this style; it may have faded from purple or crimson.

CRAVAT END

1700/1740

Flanders, Brussels, Belgium

Linen, bobbin part-lace of a type known as "Brussels" with a Droschel mesh ground; 32.1 × 41.7 cm
(12 ⅝ × 16 ⅜ in.)

Restricted gift of Mr. and Mrs. John V. Farwell III, 1987.334

When the heavily Baroque fashions originating at the court of Louis XIV (r. 1643–1715) were simplified during the late 1660s, accessories underwent similar changes. Once belonging to a set of two, this splendid piece of Brussels lace may have been made for the Sun King himself shortly before his death. This type of bobbin part-lace, initially produced in Brussels during the eighteenth century, consists of individual motifs made separately but joined together so skillfully that the seams are almost imperceptible. Worn with its mate, slightly gathered at the neck, this rectangular piece of fabric is replete with symbols signifying the elevated status of its wearer. At center are a rooster and trophies, beneath which is the king's monogram of double Ls. Surmounting this image and supported by two trumpeting angels is a baldachin, a canopy carried over important personages during processions. Armed female warriors appear to the right and left, and gracing the upper corners are the Maltese cross and the sun, the latter the emblem of Louis.

WINTER, FROM THE SEASONS

1700/1720
After a design by Charles Le Brun (French, 1619–1690)
Woven at the workshop of Étienne Le Blond (French, 1652–1727) and
Jean de La Croix (French, 1628–1712) at the Manufacture Royale des
Gobelins (French, founded 1663)
Wool and silk, slit and double interlocking tapestry weave; 540.07 × 384.81 cm (212 5/8 × 151 1/2 in.)
Gift of the Hearst Foundation in memory of William Randolph Hearst, 1954.261

Winter presents Saturn (the god of agriculture and time) and Juventas (the cupbearer
to the gods on Mount Olympus) on a large cloud. The musical instruments and the
mask at Juventas's feet allude to ballet performances and masked balls—the favored
pastimes of the French court—while Saturn holds a floral wreath that features a ballet
scene. In the foreground, a variety of winter vegetables are visible, along with a cage,
nets, a gun, and game of various kinds: the results of a successful hunt. The buildings
in the background on the right of the tapestry are identifiable as the Palais du Louvre in
Paris. The border imitates a gilt wood frame and contains shell garlands above and below cartouches that feature interlocking *L*s surmounted by a crown, a cipher of French
king Louis XIV (r. 1643–1715). The tapestry is from a series based on the Four Seasons
(*Autumn* is also in the Art Institute's collection), after a design by Charles Le Brun,
who was appointed director of the Gobelins Manufactory in 1663.

THE EMPEROR SAILING, FROM THE STORY OF THE EMPEROR OF CHINA

1716/22

After a design by Guy-Louis Vernansal (French, 1648–1729)

Woven at the Manufacture Royale de Beauvais (French, founded 1664)

Wool, silk, and silvered-and-gilt-metal-strip-wrapped silk threads, slit and double interlocking tapestry weave with some areas of 2:2 plain interlacings of silvered-and-gilt-metal-strip-wrapped-silk wefts; 385.8 × 355 cm (151 $^3/_4$ × 139 $^3/_4$ in.)

Mr. and Mrs. Charles H. Worcester Fund, 2007.22

This tapestry is part of a suite that portrays scenes from the lives of the Chinese emperor Shunzhi (r. 1644–61) and his son, the emperor Kangxi (r. 1661–1722). *The Emperor Sailing* shows the elder emperor seated in a ceremonial dragon boat as it pulls away from a quay. Members of the imperial family and their attendants watch the launch from underneath an arcade, in close proximity to a crane and a tortoise that together symbolize their well-wishes for the monarch. Philippe Behagle, then director of the Beauvais tapestry workshop, commissioned the design of this tapestry suite in the mid-1680s to cater to the French court's increasing fascinating with China. As an allegory of good governance, the series makes manifest the parallels, first propounded by French Jesuit missionaries in China, between Louis XIV and Kangxi.

THE PHEASANTS, FROM VERDURES OF THE VATICAN

1783/89
Designed by Jean-Démosthène
Dugourc (French, 1749–1825)
Woven by Camille Pernon et Cie.
(French, late 18th–early 19th
century)

Silk, satin weave with plain interlacings of
secondary binding warps and brocading wefts;
embroidered with silk in chain (tambour work)
and satin stitches; 242.5 × 44.5 cm (95 ¼ ×
17 ½ in.)

Restricted gift of Mrs. Chauncey B. Borland,
1945.12

Perhaps the last great name connected
with the French silk industry in the late
eighteenth and early nineteenth centuries
is that of Jean-Démosthène Dugourc.
A designer of costumes and stage decorations for the French opera, he was also
the superintendent of buildings and
designer of Garde-Meuble for the Duc
d'Orléans. Dugourc was the most outstanding interior decorator of his time,
and from 1774 to 1790 he produced designs for the silk manufacturer Camille
Pernon of Lyon. Educated in Italy for
a time, Dugourc was familiar with the
classical antique motifs that Raphael
had revived in his fresco decorations for
the Vatican Loggie, part of the papal
palace in Rome. In fact, the French designer titled a group of textile patterns
Verdures of the Vatican. The Pheasants,
which was designed for the Spanish royal
palace in Madrid, is part of this series.
The elaborate composition encompasses
a lavish, symmetrical interplay of birds,
baskets, strings of pearls, garlands, and
ribbons—all realized with the excellence
of workmanship that made French silks
so desirable.

BED RUG

1796

Made by Hannah Johnson (American, 1770–1848)

Wool, plain weave; with cut pile formed by wool yarns embroidered in looped running stitches; 249.4 × 246.1 cm (98 1/4 × 97 in.)

Restricted gift of the Needlework and Textile Guild, 1944.27

It is not surprising that early American textiles reflect the strong influence of European, especially English, designs and techniques. Materials were scarce and making utilitarian objects such as bedcoverings depended entirely on raw products that could be raised by a family or community. Yet indigenous forms of American needlework did develop, as can be seen in this masterful bed rug. Although the coiling tendrils of its design are reminiscent of motifs that appear in sixteenth- and seventeenth-century English textiles, their application to a bedcovering and the technique of looped running stitches embroidered through a wool support fabric are typically American. The term *rugge* or *rugg* appears in colonial inventories, where it refers to a woven yardage fabric used to make bedcovers. Such pieces were unique to the Connecticut River Valley. The information provided by the needlework contributes to the rarity of this piece: the initials *H. J.* refer to its maker, Hannah Johnson, the daughter of Ebenezer and Anna Johnson. It is dated 1796 and carries the number 26, which indicates that Johnson was twenty-six years old when she made it.

FURISODE
Japan, late Edo period (1789–1868), 1801/68

Silk, 4:1 satin damask weave (*rinzu*); embroidered with silk and gold-leaf-over-lacquered-paper-strip-wrapped silk in satin stitches; laid work and couching, and padded couching; lined with silk, plain weave; 183.8 × 128.8 cm (72 ¼ × 50 ¾ in.)

Gift of Gaylord Donnelley in memory of Frances Gaylord Smith, 1991.637

This *furisode*, a long-sleeved garment worn by children and unmarried women on special occasions, belonged to a family whose crest was the *tachibana*, the flower of the Mandarin orange. Made of *rinzu* (a soft, lustrous silk), it probably was used as an *uchikake* (outer coat). The red fabric is woven in a pattern that combines geometric and floral forms. A blossoming plum tree embroidered with gold and white silk thread spreads its branches from hem to shoulder. The carefully embroidered blooming tree shows the influence of Western art on Japanese design. Needlework typical of this period was used to portray illusionistically the contours of the tree trunk. First the edges of the trunk were padded with a heavy thread; then, over this padding, gold-wrapped thread was couched with red silk thread.

WOMAN'S ROBE
Bukhara, Uzbekistan, 1840/60

Silk and cotton, warp-resist-dyed (warp ikat) plain weave; pieced; main lining: cotton, plain weave, printed; center opening lining: silk and cotton, warp-faced plain weave; bottom edge lining: cotton, plain weave; cuff lining: cotton, twill weave; edging: silk, warp twining; 134 × 167.5 cm (52 ¹³/₁₆ × 54 in.)

Gift of Guido Goldman, 2005.606

This woman's robe exemplifies the long tradition of ikat production in Central Asia, specifically, in Bukhara, Uzbekistan, once an active center along the ancient Silk Road. Among the many uses of ikats was their role as a component of a woman's dowry. A woman would have worn this robe at weddings and other special occasions, and at her funeral it would have been draped over her bier. The choice of fabric was determined by a woman's age and status. In general, young women wore bright colors and large patterns, while older women dressed in more sober hues. Most women wore garments made of inexpensive native cotton fabrics, but wealthy women owned robes made of silk and cotton-wefted ikat fabric. Ikat is an ancient technique involving precise and repeated tying (binding) and dyeing of threads or yarns before they are woven. The warp threads are dyed, while the weft threads usually remain solid in color. These threads intersect at right angles during the weaving process; the results are complex patterns in dazzling color combinations that produce a slightly blurred visual effect known by the Persian word *abr* ("cloud").

CARPET

1887

Designed by William Morris (English, 1834–1896); produced by Morris &
Company; woven at Merton Abbey Works (British, 1875–1940)

Cotton and wool, plain weave with supplementary wrapping wefts forming "Ghiordes knots" cut pile;

472.3 × 333.4 cm (186 × 131 1/4 in.)

Gift of Mrs. Charles F. Batchelder, 1974.524

This carpet was among the original furnishings of the John J. Glessner House on
Prairie Avenue in Chicago, which was designed by the architect Henry Hobson
Richardson (1838–1886) and completed in 1887. The carpet was located in the hall
of the house and was one of the many furnishing textiles designed by Morris and
other eminent Arts and Crafts textile designers and manufacturers of the period.

The design and craftsmanship of decorative objects were of the utmost importance to Morris. His dedicated interest in understanding, practicing, and mastering
textile-manufacturing techniques, coupled with his belief in the benefits of beauty in
everyday life, made him and his firm among the most celebrated in British history. In
the 1870s Morris began designing hand-knotted and machine-made carpets. He had
long been interested in historical carpets, and many could be found in his personal
collection. Here Morris looked to Turkish and Persian rugs for inspiration, utilizing
a layout with a central medallion set in a field of interlacing stylized flowers and
foliage framed by a border of continuous palmettes.

TALISMANIC TEXTILE
Probably Senegal, late 19th/early 20th century
Four panels joined: cotton, plain weave; painted; amulets of animal hide and felt attached by knotted strips of leather; 255.2 × 178.8 cm (100 ¹/₂ × 70 ³/₈ in.)
African and Amerindian Purchase Endowment, 2000.326

In Sufism, a form of Islamic mysticism that is widely practiced in Senegal, the repetition of verses from the Qur'an and even of individual letters or words is a transcendent form of devotion. This textile is covered with Qur'anic verses that were likely recited as they were inscribed in tightly composed Arabic script, thereby forging a link between the written word and its sound. The calligraphy is arranged in a fluid checkerboard pattern and organized around a series of painted shapes. The checkered motifs evoke magic squares, arrangements of numbers that, when added together in any direction, always amount to the same sum. In Sufism, such numerological devices are held to be a powerful reflection of divine mystery. Like words, they are filled with sacred blessings, or *baraka*. The elongated quadruped figure may represent a lizard, a spirit, or a stylized rendering of the name Muhammad. Attached amulets further punctuate the textile. These commonly encase small squares of folded paper bearing sacred writing. Across Senegal, learned Sufi practitioners applied their esoteric knowledge of sacred writing to the therapeutic practices of divination, healing, and spiritual protection. This textile was likely prepared by a practitioner who lent or rented it to clients as needed.

POPPYHEADS (DRESS OR FURNISHING FABRIC) (DETAIL)

1900

Designed by Koloman Moser (Austrian, 1868–1918)

Produced by Johann Backhausen und Söhne (Austrian, founded 1849)

Silk, wild silk, and cotton; satin weave self-patterned by ground weft floats; 182.9 × 113 cm (72 × 44 ½ in.)

Restricted gift of Mrs. Julian Armstrong, Jr., 1986.963

Koloman Moser, a prominent Viennese designer, cofounded the Wiener Werkstatte (1903–32), a forward-looking Viennese design workshop. Prior to 1903 he was an influential member of the Moderne Movement in Vienna. Moser was also a founder of the Vienna Secession, the association of young artists who had broken away from the Wiener Künstlerhaus, the accepted artistic forum of the time. *Poppyheads*, designed by Moser three years before the Wiener Werkstätte was formed, foreshadowed the kind of elegant textile designs he would produce at the Werkstätte. The attenuated lines coupled with the simplification and abstraction of organic forms demonstrate a new aesthetic vision of the time shared by artists and designers in Vienna and Glasgow. Moser's design was produced in various colors by the Viennese firm of Johann Backhausen und Söhne, which was closely linked to the Werkstätte and is still in business today. The textile was intended for upholstery or curtain fabric, ideally for rooms whose design and furnishings would be produced as total environments by Werkstätte artists.

WATERS ABOVE THE FIRMAMENT
1976
Lenore Tawney (American, 1907–2007)

Linen, warp-faced weft-ribbed plain weave with discontinuous wefts; 18th/19th-century manuscript pages cut into strips, attached, and painted with Liquitex acrylic paint; braided, knotted, and cut warp fringe; 397.6 × 369 cm (156 $^1/_2$ × 145 $^1/_4$ in.)

H. L. and Mary T. Adams, Harriott A. Fox, and Mrs. Siegfried G. Schmidt endowments; restricted gift of Laurance H. Armour, Jr., and Margot G. Armour Family Foundation, Mrs. William G. Swartchild, Jr., Joan Rosenberg, Joseph W. Fell, and the Textile Society, 1983.203

Lenore Tawney's *Waters above the Firmament* owes its striking character to the simplicity of its basic concept: a large circle set into a square. This simplicity is complicated by the weight Tawney has given to the upper half of the circle, in which the warps are made of paper and fabric coated in thick blue paint. Here Tawney, known for her pioneering exposure of the warp (vertical thread element), provided a variant on that theme: she wove the circle with slits that open at regular half-inch intervals, emphasizing a third dimension, a device she utilized in many of her weavings. Trained in sculpture at the Institute of Design in Chicago and an alumna of the School of the Art Institute, Tawney's exploration of weaving as a sculptural enterprise fits well within her body of work, which also includes laminated boxes and collages as well as constructions composed of such materials as eggshells and chairs.

INDEX OF ARTISTS, CULTURES, AND MAKERS

PHOTOGRAPHY CREDITS

Details

P. 6: Art Institute of Chicago Michigan Avenue entrance
P. 9: Martin Johnson Heade, *Magnolias on Light Blue Velvet Cloth*
(detail), 1885/95 (p. 14)
P. 45: *Portrait Bust of a Woman* (detail), Roman, mid-2nd century AD
(p. 58)
P. 61: Hulger and Samuel Wilkinson Design, *Plumen 001* (detail),
2010 (p. 77)
P. 79: Olowe of Ise, *Veranda Post of Enthroned King and Senior Wife (Opo
ogoga)* (detail), early/mid-19th century (p. 84)
P. 87: *Ceremonial Knife (Tumi)* (detail), Chimú; north coast, Peru,
1100/1450 (p. 89)
P. 95: *Shiva as Lord of the Dance (Nataraja)* (detail), Tamil Nadu, India,
10th/11th century (p. 114)
P. 125: Sèvres Porcelain Manufactory, *Londonderry Vase* (detail), 1813
(p. 137)
P. 143: El Greco (Domenikos Theotokopoulos), *The Assumption of the
Virgin* (detail), 1577–79 (p. 156)
P. 195: Sigmar Polke, *Watchtower with Geese* (detail), 1987–88 (p. 259)
P. 281: Alfred Stieglitz, *Georgia O'Keeffe—Hands and Thimble* (detail),
1919 (p. 287)
P. 303: James McNeill Whistler, *Green and Blue: The Dancer* (detail),
c. 1893 (p. 317)
P. 331: *Furisode* (detail), Japanese, 1801/68 (p. 343)